Birnbaum's 95
Chicago

A BIRNBAUM TRAVEL GUIDE

Alexandra Mayes Birnbaum
EDITORIAL CONSULTANT

Lois Spritzer
Editorial Director

Laura L. Brengelman
Managing Editor

Mary Callahan
Senior Editor

David Appell
Patricia Canole
Gene Gold
Jill Kadetsky
Susan McClung
Associate Editors

HarperPerennial
A Division of HarperCollinsPublishers

To Stephen, who merely made all this possible.

FIRST EDITION

ISSN 0749-2561 (Birnbaum Travel Guides)
ISSN 1056-4365 (Chicago)
ISBN 0-06-278186-3 (pbk.)

95 96 97 ❖/RRD 5 4 3 2 1

Cover design © Drenttel Doyle Partners
Cover photograph © Paul Hurd/AllStock
Water Tower and Sears Tower, Chicago

BIRNBAUM TRAVEL GUIDES

Bahamas, and Turks & Caicos
Berlin
Bermuda
Boston
Canada
Cancun, Cozumel & Isla Mujeres
Caribbean
Chicago
Country Inns and Back Roads
Disneyland
Eastern Europe
Europe
Europe for Business Travelers
France
Germany
Great Britain
Hawaii
Ireland
Italy
London
Los Angeles
Mexico
Miami & Ft. Lauderdale
Montreal & Quebec City
New Orleans
New York
Paris
Portugal
Rome
San Francisco
Santa Fe & Taos
South America
Spain
United States
USA for Business Travelers
Walt Disney World
Walt Disney World for Kids, By Kids
Washington, DC

Contributing Editors

Mary Dempsey
Connie Goddard
Laura Nash

Maps

Mark Carlson
Susan Carlson

Contents

Getting Ready to Go

Practical information for planning your trip.

The City

A thorough, qualitative guide to Chicago, highlighting the city's attractions, services, hotels, and restaurants.

Diversions

A selective guide to a variety of unexpected pleasures, pinpointing the best places to pursue them.

Exceptional Pleasures and Treasures

Directions

Fourteen of the most delightful walks through Chicago.

Foreword

Dyed in the wool New Yorker that I am, if I couldn't live smack in the middle of Manhattan, I'd choose Chicago. I used to regale my husband, Steve Birnbaum, with encomiums to the architecture and ambience of Chicago, all in an effort to convince him that the aesthetic aspects of the so-called Second City (now, by population count, actually the third) should be drawing him back again and again. But culture wasn't the magnet for him.

Steve went to Chicago to eat. That's it, plain and simple, and it is not in the least hyperbolic to report that as he deplaned from O'Hare Airport he mentally tucked a napkin under his chin. Oh, he liked Chicago's citizenry a lot, and he agreed with me that the skyline is at least as impressive as advertised, and the lakeshore setting is spectacular, but mention Chicago's extraordinary spectrum of menus and you really got his attention.

Now truth to tell, food also draws *me* to Chicago's dining tables. In a restaurant world that has gone more than a little bonkers in offering nouvelle nonsense as a substitute for real food, Chicago has kept its head on straight. For folks who prefer straightforward meals to small portions of radicchio slathered in raspberry sauce, Chicago is a gastronomic shrine. And, Chicago has a way of showing visitors just what truly is important in life.

That's why we've tried to create a guide to Chicago that's specifically organized, written, and edited for today's demanding traveler, one for whom qualitative information is infinitely more desirable than mere quantities of unappraised data. We realize that it's impossible for any single travel writer to visit thousands of restaurants (and nearly as many hotels) in any given year and provide accurate appraisals of each. And even if it were physically possible for one human being to survive such an itinerary, it would of necessity have to be done at a dead sprint, and the perceptions derived therefrom would probably be less valid than those of any other intelligent individual visiting the same establishments. It is, therefore, both impractical and undesirable (especially in a large, annually revised and updated guidebook *series* such as we offer) to have only one person provide all the data on the entire world. Instead, we have chosen what we like to describe as the "thee and me" approach to restaurant and hotel evaluation and, to a more limited degree, to the sites and sights we have included in the other sections of our text. What this really reflects is a personal sampling tempered by intelligent counsel from informed local sources.

This guidebook is directed to the "visitor," and such elements as restaurants have been specifically picked to provide the visitor with a representative, enlightening, and, above all, pleasant experience. Since so many extraneous considerations can affect the reception and service accorded a regular restaurant patron, our choices can in no way be construed as an exhaustive guide to resident dining. We think we've listed all the best places, in various price ranges, but they were chosen with a visitor's enjoyment in mind.

Other evidence of how we've tried to tailor our text to reflect modern travel habits is apparent in the section we call DIVERSIONS. Where once it was common for travelers to spend an urban visit seeing only the obvious sights, today's traveler is more likely to want to pursue a special interest or to venture off the beaten path. In response to this trend, we have collected these exceptional experiences so that it is no longer necessary to wade through a pound or two of superfluous prose just to find exceptional pleasures and treasures.

Finally, I also should point out that every good travel guide is a living enterprise; that is, no part of this text is carved in stone. In our annual revisions, we refine, expand, and further hone all our material to serve your travel needs better. To this end, no contribution is of greater value to us than your personal reaction to what we have written, as well as information reflecting your own experiences while using the book. Please write to us at 10 E. 53rd St., New York, NY 10022.

We sincerely hope to hear from you.

Alexandra Mayes Birnbaum

ALEXANDRA MAYES BIRNBAUM, editorial consultant to the *Birnbaum Travel Guides*, worked with her late husband, Stephen Birnbaum, as co-editor of the series. She has been a world traveler since childhood and is known for her travel reports on radio on what's hot and what's not.

Chicago

How to Use This Guide

A great deal of care has gone into the special organization of this guidebook, and we believe it represents a real breakthrough in the presentation of travel material.

Our text is divided into four basic sections, in order to present information in the best way on every possible aspect of a vacation to Chicago. Our aim is to highlight what's where and to provide basic information—how, when, where, how much, and what's best—to assist you in making the most intelligent choices possible.

Here is a brief summary of what you can expect to find in each section. We believe that you will find both your travel planning and en route enjoyment enhanced by having this book at your side.

GETTING READY TO GO

A mini-encyclopedia of practical travel facts with all the precise data necessary to create a successful trip to Chicago. Here you will find how to get where you're going, plus selected resources—including useful publications, and companies and organizations specializing in discount and special-interest travel—providing a wealth of information and assistance useful both before and during your trip.

THE CITY

Our individual report on Chicago offers a short-stay guide, including an essay introducing the city as a historic entity and as a contemporary place to visit; an *At-a-Glance* section that's a site-by-site survey of the most important, interesting, and unique sights to see and things to do; *Sources and Resources,* a concise listing of pertinent tourism information, such as the address of the local tourist office, which sightseeing tours to take, where to find the best nightspot or hail a taxi, which shops have the finest merchandise and/or the most irresistible bargains, and where the best museums and theaters are to be found; and *Best in Town,* which lists our cost-and-quality choices of the best places to eat and sleep on a variety of budgets.

DIVERSIONS

This section is designed to help travelers find the best places in which to engage in a variety of exceptional experiences, without having to wade through endless pages of unrelated text. In every case, our particular suggestions are intended to guide you to that special place where the quality of experience is likely to be highest.

DIRECTIONS

Here are 14 walks and drives that cover Chicago, its main thoroughfares and side streets, its most spectacular landmarks and parks, and its most compelling outlying communities.

To use this book to full advantage, take a few minutes to read the table of contents and random entries in each section to get a firsthand feel for how it all fits together. You will find that the sections of this book are building blocks designed to help you put together the best possible trip. Use them selectively as a tool, a source of ideas, a reference work for accurate facts, and a guidebook to the best buys, the most exciting sights, the most pleasant accommodations, the tastiest foods—*the best travel experience* that you can possibly have.

Getting Ready to Go

Getting Ready to Go

When to Go

Chicago receives the most visitors from June to September. The best time to see the city, however, may be in autumn, when the days generally are clear and brisk. The cool spring season also is a pleasant time to visit. Summers can be muggy and rainy, although temperatures rarely climb above the 80s. Chicago's winters are formidable, with heavy snowfall, and a combination of cold temperatures and blustery winds that can create windchill factors well below zero.

In Chicago, there are no real off-season periods when attractions are closed, and prices stay pretty much within the same range year-round. Hotel bargains are more likely to appear on weekends (when business travel is slow) than during any particular season of the year, although some special rates are offered during the winter. (For information, see *Best in Town* in THE CITY.)

If you have a touch-tone phone, you can call *The Weather Channel Connection* (phone: 900-WEATHER) for current weather forecasts. This service, available from *The Weather Channel* (2600 Cumberland Pkwy., Atlanta, GA 30339; phone: 404-434-6800), costs 95¢ per minute; the charge will appear on your phone bill.

Traveling by Plane

SCHEDULED FLIGHTS

Leading airlines offering flights to Chicago's *O'Hare International Airport* and *Midway Airport* include *America West, American, American Eagle, Continental, Delta, Delta Connection, Northwest, Southwest Airlines, TWA, TWA Express, United, United Express, USAir,* and *USAir Express.*

FARES The great variety of airfares can be reduced to the following basic categories: first class, business class, coach (also called economy or tourist class), excursion or discount, and standby, as well as various promotional fares. For information on applicable fares and restrictions, contact the airlines listed above or ask your travel agent. Most airfares are offered for a limited time. Once you've found the lowest fare for which you can qualify, purchase your ticket as soon as possible.

RESERVATIONS Reconfirmation is not generally required on domestic flights, although it is wise to call ahead to make sure that the airline has your reservation and any special requests in its computer.

SEATING Airline seats usually are assigned on a first-come, first-served basis at check-in, although you may be able to reserve a seat when purchasing your ticket. Seating charts sometimes are available from airlines and also are included in the *Airline Seating Guide* (Carlson Publishing Co., 11132 Los Alamitos Blvd., Los Alamitos, CA 90720; phone: 310-493-4877).

SMOKING US law prohibits smoking on flights scheduled for six hours or less within the US and its territories on both domestic and international carriers. A free wallet-size guide that describes the rights of nonsmokers under current regulations is available from *ASH* (*Action on Smoking and Health;* DOT Card, 2013 H St. NW, Washington, DC 20006; phone: 202-659-4310).

SPECIAL MEALS When making your reservation, you can request one of the airline's alternate menu choices for no additional charge. Though not always required, it is a good idea to reconfirm your request the day before departure.

BAGGAGE On major airlines, passengers usually are allowed to carry on board one bag that will fit under a seat or in an overhead bin and to check two bags in the cargo hold. Specific regulations regarding dimensions and weight restrictions vary among airlines, but a checked bag usually cannot exceed 62 inches in combined dimensions (length, width, and depth), or weigh more than 70 pounds. There may be charges for additional, oversize, or overweight luggage, and for special equipment or sporting gear. Check that the tags the airline attaches are correctly coded for your destination.

CHARTER FLIGHTS

By booking a block of seats on a specially arranged flight, charter operators frequently can offer travelers bargain airfares. If you do fly on a charter, however, read the contract's fine print carefully. Federal regulations permit charter operators to cancel a flight or assess surcharges of as much as 10% of the airfare up to 10 days before departure. You usually must book in advance, and once booked, no changes are permitted, so buy trip cancellation insurance. Also, make your check out to the company's escrow account, which provides some protection for your investment in the event that the charter operator fails. For further information, consult the publication *Jax Fax* (397 Post Rd., Darien, CT 06820; phone: 203-655-8746; fax: 203-655-6257).

DISCOUNTS ON SCHEDULED FLIGHTS

COURIER TRAVEL In return for arranging to accompany some kind of freight, a traveler pays only a portion of the total airfare (and sometimes a small registration fee). One agency that matches up would-be couriers with courier companies is *Now Voyager* (74 Varick St., Suite 307, New York, NY 10013; phone: 212-431-1616; fax: 212-334-5243).

Courier Companies

Discount Travel International (169 W. 81st St., New York, NY 10024; phone: 212-362-3636; fax: 212-362-3236; and 801 Alton Rd., Suite 1, Miami Beach, FL 33139; phone: 305-538-1616; fax: 305-673-9376).

F.B. On Board Courier Club (10225 Ryan Ave., Suite 103, Dorval, Quebec H9P 1A2, Canada; phone: 514-633-0740; fax: 514-633-0735).

Halbart Express (147-05 176th St., Jamaica, NY 11434; phone: 718-656-8279; fax: 718-244-0559).

Midnite Express (925 W. Hyde Park Blvd., Inglewood, CA 90302; phone: 310-672-1100; fax: 310-671-0107).

Way to Go Travel (6679 Sunset Blvd., Hollywood, CA 90028; phone: 213-466-1126; fax: 213-466-8994).

Publications

Insiders Guide to Air Courier Bargains, by Kelly Monaghan (The Intrepid Traveler, PO Box 438, New York, NY 10034; phone: 212-569-1081 for information; 800-356-9315 for orders; fax: 212-942-6687).

Travel Unlimited (PO Box 1058, Allston, MA 02134-1058; no phone).

CONSOLIDATORS AND BUCKET SHOPS These companies buy blocks of tickets from airlines and sell them at a discount to travel agents or directly to consumers. Since many bucket shops operate on a thin margin, be sure to check a company's record with the *Better Business Bureau*—before parting with any money.

Council Charter (205 E. 42nd St., New York, NY 10017; phone: 800-800-8222 or 212-661-0311; fax: 212-972-0194).

International Adventures (60 E. 42nd St., Room 763, New York, NY 10165; phone: 212-599-0577; fax: 212-599-3288).

Travac Tours and Charters (989 Ave. of the Americas, New York, NY 10018; phone: 800-872-8800 or 212-563-3303; fax: 212-563-3631).

Unitravel (1177 N. Warson Rd., St. Louis, MO 63132; phone: 800-325-2222 or 314-569-0900; fax: 314-569-2503).

LAST-MINUTE TRAVEL CLUBS Members of such clubs receive information on imminent trips and other bargain travel opportunities. There usually is an annual fee, although a few clubs offer free membership. Despite the names of some of the clubs listed below, you don't have to wait until literally the last minute to make travel plans.

Discount Travel International (114 Forrest Ave., Suite 203, Narberth, PA 19072; phone: 215-668-7184; fax: 215-668-9182).

FLY ASAP (PO Box 9808, Scottsdale, AZ 85252-3808; phone: 800-FLY-ASAP or 602-956-1987; fax: 602-956-6414).

Last Minute Travel (1249 Boylston St., Boston, MA 02215; phone: 800-LAST-MIN or 617-267-9800; fax: 617-424-1943).

Moment's Notice (425 Madison Ave., New York, NY 10017; phone: 212-486-0500/1/2/3; fax: 212-486-0783).

Spur of the Moment Cruises (411 N. Harbor Blvd., Suite 302, San Pedro, CA 90731; phone: 800-4-CRUISES or 310-521-1070 in California; 800-343-1991 elsewhere in the US; 24-hour hotline: 310-521-1060; fax: 310-521-1061).

Traveler's Advantage (3033 S. Parker Rd., Suite 900, Aurora, CO 80014; phone: 800-548-1116 or 800-835-8747; fax: 303-368-3985).

Vacations to Go (1502 Augusta Dr., Suite 415, Houston, TX 77057; phone: 713-974-2121 in Texas; 800-338-4962 elsewhere in the US; fax: 713-974-0445).

Worldwide Discount Travel Club (1674 Meridian Ave., Miami Beach, FL 33139; phone: 305-534-2082; fax: 305-534-2070).

GENERIC AIR TRAVEL These organizations operate much like an ordinary airline standby service, except that they offer seats on not one but several scheduled and charter airlines. One pioneer of generic flights is *Airhitch* (2790 Broadway, Suite 100, New York, NY 10025; phone: 212-864-2000).

BARTERED TRAVEL SOURCES Barter—the exchange of commodities or services in lieu of cash payment—is a common practice among travel suppliers. Companies that have obtained travel services through barter may sell these services at substantial discounts to travel clubs, who pass along the savings to members. One organization offering bartered travel opportunities is *Travel World Leisure Club* (225 W. 34th St., Suite 909, New York, NY 10122; phone: 800-444-TWLC or 212-239-4855; fax: 212-564-5158).

CONSUMER PROTECTION

Passengers whose complaints have not been satisfactorily addressed by the airline can contact the *US Department of Transportation* (*DOT;* Consumer Affairs Division, 400 Seventh St. SW, Room 10405, Washington, DC 20590; phone: 202-366-2220). Also see *Fly Rights* (Publication #050-000-00513-5; *US Government Printing Office,* PO Box 371954, Pittsburgh, PA 15250-7954; phone: 202-783-3238; fax: 202-512-2250). If you have safety-related questions or concerns, write to the *Federal Aviation Administration* (*FAA;* 800 Independence Ave. SW, Washington, DC 20591) or call the *FAA Consumer Hotline* (phone: 800-322-7873).

On Arrival

FROM THE AIRPORTS TO THE CITY

O'Hare International Airport is about 25 miles west of the Loop, downtown Chicago's central business district. Depending on traffic, the trip takes from 40 to 60 minutes by cab and costs between $20 and $25. *Continental Air Transport* (phone: 312-454-7800) provides van service between *O'Hare* and major hotels in the Loop; the one-hour trip costs $14.50 one-way ($25.50 round-trip). *Continental* also provides service between the airport and the Chicago suburbs ($15.15 one-way; no round-trip fare). The *Blue Line "L"* train, operated by the *Chicato Transit Authority* (*CTA;* phone: 312-836-7000) is the most economical way to travel between *O'Hare* and downtown Chicago. The 40- to 45-minute trip costs only $1.50.

Midway Airport lies 11 miles south of the Loop, a 10- to 20-minute trip by taxi ($10 to $15). Van service between the airport and most major downtown hotels also is provided by *Continental Air Transport* ($10.75 one-way, $19 round-trip), and takes about 45 minutes. The *CTA's Orange Line "L"* train runs between *Midway* and downtown weekdays and Saturdays from 5 AM to 11 PM, and Sundays from 8:30 AM to 11 PM. The 30-minute trip costs $1.50.

RENTING A CAR

You can rent a car through a travel agent or national rental firm before leaving home, or from a regional or local company once in Chicago. Reserve in advance.

Most car rental companies require a credit card, although some will accept a substantial cash deposit. The minimum age to rent a car is set by the company; some also may impose special conditions on drivers above a certain age. In most states, you are given the option of paying for collision damage waiver (CDW) protection, which adds to the cost of renting a car, but releases you from financial liability for the vehicle. In Illinois, however, car rental companies are *required* to include CDW in basic rates—so you won't have a choice—and prices are higher by the amount of this otherwise separate charge. Additional costs include drop-off charges or one-way service fees.

Car Rental Companies

Ace Rent A Car (phone: 800-243-3443).
Agency Rent-A-Car (phone: 800-321-1972).
Airways Rent-A-Car (phone: 800-952-9200 or 708-671-7070).
Alamo (phone: 800-327-9633 or 708-671-7662).
Avis (phone: 800-331-1212).
Budget (phone: 800-527-0700, 708-955-1900, or 312-686-6800).
Dependable Auto Rental (phone: 312-767-6646).
Dollar Rent A Car (phone: 800-800-4000, 312-735-7200, or 312-694-2200).
Econo-Car (phone: 312-951-6262, 312-939-6001, or 312-226-1828).
Enterprise Rent-A-Car (phone: 800-325-8007).
Hertz (phone: 800-654-3131).
National (phone: 800-CAR-RENT).
Paragon Auto Leasing (phone: 312-622-7660).
Payless (phone: 800-PAYLESS).

Premier Car Rental (phone: 800-449-8200 or 708-616-0005).
Pride Car & Truck Rental (phone: 312-622-6655 or 708-678-7766).
Sears (phone: 800-527-0770).
Snappy Car Rental (phone: 800-669-4802).
Thrifty (phone: 800-367-2277).

NOTE

Rent-A-Wreck (phone: 800-421-7253 for locations of franchises nation-wide; 312-585-7344 or 312-281-4242 for local Chicago offices) rents cars that are well worn but (presumably) mechanically sound.

Package Tours

A package is a collection of travel services that can be purchased in a single transaction. Its principal advantages are convenience and economy—the cost usually is lower than that of the same services purchased separately. Tour programs generally can be divided into two categories: escorted or locally hosted (with a set itinerary) and independent (usually more flexible).

When considering a package tour, read the brochure *carefully* to determine exactly what is included and any conditions that may apply, and check the company's record with the *Better Business Bureau.* The *United States Tour Operators Association* (*USTOA;* 211 E. 51st St., Suite 12B, New York, NY 10022; phone: 212-750-7371; fax: 212-421-1285) also can be helpful in determining a package tour operator's reliability. As with charter flights, to safeguard your funds, always make your check out to the company's escrow account.

Many tour operators offer packages focused on special interests such as the arts, local history, sports, and other recreations. *All Adventure Travel* (5589 Arapahoe St., Suite 208, Boulder, CO 80303; phone: 800-537-4025 or 303-440-7924; fax: 303-440-4160) represents such specialized packagers. Many also are listed in the *Specialty Travel Index* (305 San Anselmo Ave., Suite 313, San Anselmo, CA 94960; phone: 415-459-4900 in California; 800-442-4922 elsewhere in the US; fax: 415-459-4974). In addition, a number of companies offer half- or full-day sightseeing tours in and around Chicago.

Package Tour Operators

Adventure Tours (10612 Beaver Dam Rd., Hunt Valley, MD 21030-2205; phone: 410-785-3500 in Baltimore, 800-638-9040 elsewhere in the US; fax: 410-584-2771).

American Airlines FlyAAway Vacations (offices throughout the US; phone: 800-321-2121).

Certified Vacations (110 E. Broward Blvd., Ft. Lauderdale, FL 33302; phone: 800-233-7260 or 305-522-1440; fax: 305-357-4687).

Collette Tours (162 Middle St., Pawtucket, RI 02860; phone: 800-752-2655 in New England; 800-832-4656 elsewhere in the US; fax: 401-727-4745).

Contiki Holidays (300 Plaza Alicante, Suite 900, Garden Grove, CA 92640; phone: 800-266-8454 or 714-740-0808; fax: 714-740-0818).

Continental Grand Destinations (offices throughout the US; phone: 800-634-5555).

Dan Dipert Tours (PO Box 580, Arlington, TX 76004-0580; phone: 800-433-5335 or 817-543-3710; fax: 817-543-3729).

Domenico Tours (751 Broadway, Bayonne, NJ 07002; phone: 800-554-8687, 201-823-8687, or 212-757-8687; fax: 201-823-1527).

Globus/Cosmos (5301 S. Federal Circle, Littleton, CO 80123; phone: 800-221-0090, 800-556-5454, or 303-797-2800; fax: 303-347-2080).

GOGO Tours (69 Spring St., Ramsey, NJ 07446-0507; phone: 201-934-3759).

Kerrville Tours (PO Box 79, Shreveport, LA 71161-0079; phone: 800-442-8705 or 318-227-2882; fax: 318-227-2486).

Le Ob's Tours (4635 Touro St., New Orleans, LA 70122-3933; phone: 504-288-3478; fax: 504-288-8517).

Marathon Tours (108 Main St., Charlestown, MA 02129; phone: 800-444-4097 or 617-242-7845; fax: 617-242-7686).

Maupintour (PO Box 807, Lawrence, KS 66044; phone: 800-255-4266 or 913-843-1211; fax: 913-843-8351).

Panorama Tours (600 N. Sprigg St., Cape Girardeau, MO 63701; phone: 800-962-8687 in Missouri and adjacent states; 314-335-7824 elsewhere in the US; fax: 314-335-7824).

Saga International Holidays (222 Berkeley St., Boston, MA 02116; phone: 800-343-0273 or 617-262-2262).

Tours and Travel Odyssey (230 E. McClellan Ave., Livingston, NJ 07039; phone: 800-527-2989 or 201-992-5459; fax: 201-994-1618).

TravelTours International (250 W. 49th St., Suite 600, New York, NY 10019; phone: 800-767-8777 or 212-262-0700; fax: 212-944-5854).

Trek America (PO Box 470, Blairstown, NJ 07825; phone: 800-221-0596 or 908-362-9198; fax: 908-362-9313).

United Airlines Vacations (PO Box 24580, Milwaukee, WI 53224-0580; phone: 800-328-6877).

Companies Offering Day Tours

A Admiral's Sight-Seeing Cruise Line (PO Box 811493, Chicago, IL 60681; phone: 312-641-7245; fax: 312-641-7246).

American Sightseeing Tours and Chicago Gray Line (*Palmer House Hilton*, 17 E. Monroe St., Chicago, IL 60605; phone: 800-621-4153, 312-427-3100, or 312-427-3107; fax: 312-427-9588).

Antique Coach and Carriage (1523 N. Kingsbury St., Chicago, IL 60622; phone: 312-735-9400).

Chicago Architecture Foundation Tour Center (224 S. Michigan Ave., Chicago, IL 60604; phone: 312-922-TOUR or 312-922-3432; fax: 312-922-0481).

Chicago from the Lake (455 E. Illinois St., Suite 361, Chicago, IL 60611; phone: 312-527-2002; fax: 312-527-2313).

Chicago Motor Coach (750 S. Clinton St., Chicago, IL 60607; phone: 312-922-8919; fax: 312-922-9105).

Chicago Supernatural Tours (PO Box 29054, Chicago, IL 60629; phone: 708-499-0300).

Historic Pullman Foundation (11111 S. Forrestville Ave., Chicago, IL 60628-4649; phone: 312-785-8181; fax: 312-785-8182).

J. C. Cutters (1428 N. Orleans, Chicago, IL 60610; phone: 312-664-6014; fax: 312-664-6103).

My Kind of Tour (PO Box 924, Ravinia Station, Highland Park, IL 60035; phone: 708-432-7003; fax: 708-432-7703).

Mercury Cruise Line (Michigan Ave. and Wacker Dr., Chicago, IL 60601; phone: 312-332-1353).

Odyssey Cruises (401 E. Illinois St., Suite 425, Chicago, IL 60611; phone: 312-321-7600; fax: 312-321-7610).

Shoreline Sightseeing (474 N. Lakeshore Dr., Suite 3412, Chicago, IL 60611; phone: 312-222-9328; fax: 312-321-0632).

Spirit of Chicago (455 E. Illinois St., Suite 461, Chicago, IL 60611; phone: 312-836-7899; fax: 312-836-7889).

Untouchable Tours (PO Box 43185, Chicago, IL 60643; phone: 312-881-1195; fax: 312-881-7384).

Wendella Sightseeing Boats (400 N. Michigan Ave., Chicago, IL 60611; phone: 312-337-1446; fax: 312-728-0220).

Insurance

The first person with whom you should discuss travel insurance is your own insurance broker. You may discover that the insurance you already carry protects you adequately while traveling and that you need little additional coverage. If you charge travel services, the credit card company also may provide some insurance coverage (and other safeguards).

Types of Travel Insurance

Automobile insurance: Provides collision, theft, property damage, and personal liability protection while driving.

Baggage and personal effects insurance: Protects your bags and their contents in case of damage or theft at any point during your travels.

Default and/or bankruptcy insurance: Provides coverage in the event of default and/or bankruptcy on the part of the tour operator, airline, or other travel supplier.

Flight insurance: Covers accidental injury or death while flying.

Personal accident and sickness insurance: Covers cases of illness, injury, or death in an accident while traveling.

Trip cancellation and interruption insurance: Guarantees a refund if you must cancel a trip; may reimburse you for additional travel costs incurred in catching up with a tour or traveling home early.

Combination policies: Include any or all of the above.

Disabled Travelers

Make travel arrangements well in advance. Specify to all services involved the nature of your disability to determine if there are accommodations and facilities that meet your needs. For information on accessibility and services for the disabled in Chicago, contact the *Mayor's Office for People with Disabilities* (City Hall, Rm. 1111, 121 N. LaSalle St., Chicago, IL 60602; phone: 312-744-MOPD; TDD: 312-744-7833). The *City of Chicago* provides a 24-hour TDD information line for the hearing impaired (TDD: 312-744-8599), as does the *Mayor's Office of Special Events* (TDD: 312-744-2964).

Transit maps that identify wheelchair-accessible train stations are available at the city's airports and train stations, and can be ordered directly from the *Chicago Transit Authority (CTA;* 222 Merchandise Mart Plaza, Chicago, IL 60654; phone: 312-836-7000). Van service for disabled residents, also provided by the *CTA,* is available to visitors; to register, call 312-521-1154 at least five days in advance of your trip (no mail registration).

Organizations

ACCENT on Living (PO Box 700, Bloomington, IL 61702; phone: 800-787-8444 or 309-378-2961; fax: 309-378-4420).

Access: The Foundation for Accessibility by the Disabled (PO Box 356, Malverne, NY 11565; phone/fax: 516-887-5798).

American Foundation for the Blind (15 W. 16th St., New York, NY 10011; phone: 800-232-5463 or 212-620-2147; fax: 212-727-7418).

Information Center for Individuals with Disabilities (Ft. Point Pl., 27-43 Wormwood St., Boston, MA 02210; phone: 800-462-5015 in Massachusetts; 617-727-5540 elsewhere in the US; TDD: 617-345-9743; fax: 617-345-5318).

Mobility International (main office: 228 Borough High St., London SE1 1JX, England; phone: 44-171-403-5688; fax: 44-171-378-1292; US office: *MIUSA,* PO Box 10767, Eugene, OR 97440; phone/TDD: 503-343-1284; fax: 503-343-6812).

Moss Rehabilitation Hospital Travel Information Service (telephone referrals only; phone: 215-456-9600; TDD: 215-456-9602).

National Rehabilitation Information Center (8455 Colesville Rd., Suite 935, Silver Spring, MD 20910; phone: 301-588-9284; fax: 301-587-1967).

Paralyzed Veterans of America (*PVA;* PVA/ATTS Program, 801 18th St. NW, Washington, DC 20006; phone: 202-872-1300 in Washington, DC; 800-424-8200 elsewhere in the US; fax: 202-785-4452).

Royal Association for Disability and Rehabilitation (*RADAR;* 12 City Forum, 250 City Rd., London EC1V 8AF, England; phone: 44-171-250-3222; fax: 44-171-250-0212).

Society for the Advancement of Travel for the Handicapped (*SATH;* 347 Fifth Ave., Suite 610, New York, NY 10016; phone: 212-447-7284; fax: 212-725-8253).

Travel Industry and Disabled Exchange (*TIDE;* 5435 Donna Ave., Tarzana, CA 91356; phone: 818-368-5648).

Publications

Access Travel: A Guide to the Accessibility of Airport Terminals (Consumer Information Center, Dept. 578Z, Pueblo, CO 81009; phone: 719-948-3334).

Air Transportation of Handicapped Persons (Publication #AC-120-32; *US Department of Transportation,* Distribution Unit, Publications Section, M-443-2, 400 Seventh St. SW, Washington, DC 20590; phone: 202-366-0039).

The Diabetic Traveler (PO Box 8223 RW, Stamford, CT 06905; phone: 203-327-5832; fax: 203-975-1748).

Directory of Travel Agencies for the Disabled and *Travel for the Disabled,* both by Helen Hecker (Twin Peaks Press, PO Box 129, Vancouver, WA 98666; phone: 800-637-CALM or 206-694-2462; fax: 206-696-3210).

Guide to Traveling with Arthritis (Upjohn Company, PO Box 989, Dearborn, MI 48121; phone: 800-253-9860).

The Handicapped Driver's Mobility Guide (*American Automobile Association,* 1000 AAA Dr., Heathrow, FL 32746-5080; phone: 407-444-7000; fax: 407-444-7380).

Handicapped Travel Newsletter (PO Box 269, Athens, TX 75751; phone/fax: 903-677-1260).

Handi-Travel: A Resource Book for Disabled and Elderly Travellers, by Cinnie Noble (*Canadian Rehabilitation Council for the Disabled,* 45 Sheppard Ave. E., Suite 801, Toronto, Ontario M2N 5W9, Canada; phone/TDD: 416-250-7490; fax: 416-229-1371).

Incapacitated Passengers Air Travel Guide (*International Air Transport Association,* Publications Sales Department, 2000 Peel St., Montreal, Quebec H3A 2R4, Canada; phone: 514-844-6311; fax: 514-844-5286).

Ticket to Safe Travel (*American Diabetes Association,* 1660 Duke St., Alexandria, VA 22314; phone: 800-232-3472 or 703-549-1500; fax: 703-836-7439).

Travel for the Patient with Chronic Obstructive Pulmonary Disease (Dr. Harold Silver, 1601 18th St. NW, Washington, DC 20009; phone: 202-667-0134; fax: 202-667-0148).

Travel Tips for Hearing-Impaired People (*American Academy of Otolaryngology,* 1 Prince St., Alexandria, VA 22314; phone: 703-836-4444; fax: 703-683-5100).

Travel Tips for People with Arthritis (*Arthritis Foundation,* 1314 Spring St. NW, Atlanta, GA 30309; phone: 800-283-7800 or 404-872-7100; fax: 404-872-0457).

Traveling Like Everybody Else: A Practical Guide for Disabled Travelers, by Jacqueline Freedman and Susan Gersten (Modan Publishing, PO Box 1202, Bellmore, NY 11710; phone: 516-679-1380; fax: 516-679-1448).

The Wheelchair Traveler, by Douglass R. Annand (123 Ball Hill Rd., Milford, NH 03055; phone: 603-673-4539).

Package Tour Operators

Accessible Journeys (35 W. Sellers Ave., Ridley Park, PA 19078; phone: 800-846-4537 or 215-521-0339; fax: 215-521-6959).

Accessible Tours/Directions Unlimited (Attn.: Lois Bonnani, 720 N. Bedford Rd., Bedford Hills, NY 10507; phone: 800-533-5343 or 914-241-1700; fax: 914-241-0243).

Beehive Business and Leisure Travel (1130 W. Center St., N. Salt Lake, UT 84054; phone: 800-777-5727 or 801-292-4445; fax: 801-298-9460).

Classic Travel Service (8 W. 40th St., New York, NY 10018; phone: 212-869-2560 in New York State; 800-247-0909 elsewhere in the US; fax: 212-944-4493).

Evergreen Travel Service (4114 198th St. SW, Suite 13, Lynnwood, WA 98036-6742; phone: 800-435-2288 or 206-776-1184; fax: 206-775-0728).

Flying Wheels Travel (143 W. Bridge St., PO Box 382, Owatonna, MN 55060; phone: 800-535-6790 or 507-451-5005; fax: 507-451-1685).

Good Neighbor Travel Service (124 S. Main St., Viroqua, WI 54665; phone: 800-338-3245 or 608-637-2128; fax: 608-637-3030).

The Guided Tour (7900 Old York Rd., Suite 114B, Elkins Park, PA 19117-2339; phone: 800-783-5841 or 215-782-1370; fax: 215-635-2637).

Hinsdale Travel (201 E. Ogden Ave., Hinsdale, IL 60521; phone: 708-325-1335 or 708-469-7349; fax: 708-325-1342).

MedEscort International (*ABE International Airport,* PO Box 8766, Allentown, PA 18105-8766; phone: 800-255-7182 or 215-791-3111; fax: 215-791-9189).

Prestige World Travel (5710-X High Point Rd., Greensboro, NC 27407; phone: 800-476-7737 or 910-292-6690; fax: 910-632-9404).

Sprout (893 Amsterdam Ave., New York, NY 10025; phone: 212-222-9575; fax: 212-222-9768).

Weston Travel Agency (134 N. Cass Ave., Westmont, IL 60559; phone: 708-968-2513 in Illinois; 800-633-3725 elsewhere in the US; fax: 708-968-2539).

NOTE

Illinois Medi-Car (395 W. Lake St., Elmhurst, IL 60126; phone: 708-530-1500; fax: 708-832-2041) and *Wheelchair Getaways* (PO Box 5191, Evanston, IL 60204; phone: 800-637-2597 or 708-853-1011; fax: 708-853-1017) both rent vans designed to accommodate disabled travelers.

Single Travelers

The travel industry is not very fair to people who vacation by themselves—they often end up paying more than those traveling in pairs. There are services catering to single travelers, however, that match travel companions, offer travel arrangements with shared accommodations, and provide information and discounts. Useful publications include *Going Solo* (Doerfer Communications, PO Box 123, Apalachicola, FL 32329; phone/fax: 904-653-8848) and *Traveling on Your Own,* by Eleanor Berman (Random House, Order Dept., 400 Hahn Rd., Westminster, MD 21157; phone: 800-733-3000; fax: 800-659-2436).

Organizations and Companies

Contiki Holidays (300 Plaza Alicante, Suite 900, Garden Grove, CA 92640; phone: 800-466-0610 or 714-740-0808; fax: 714-740-0818).

Gallivanting (515 E. 79th St., Suite 20F, New York, NY 10021; phone: 800-933-9699 or 212-988-0617; fax: 212-988-0144).

Globus/Cosmos (5301 S. Federal Circle, Littleton, CO 80123; phone: 800-221-0090, 800-556-5454, or 303-797-2800; fax: 303-347-2080).

Jane's International and Sophisticated Women Travelers (2603 Bath Ave., Brooklyn, NY 11214; phone: 718-266-2045; fax: 718-266-4062).

Marion Smith Singles (611 Prescott Pl., N. Woodmere, NY 11581; phone: 516-791-4852, 516-791-4865, or 212-944-2112; fax: 516-791-4879).

Partners-in-Travel (11660 Chenault St., Suite 119, Los Angeles, CA 90049; phone: 310-476-4869).

Singles in Motion (545 W. 236th St., Riverdale, NY 10463; phone/fax: 718-884-4464).

Singleworld (401 Theodore Fremd Ave., Rye, NY 10580; phone: 800-223-6490 or 914-967-3334; fax: 914-967-7395).

Solo Flights (63 High Noon Rd., Weston, CT 06883; phone: 800-266-1566 or 203-226-9993).

Suddenly Singles Tours (161 Dreiser Loop, Bronx, NY 10475; phone: 718-379-8800 in New York City; 800-859-8396 elsewhere in the US; fax: 718-379-8858).

Travel Companion Exchange (PO Box 833, Amityville, NY 11701; phone: 516-454-0880; fax: 516-454-0170).

Travel Companions (Atrium Financial Center, 1515 N. Federal Hwy., Suite 300, Boca Raton, FL 33432; phone: 800-383-7211 or 407-393-6448; fax: 407-451-8560).

Travel in Two's (239 N. Broadway, Suite 3, N. Tarrytown, NY 10591; phone: 914-631-8301 in New York State; 800-692-5252 elsewhere in the US).

Umbrella Singles (PO Box 157, Woodbourne, NY 12788; phone: 800-537-2797 or 914-434-6871; fax: 914-434-3532).

Older Travelers

Special discounts and more free time are just two factors that have given older travelers a chance to see the world at affordable prices. Many travel suppliers offer senior discounts—sometimes only to members of certain senior citizens organizations (which provide benefits of their own). When considering a particular package, make sure the facilities—and the pace of the tour—match your needs and physical condition.

Publications

The Mature Traveler (PO Box 50820, Reno, NV 89513-0820; phone: 702-786-7419).

The Senior Citizen's Guide to Budget Travel in the US and Canada, by Paige Palmer (Pilot Books, 103 Cooper St., Babylon, NY 11702; phone: 516-422-2225; fax: 516-422-2227).

Take a Camel to Lunch and Other Adventures for Mature Travelers, by Nancy O'Connell (Bristol Publishing Enterprises, PO Box 1737, San Leandro, CA 94577; phone: 510-895-4461 in California; 800-346-4889 elsewhere in the US; fax: 510-895-4459).

Unbelievably Good Deals & Great Adventures That You Absolutely Can't Get Unless You're Over 50, by Joan Rattner Heilman (Contemporary Books, 1200 Stetson Ave., Chicago, IL 60601; phone: 312-782-9181; fax: 312-540-4687).

Organizations

American Association of Retired Persons (*AARP;* 601 E St. NW, Washington, DC 20049; phone: 202-434-2277).

Golden Companions (PO Box 754, Pullman, WA 99163-0754; phone: 208-858-2183).

Mature Outlook (Customer Service Center, 6001 N. Clark St., Chicago, IL 60660; phone: 800-336-6330).

National Council of Senior Citizens (1331 F St. NW, Washington, DC 20004; phone: 202-347-8800; fax: 202-624-9595).

Package Tour Operators

Elderhostel (75 Federal St., Boston, MA 02110-1941; phone: 617-426-7788; fax: 617-426-8351).

Evergreen Travel Service (4114 198th St. SW, Suite 13, Lynnwood, WA 98036-6742; phone: 800-435-2288 or 206-776-1184; fax: 206-775-0728).

Gadabout Tours (700 E. Tahquitz Canyon Way, Palm Springs, CA 92262; phone: 800-952-5068 or 619-325-5556; fax: 619-325-5127).

Grand Circle Travel (347 Congress St., Boston, MA 02210; phone: 800-221-2610 or 617-350-7500; fax: 617-423-0445).

Grandtravel (6900 Wisconsin Ave., Suite 706, Chevy Chase, MD 20815; phone: 800-247-7651 or 301-986-0790; fax: 301-913-0166).

Interhostel (*University of New Hampshire,* Division of Continuing Education, 6 Garrison Ave., Durham, NH 03824; phone: 800-733-9753 or 603-862-1147; fax: 603-862-1113).

Mature Tours (c/o *Solo Flights,* 63 High Noon Rd., Weston, CT 06883; phone: 800-266-1566 or 203-226-9993).

OmniTours (104 Wilmot Rd., Deerfield, IL 60015; phone: 800-962-0060 or 708-374-0088; fax: 708-374-9515).

Saga International Holidays (222 Berkeley St., Boston, MA 02116; phone: 800-343-0273 or 617-262-2262; fax: 617-375-5950).

Money Matters

CREDIT CARDS AND TRAVELER'S CHECKS

Most major credit cards enjoy wide domestic and international acceptance; however, not every hotel, restaurant, or shop in Chicago accepts all (or in some cases any) credit cards. It's also wise to carry traveler's checks while on the road, since they are widely accepted and replaceable if stolen or lost. You can buy traveler's checks at banks and some are available by mail or phone. Keep a separate list of all traveler's checks (noting those that you have cashed) and the names and numbers of your credit cards. Both traveler's check and credit card companies have international numbers to call for information or in the event of loss or theft.

CASH MACHINES

Automated teller machines (ATMs) are increasingly common worldwide, and most banks participate in international ATM networks such as *CIR-*

RUS (phone: 800-4-CIRRUS) and *PLUS* (phone: 800-THE-PLUS). Cardholders can withdraw cash from any machine in the same network using either a "bank" card or, in some cases, a credit card. Additional information on ATMs and networks can be obtained from your bank or credit card company.

SENDING MONEY

Should the need arise, you can have money sent to you in Chicago via the services provided by *American Express MoneyGram* (phone: 800-926-9400 for information; 800-866-8800 for money transfers) or *Western Union Financial Services* (phone: 800-325-6000 or 800-325-4176).

Time Zone

Chicago is in the central time zone. Daylight saving time is observed from the first Sunday in April until the last Sunday in October.

Business and Shopping Hours

Chicago maintains business hours that are fairly standard throughout the US: 9 AM to 5 PM, Mondays through Fridays. Although banks usually are open weekdays from 9 AM to 3 PM, many stay open until 5:30 or 6 PM at least one day a week and some also offer Saturday morning hours. Retail stores usually are open Mondays through Saturdays from 9:30 or 10 AM to 5:30 or 6 PM; many also are open on Sundays, usually from around 10 AM to 5 PM. Malls and larger department stores may stay open as late as 9 or 10 PM at least one day a week.

Mail

Chicago's main post office (433 W. Van Buren St., Chicago, IL 60607; phone: 312-765-3585) is open weekdays from 7 AM to 9 PM and Saturdays from 8 AM to 5 PM. Other conveniently located branches include the Loop Station post office (211 S. Clark St., Chicago, IL 60604; phone: 312-427-4225), which is open weekdays from 7 AM to 7 PM, and the Ontario Street Station (227 E. Ontario St., Chicago, IL 60611; phone: 312-642-7697), which is open weekdays from 8 AM to 6 PM. For other branches, call the main post office or check the yellow pages.

Stamps also are available at most hotel desks, some stores, and from public vending machines. For rapid, overnight delivery to other cities, use *Express Mail* (available at post offices), *Federal Express* (phone: 800-238-5355), or *DHL Worldwide Express* (phone: 800-225-5345).

You can have mail sent to you care of your hotel (marked "Guest Mail, Hold for Arrival") or to the main post office (sent "c/o General Delivery" to the address above). Some *American Express* offices in Chicago also will hold mail for customers ("c/o Client Letter Service"); information is provided in their pamphlet *Travelers' Companion.*

Telephone

The area code for Chicago is 312; the adjoining suburbs are in the 708 area code. To make a long-distance call, dial 1 + the area code + the local number. The nationwide number for information is 555-1212; you also can dial 411 for local information. If you need a number in another area code, dial 1 + the area code + 555-1212. (If you don't know the area code, dial 555-1212 or 411 for directory assistance.) The nationwide number for emergency assistance is 911.

Although you can use a telephone company calling card number on any phone, pay phones that take major credit cards (*American Express, MasterCard, Visa,* and so on) are increasingly common. Also available are combined telephone calling/bank credit cards, such as the *AT&T Universal Card* (PO Box 44167, Jacksonville, FL 32231-4167; phone: 800-423-4343). Similarly, *Sprint* (8140 Ward Pkwy., Kansas City, MO 64114; phone: 800-THE-MOST or 800-800-USAA) offers the *VisaPhone* program, through which you can add phone card privileges to your existing *Visa* card. Companies offering long-distance phone cards without additional credit card privileges include *AT&T* (phone: 800-CALL-ATT), *Executive Telecard International* (4260 E. Evans Ave., Suite 6, Denver, CO 80222; phone: 800-950-3800), *MCI* (323 Third St. SE, Cedar Rapids, IA 52401; phone: 800-444-4444; and 12790 Merit Dr., Dallas, TX 75251; phone: 800-444-3333), *Metromedia Communications* (1 International Center, 100 NE Loop 410, San Antonio, TX 78216; phone: 800-275-0200), and *Sprint* (address above).

Hotels routinely add surcharges to the cost of phone calls made from their rooms. Long-distance telephone services that may help you avoid this added expense are provided by a number of companies, including *AT&T* (International Information Service, 635 Grant St., Pittsburgh, PA 15219; phone: 800-874-4000), *MCI* (address above), *Metromedia Communications* (address above), and *Sprint* (address above). Note that even when you use such long-distance services, some hotels still may charge a fee for line usage.

Useful resources for travelers include the *AT&T 800 Travel Directory* (phone: 800-426-8686 for orders), the *Toll-Free Travel & Vacation Information Directory* (Pilot Books, 103 Cooper St., Babylon, NY 11702; phone: 516-422-2225; fax: 516-422-2227), and *The Phone Booklet* (Scott American Corporation, PO Box 88, W. Redding, CT 06896; no phone).

Medical Aid

In an emergency: Dial 911 for assistance, 0 for an operator, or go directly to the emergency room of the nearest hospital.

Hospitals

Michael Reese Hospital & Medical Center (29th Pl. and Cottage Grove; phone: 312-791-2000).

Northwestern Memorial Hospital (233 E. Superior St. at Fairbanks Ct.; phone: 312-908-5222).

Rush-Presbyterian St. Luke's Medical Center (1653 W. Congress Pkwy.; phone: 312-942-5000).

24-Hour Pharmacies

Walgreens: 757 N. Michigan Ave. (phone: 312-664-4000).

Walgreens: 1601 N. Wells (phone: 312-642-4008).

Additional Resources

International SOS Assistance (PO Box 11568, Philadelphia, PA 19116; phone: 800-523-8930 or 215-244-1500; fax: 215-244-2227).

Medic Alert Foundation (2323 Colorado Ave., Turlock, CA 95382; phone: 800-ID-ALERT or 209-668-3333; fax: 209-669-2495).

Travel Care International (*Eagle River Airport,* PO Box 846, Eagle River, WI 54521; phone: 800-5-AIR-MED or 715-479-8881; fax: 715-479-8178).

Legal Aid

If you don't have, or cannot reach, your own attorney, most cities offer legal referral services maintained by county bar associations. These services ensure that anyone in need of legal representation gets it and can match you with a local attorney. For legal assistance in Chicago, call the *Chicago Bar Association Lawyer Referral Service* (phone: 312-554-2001; fax: 312-554-2054). If you must appear in court, you are entitled to court-appointed representation if you can't obtain a lawyer or can't afford one.

For Further Information

Tourist information is available from the *Chicago Office of Tourism* (mailing address and walk-in *Visitor Information Center:* 78 E. Washington St., Chicago, IL 60602; phone: 800-487-2446 or 312-744-2400; fax: 312-744-2359; additional *Visitor Information Centers:* 77 E. Randolph St.; phone: 312-744-0528; and 806 N. Michigan; phone: 312-380-5748). Tourist information also can be obtained from the *Chicago Convention and Tourism Bureau* (2301 S. Lakeshore Dr., Chicago, IL 60616-1490; phone: 312-567-8500; fax: 312-567-8533). Through their automated "FaxBack" phone service (phone: 312-567-8528), you can have information on specific topics faxed to you.

The *Illinois Bureau of Tourism* (mail and phone inquiries only: *James R. Thompson Center,* 100 W. Randolph, Suite 3-400, Chicago, IL 60601; phone: 800-223-0121 or 312-814-4733; fax: 312-814-6175) also can provide information on Chicago. For other sources of local tourist information, see *Sources and Resources* in THE CITY.

The City

Chicago

Ask a resident if Chicago has a soul, and you're likely to be greeted with a laugh. The third-largest city in the country (the city proper has just under three million people; the metropolitan area, more than six million), Chicago carries a long-standing reputation as a tough meat-and-potatoes town—"Hog Butcher to the World," as Carl Sandburg sang—and locals refuse to acknowledge that there is a vibrant cultural and intellectual life here. One of the world's great cities, Chicago nonetheless suffers from an inferiority complex, one that stems from endless, inevitable comparisons to New York and, more recently, to Los Angeles, which has wrested away its "Second City" title.

In fact, there is a unique allure to Chicago. It is a vibrant, hip smorgasbord of theaters, award-winning restaurants, blues bars, museums, after-hours clubs, and world class hotels that stretch like a long, beckoning finger north along Lake Michigan, from the Loop (downtown Chicago's central business district) past Lincoln Park. It has inspired a Broadway musical, scores of stories and poems, and countless popular songs, and has been the subject of endless numbers of Hollywood films. All of which may seem especially ironic if you consider that nobody really knows whether the Indian word *checagou* means "great and powerful," "wild onion," or "skunk."

Chicago spreads along 29 miles of carefully groomed lakeshore. Respecting Lake Michigan, the people of Chicago have been careful not to destroy the property near the water with heavy manufacturing or industry. The lake is a source of water, as well as a port of entry for steamships and freighters coming from Europe via the St. Lawrence Seaway. Tens of millions of tons of freight are handled by Chicago's ports every year, and the city is still one of the world's largest railroad centers. The *Chicago Board of Trade* is the nation's most important grain market, and *O'Hare International,* its busiest airport.

Nuclear research and the electronics industry came of age here. In 1942, the world's first self-sustaining nuclear chain reaction was achieved at the *University of Chicago.* Half the radar equipment used during World War II was made here, too. Chicago is *Second City,* the comedy club that spawned John Belushi, Joan Rivers, and Bill Murray, among others. Chicago is *Wrigley Field* and the long-suffering *Cubs.* Chicago is the *Goodman Theatre* and the *Hubbard Street Dance Company* and the symphony and bold Helmut Jahn architecture. It is barbecued ribs and stuffed pizza, David Mamet and John Malkovich, Mike Royko and Oprah Winfrey. It is Buddy Guy wailing the blues.

People from all over the world have come here to live. In 1890, 80% of all Chicago residents were immigrants or children of immigrants. There are more Poles in Chicago than in any Polish city except Warsaw, as well as sizable contingents from Germany, Italy, Sweden, and Ireland. People talk about "ethnic Chicago," which means you can find neighborhoods that will make you think you're in a foreign country. Chinatown stretches along Wentworth Avenue. Little Saigon occupies several blocks of Argyle Street, and a Korean neighborhood fills West Lawrence Avenue. Enclaves of Ukrainians and Irish live on the southwest side. The Greeks can be found on South Halsted Street; Lithuanians around Marquette Park; Mexicans in Pilsen; and Italians in an area surrounded by the *University of Illinois at Chicago.* Polonia, which looks like a set for a 1930s Polish version of *West Side Story,* meanders mostly along Milwaukee Avenue. Nearly every nationality has a museum, and at least some of its customs have become public domain as well. There's a splendid array of inexpensive ethnic restaurants where you can get a whole meal for the price of an appetizer in a ritzier place.

This cosmopolitan center had unprepossessing beginnings. Jacques Marquette and Louis Joliet, the French explorers who provided the first record of the area, knew it as the Chicago Portage, one landmark on their route to Lake Michigan from the Mississippi. A trading post was established in 1679. In the 1812 Fort Dearborn Massacre, 53 people were killed by Indians. Eighteen years later, the first parcels of land were sold—$40 to $60 per 15,000-square-foot plot. The city, incorporated in 1837, began to look as if it might amount to something when the *Union Pacific Railroad* connected it to San Francisco in 1869; two years later, on October 8, 1871, it was in ashes. Burning at the rate of 65 acres per hour ($125,000 of damage per minute) and aided by a furious southwest wind, the Great Fire took 250 lives, made 90,000 homeless, melted 15,000 water service pipes, and left 1,688 acres in rubble. The total damage was estimated at $196 million.

As San Francisco would do after its 1906 earthquake, Chicago simply began to rebuild. And in the process, over the next 50 years, a new urban architecture was born. Building quickly and furiously upon four square miles of charcoal, and abetted by clients whose aesthetics derived from their interest in the profits to be gained from efficient buildings rather than the glory to be garnered from neoclassical palaces, Chicago architects *invented* the skyscraper. Frank Lloyd Wright then pioneered the ground-hugging, Prairie-style house that has become the prototype for the suburban, single-family dwelling units we know today. In 1909, architect Daniel Burnham laid out an elegant plan for the city, whose motto became *urbs in horto* ("city in a garden"). Today, 561 parks (including 32 clean public beaches) stretch across Chicago's 7,332 acres, and there are 66,993 acres of trail-crossed forest preserves on the city's outskirts.

That the beaches are still clean and the forest acreage still pretty much unspoiled is a credit to the city planners, who have, over the years, managed to keep Chicago vibrant even as other downtown areas around the country have declined. While buildings elsewhere were pulled down to make way for parking lots, Chicago built a handful of skyscrapers set on pedestrian plazas studded with magnificent pieces of sculpture by Alexander Calder, Marc Chagall, Pablo Picasso, Claes Oldenburg, Joan Miró, and others. Lively lunchtime programs keep the plazas thronged with sightseers and Loop office workers alike in the summer.

If you haven't seen Chicago for a while, you're likely to be astounded. During the 1980s, the city underwent the greatest building boom it had seen since the 1920s. Along the lakeshore, new apartment buildings testify to the growing number of wealthy Chicagoans who are returning to live downtown (it's the departure of the working class that accounts for the city's drop in population). In the Loop, new postmodern office buildings compete with the steel and glass towers of a generation ago and with the classics that gave Chicago its tradition of architectural distinction. The *Harold Washington Library Center,* built in 1991 and named for the former mayor, has added to the city's architectural reputation with its combination of Beaux Arts design and the powerful, heavy masonry that traditionally has characterized Chicago edifices. North Michigan Avenue has been transformed into an extensive—and exclusive—shopping strip. Lincoln Park, once sleepy and isolated, has reemerged as one of the nation's most intriguing residential neighborhoods—or a series of them, each with its own distinct character.

The changes aren't just in how the city looks, but also in how it feels about itself. No longer content with the "Second City" label, the directors of Chicago's major cultural attractions are putting on productions that do the city proud. As the nation's leading convention center, Chicago attracts large numbers of businesspeople. Its colleges and universities have long since shed a provincial image and can compete intellectually and academically with the best Eastern and Western schools. Even Chicago's politics have improved with age; though raucously inclined political reporters and incompetent aldermen still feed on each other, the city is run like a thoroughly modern metropolis rather than the fiefdom it once was.

So Chicago is quite a city, from its tony Gold Coast along the shore of Lake Michigan to its diverse ethnic neighborhoods; from the Rush Street bars to the shops and galleries of its Magnificent Mile. It's got the *Chicago Symphony Orchestra,* the *Lyric Opera,* and the *Art Institute,* with its world-famous collection of Impressionist and Postimpressionist paintings. It's got jazz and blues until the wee hours of the morning. And if it's the kind of place that makes you want to sing—well, you won't be the first.

Chicago At-a-Glance

SEEING THE CITY

The 110-story *Sears Tower* (Wacker and Adams Sts.; phone: 875-9696) maintains a *Skydeck* on the 103rd floor. It's open daily; admission charge (also see *Special Places*). For a view from the north, visit the *John Hancock*

Building (875 Michigan Ave.); the fifth-tallest building in the world, it's fondly nicknamed "Big John." On the 95th floor are a bar and restaurant (closed Saturday lunch; phone: 787-9596). The observation deck is open daily; admission charge (phone: 751-3681).

SPECIAL PLACES

A sophisticated public transport system makes it easy to negotiate Chicago's streets. You can explore the Loop, the lakefront, and suburbs by El train, subway, and bus (see *Getting Around*). In addition, Chicago's grid plan and street numbering system even make it easy for newcomers to find their way around. State Street is the north-south axis, Madison Street the east-west axis: 1200 North on any street is at Division Street; 800 West is at Halsted Street.

THE LOOP

The Loop generally refers to Chicago's central business district, which is circled by the elevated train known as the "El." (Also see *Walk 1: The Loop—A Heritage in Stone and Steel* in DIRECTIONS.)

ARCHICENTER The *Exhibition Gallery* has changing shows that span a wide range of architectural topics. Run by the *Chicago Architecture Foundation,* the *ArchiCenter* also offers a variety of tours. Guided walking tours of the Loop (and other neighborhoods) are conducted daily May through November, Fridays through Mondays the rest of the year. The "Chicago Highlights" bus tour is offered on Saturdays year-round. There's a charge for the tours. 224 S. Michigan Ave. (phone: 922-3432).

ART INSTITUTE OF CHICAGO El Greco's *Assumption of the Virgin,* Seurat's *A Sunday on La Grand Jatte–1884,* and Grant Wood's *American Gothic* are among the works in this museum's outstanding collections, which also include excellent Impressionist and Postimpressionist works, Japanese prints, Chinese sculpture and bronzes, European and American prints and drawings, decorative arts and sculpture, and more housed in the impressive *Rice Building.* The *American Galleries* are wonderfully conceived to show off the development of US culture; the Chagall stained glass windows and the *Trading Room,* from the old *Chicago Stock Exchange Building,* are not to be missed. The photography department is one of the most sophisticated facilities of its kind in the world. The renovated *Galleries of Modern Art 1900–1950* display outstanding examples of European and American art, including Edward Hopper's *Nighthawks,* Vincent Van Gogh's *Bedroom at Arles,* and Toulouse-Lautrec's *Ballet Dancers,* as well as one of the major Surrealist collections in the world. Open daily. Admission charge except on Tuesdays. Michigan Ave. at Adams St. (phone: 443-3600 or 443-3500 for recorded information).

AUDITORIUM THEATER Brilliant Chicago architect Louis Sullivan died penniless, but this 104-year-old landmark, one of his most important works, still stands.

Hand-painted murals and gold leaf abound here, and the interior—which houses a 2,412- to 3,661-seat theater (depending on the production), a hotel, and an office center—features 55 million pieces of mosaic tile. There's not a bad seat in the house. During World War II this theater was turned into a bowling alley, but a major fund-raising effort in the mid-1960s brought about a restoration. Now used for a variety of cultural functions, from stage plays to pop concerts, the theater's recent offerings have included such blockbusters as *The Phantom of the Opera* and *Les Misérables.* Tours are offered for groups of 10 or more, but individuals can join, if space is available. There's a charge for the tours. 50 E. Congress Pkwy. (phone: 922-4046 or 559-1212 for performance information).

CHICAGO BOARD OF TRADE The largest grain exchange in the world, this Art Deco treasure was built in 1930 and, half a century later, gained a new trading floor to accommodate expanding markets. Stand in the visitors' gallery and watch traders gesticulating on the floor, runners in colored jackets delivering orders, and an electronic record of all the trades displayed overhead. Free tours and a 15-minute movie run throughout the morning. Closed afternoons and weekends. No admission charge. 141 W. Jackson Blvd. at LaSalle St. (phone: 435-3590).

CHICAGO CULTURAL CENTER This 1897 Italian Renaissance–style building originally served as the *Chicago Public Library.* Its impressive interior, including green and white marble, elaborate mosaics, and a Louis Tiffany stained glass dome, is a fitting backdrop for a continuous schedule of dance performances, concerts, art exhibits, photography shows, lectures, and films. The city presents more than 500 free programs and exhibits at the center annually. The *Museum of Broadcast Communications* is also housed here (see below). Open daily. No admission charge. 78 E. Washington St. (phone: 346-3278 for recorded message; 744-6630 for general information).

CHICAGO MERCANTILE EXCHANGE AND INTERNATIONAL MONETARY MARKET The spectacle is much the same as at the *Board of Trade,* only here you can sit down. Opened in 1898 as the Butter and Egg Board, today more than 4,000 traders and staff crowd the trading floor daily. Visitors can watch the auction from a fourth floor gallery. Each commodity has its own opening and closing time. Free tours are available and must be scheduled in advance. Closed weekends. No admission charge. 30 S. Wacker Dr. (phone: 930-8249).

CHICAGO THEATER Restored to its 1920s splendor, this stage offers pop music concerts, contemporary dramas, and musicals against a Baroque backdrop of marble and crystal chandeliers. Even if you aren't going for the show, stop by for a look at its interior. 175 N. State St. (phone: 443-1130).

GRANT PARK A favorite spot for summer music festivals, the park, located south of Randolph Street (bordered by Randolph Street, Lake Shore Drive,

Michigan Avenue, and Roosevelt Road), offers an incredible view of the Chicago skyline. Near the intersection of Columbus Avenue and Congress Parkway, stop by the *Buckingham Fountain*, the world's largest lighted fountain—with a computerized 135-foot-high water display that spouts daily from May through September. The fountain was modeled after the *Latona Fountain* at *Versailles*, but it is twice the size; the formal gardens are just steps away. Between S. Michigan Ave. and Lake Shore Dr., south of Randolph St. (phone: 294-2307).

HAROLD WASHINGTON LIBRARY CENTER Named for the city's late Mayor Washington, it's the largest municipal library facility in the world (in square footage); it's also expansive and comfortable to use and chock-full of an amazing array of contemporary art. The ornamental rose-brick façade has received its share of criticism as well as praise, but it does add warmth to a dreary corner of the Loop. Across the street to the north is a lovely little park, its design inspired by a Magritte painting. Closed Sundays. 400 S. State St. (phone: 747-4999).

MARSHALL FIELD'S Chicago's most famous department store. When it was built in 1892—before electric lighting was common—it was designed in sections, with shopping areas on balconies overlooking a skylit central courtyard. Later, the skylights were covered, one with a vivid blue and gold Louis Tiffany mosaic visible by entering on the corner of Washington and State Streets. On the seventh floor is a marvelous food court, including the famed *Walnut Room* (a special treat at *Christmas*) and the *Crystal Palace*, which serves unbelievable ice cream sundaes (Frango mint ice cream—a subtle mix of coffee, chocolate, malt, and mint—is a tradition, as are its chocolate candies). Open daily. Wabash, State, Randolph, and Washington Sts. (phone: 335-7700).

MUSEUM OF BROADCAST COMMUNICATIONS This facility traces the city's role in the broadcast industry using an extensive tape library and exhibits. In the museum's *Kraft Television Theatre*, you can watch old commercials and vintage prime-time shows. On weekends, visitors to the museum's news center can "anchor" a newscast, then watch it on video (call ahead to reserve camera time). The museum's shop, *Commercial Break*, sells ABC Sports jackets and David Letterman T-shirts, along with other media-related items. Open daily. No admission charge. In the *Chicago Cultural Center*, 78 E. Washington St. (phone: 629-6000).

PRINTER'S ROW Architecture buffs will find a haven among the restored buildings, jazz and blues clubs, bookstores, and galleries just south of the Loop on South Dearborn Street and South Plymouth Court. The *Hyatt Printer's Row*, housed in a building on the National Register of Historic Places, also graces the area. Every June along South Dearborn Street and South Plymouth Court, there is a two-day *Printer's Row Book Fair* with exhibits dedicated to all aspects of printing and publishing. While in the neighborhood, stop for a drink or an elegant dinner at the *Printer's Row* restaurant (see *Eating Out*), or have a snack at the *Upfront* (161 W. Harrison St.; phone: 554-1991)—everything you always wanted in a sports bar and more, including a ticket service for local sporting events. Also a jazz spot, the spacious wood-floored *Upfront* has pool tables and dart boards, all housed in the elegant *Patten Building.* For more information about this area see *Walk 2: Printer's Row and South Loop* in DIRECTIONS.

NAVY DEVELOPMENT/SKYLINE STAGE THEATER At the beginning of this century, the *Navy Pier* was the place where Chicago families boarded boats for a summer outing. Long neglected, the pier is enjoying a renaissance, this time as a multipurpose development which includes the new, 1,500-seat *Skyline Stage Theater*, site of stage shows and concerts plus ballet performances and children's theater. Among the other additions to the complex—scheduled for completion this March—are the *Family Pavilion,* with shops and restaurants; a 15-story Ferris wheel; and a carousel. For theater tickets, phone *Ticketmaster* at 559-1212; for information on the pier, dial 791-PIER.

SEARS TOWER At 1,454 feet and 110 stories, it's the world's tallest building; it also boasts the world's fastest elevator (it travels more than 20 miles per hour and takes only 55 seconds to get to the 103rd floor). Some 16,500 people use the building each day. The tower, which consists of nine staggered square tubes, was completed in 1974. The arched glass entryway was added in 1985 and generated another of Chicago's seemingly endless architectural controversies. Some thought the plaza too stark without the addition; others, particularly architectural purists, thought it glitzed up a building that made a strong enough statement on its own. Check out the Calder *Universe* sculpture and see the ground-floor audiovisual show about Chicago before heading for the *Skydeck* on the 103rd floor. The *Skydeck* is open daily; admission charge. 233 S. Wacker Dr., between Adams St. and Jackson Blvd. (phone: 875-9696, *Skydeck*).

NEAR SOUTH SIDE

ADLER PLANETARIUM Exhibitions here include everything from surveying and navigating instruments to modern space exploration devices, plus a real moon rock and an antique instrument collection that is considered the best in the Western Hemisphere and one of the top three in the world. You can see it all before or after the sky show, which is the reason that most people come. There are new shows every six months, one for adults and one for children five years old and younger. Open daily. Admission charge for the sky shows only. 1300 S. Lake Shore Dr. on Museum Point (phone: 322-0304).

FIELD MUSEUM OF NATURAL HISTORY Not only do the outstanding collections of more than 19 million artifacts and specimens on more than nine acres make this one of the largest public museums in the US, but through ongoing field-work and basic research, the museum has become an international center for scientific study and public learning. The museum's public exhibitions have shifted over the years from conventional displays to a strategy of intro-ductory exhibits, major thematic exhibits, and resource centers. One of its most famous attractions is the pair of fighting elephants in the *Main Hall*. Other must-sees include the hands-on *Place for Wonder,* where youngsters can touch a fish skeleton from the dinosaur age and try on ethnic masks; the *Plants of the World Hall,* with reproductions of about 500 plants from around the globe; the full-scale model of a Pawnee earth lodge, where there are daily programs on Indian life; and a full-size, three-level ancient Egyptian tomb. The *Hall of Chinese Jade* and the display of Japanese lacquerware are also outstanding. Closed *Thanksgiving, Christmas,* and *New Year's Day*. Admission charge except on Thursdays. S. Lake Shore Dr. at Roosevelt Rd. (phone: 922-9410).

PRAIRIE AVENUE HISTORIC DISTRICT This area of 19th-century mansions along Prairie Avenue, between 18th and Cullerton Streets, is where Chicago's wealthy citizens once lived. The buildings that remain have been restored to their former elegance, and other historic buildings have been moved here. Standouts are the *Glessner House* (1800 S. Prairie Ave.), built by archi-tect H. H. Richardson in 1886, and the *Henry B. Clark House,* the city's old-est building, built in 1836. The *Chicago Architecture Foundation* (phone: 922-3432) runs tours of the homes every Wednesday, Friday, Saturday, and Sunday.

JOHN G. SHEDD AQUARIUM The largest aquarium in the world, it has more than 200 fish tanks and a collection of over 7,000 specimens: sturgeon from Russia, Bahamian angelfish, Australian lungfish, and a coral reef where divers feed the fish several times a day. The *Oceanarium* re-creates a Pacific Northwest coastal exhibit with whales, seals, dolphins, and otters. Closed *Christmas* and *New Year's Day*. Admission charge. Museum Point at 1200 S. Lake Shore Dr. (phone: 939-2426; 939-2438, *Oceanarium*).

NORTH MICHIGAN AVENUE

CHICAGO CHILDREN'S MUSEUM This hands-on museum for youngsters has an observation deck for viewing the city's skyline and a kid-size perspective of the city. Children can learn about architecture, try out a fully equipped mini-kitchen, and climb, ride, and fly—all at the same time—in a "Fantasy Vehicle." There is one room filled with nothing but Lego building blocks. Closed Mondays. Admission charge. 435 E. Illinois St., North Pier (phone: 527-1000).

MUSEUM OF CONTEMPORARY ART Lively changing exhibitions—retrospectives of contemporary artists as well as surveys of 20th-century art movements and avant-garde phenomena—are featured here. The museum also mounts shows by Chicago artists and sponsors symposia and other special events. Closed Mondays. Admission charge except on Tuesdays. 237 E. Ontario St. (phone: 280-5161).

PEACE MUSEUM The only one of its kind in the US, it features exhibits and special programs at a variety of sites throughout the city on issues related to war, peace, and nonviolence. Closed Sundays and Mondays. Admission charge. 350 W. Ontario St. (phone: 440-1860).

TERRA MUSEUM OF AMERICAN ART The permanent collection here reads like a *Who's Who in American Art* over the past two centuries, including works by Mary Cassatt, Winslow Homer, John Singer Sargent, William Merritt Chase, Samuel F. B. Morse, Edward Hopper, and Andrew Wyeth. Morse, inventor of the Morse code, painted the *Gallery of the Louvre,* a huge canvas recreating dozens of paintings from the *Louvre.* One of the few museums in the country dedicated solely to American art and artists, it also has visiting exhibits. Closed Mondays. Admission charge. 666 N. Michigan Ave. (phone: 664-3939).

WATER TOWER AND WATER TOWER PUMPING STATION Now landmarks, these distinctive matching castle-like structures are the only survivors of the Great Fire of 1871. The *Water Tower* (N. Michigan Ave. and Pearson St.), which masks a 135-foot-tall standpipe, now houses the *Chicago Office of Tourism* (see *Tourist Information,* below). Across Michigan Avenue is the *Water Tower Pumping Station* (803 N. Michigan Ave.), which now is the home of *Here's Chicago,* a multimedia show about the city. The show is presented daily except holidays; there's an admission charge (phone: 467-7114).

WATER TOWER PLACE This incredible, vertical shopping mall gets busier and better every year. Asymmetrical glass-enclosed elevators shoot up through a seven-story atrium, past shops selling dresses, books, and gift items, plus restaurants and a movie theater. Branches of *Marshall Field's, FAO Schwarz,* and *Lord & Taylor* are here, along with the lovely *Ritz-Carlton* hotel, reaching 20 stories above its 12th-floor lobby in the tower. The hotel's skylit *Greenhouse* is great for tea or cocktails after a hard day of shopping. N. Michigan Ave. at Pearson St.

NORTH SIDE

BIOGRAPH THEATRE A legend, although not as a theater; it was here in 1934 that the Lady in Red (Anna Sage) turned bank robber John Dillinger over to the federal agents who then shot him, ending a massive manhunt for the FBI's "Public Enemy No. 1." Today the theater shows foreign and contemporary films. 2433 N. Lincoln Ave. (phone: 348-4123).

CHICAGO ACADEMY OF SCIENCES This museum features particularly lively exhibitions about the natural history of the Great Lakes area; the reconstruction of a 300-million-year-old forest that once stood near the present site, complete with gigantic insects and carnivorous dragonflies, is especially interesting. A "walk-through" cave and canyon are other highlights. Closed *Christmas.* Admission charge except on Mondays. In *Lincoln Park* at 2001 N. Clark St. (phone: 549-0606).

CHICAGO HISTORICAL SOCIETY Pioneer crafts demonstrations and a slide show about the Chicago Fire make this one of the city's most fascinating museums. New galleries focus on Chicago's beginnings and explore 19th-century American life through furniture and decorative objects. Closed *Thanksgiving, Christmas,* and *New Year's Day.* Admission charge except on Mondays. N. Clark St. and North Ave. (phone: 642-4600).

GRACELAND CEMETERY Buried here are hotel barons, steel magnates, architects Louis Sullivan and Daniel Burnham—enshrined in tombs and miniature temples, and overlooking islands, lakes, hills, and other scenic views. The ranks of Chicago's rich and famous interred here also include George Pullman, inventor of the sleeper railcar, Cyrus McCormick, who invented the harvester, and merchant Marshall Field. The *Getty Tomb,* designed by Sullivan, is a must stop. On most Sundays in August, September, and October, the *Chicago Architecture Foundation* sponsors two-hour tours of the cemetery. There's a charge for the tour. Call the foundation in advance for details (phone: 922-3432). N. Clark St. and Irving Park Rd.

LILL STREET With more than 40 professional potters working in dozens of studios, this is the largest ceramics center in the Midwest. Visitors can watch the artisans or buy some of their work. *Lill Street* potters offer classes, including a one-day family clay workshop. 1021 W. Lill St. (phone: 477-6185).

LINCOLN PARK CONSERVATORY This botanical delight features changing floral displays and a magnificent permanent collection that includes orchids, a 50-foot African fiddle-leaf rubber tree with giant leaves, fig trees, and more ferns than you can shake a stick at. Closed *Christmas.* No admission charge. In *Lincoln Park,* Stockton Dr. at Fullerton Ave. (phone: 294-4770).

LINCOLN PARK ZOO The best thing about this zoo is that it has the largest group of great apes in captivity, all happily coexisting in a *Great Ape House.* There's also a *Lion House,* a *Bird House,* and the standard houses of monkey, tiger, bear, and bison, plus the zoo's popular farm. Next door, a building restored to its early 20th-century charm now houses the *Café Brauer* (phone: 294-4660), with a fine view of the park and the Chicago skyline, as well as an office for bike and skate rentals, a small cafeteria, and the *Ice Cream Shoppe,* which dishes out old-fashioned ice cream creations. Open daily. No admission charge. 2200 Cannon Dr., *Lincoln Park* (phone: 294-4660).

SOUTH SIDE

MUSEUM OF SCIENCE AND INDUSTRY Chicago's most popular attraction has computers to question, buttons to push, rides to ride, and much more. There are some 2,000 exhibitions in 75 major halls examining the principles of science and technology (as well as other subjects). High points: Colleen Moore's fairy castle of a dollhouse, and the Sears circus exhibit, full of dioramas of circus scenes, piped-in circus music, and a dynamic short film (the kind you want to sit through twice in a row). The working coal mine, the walk-through human heart, and the German *U-505* submarine are every bit as much fun as they always have been. And there also are exhibits on chemistry, physics, geology, the brain, the post office, anesthesiology, and the life sciences, as well as a *Business Hall of Fame* and an exciting section on computers. The *Henry Crown Space Center* features the *Omnimax Theater* and space exhibitions. (Be warned, it's a madhouse on weekends.) Closed *Christmas.* Admission charge except Thursdays. S. Lake Shore Dr. at E. 57th St. (phone: 684-1414).

ORIENTAL INSTITUTE MUSEUM This collection of art, archaeological artifacts, and textiles from the ancient Near East boasts a colossal statue of Tutankhamen and a winged bull with a human head from Assyria. Run by the *University of Chicago,* the museum offers guided tours and free films on Sunday afternoons. Closed Mondays. No admission charge. 1155 E. 58th St. (phone: 702-9521).

PULLMAN COMMUNITY Founded by George Pullman in 1880 as the nation's first company town, this early example of comprehensive urban planning is now a city, state, and national landmark. Walking tours conducted on the first Sunday of the month from May through October tell the story in detail; at other times, find the *Greenstone Church* and other important sites on maps available at the *Florence* hotel, a Pullman-era structure that serves as a visitors' center of sorts (and provides lunch on weekdays, breakfast and lunch on Saturdays, and brunch on Sundays). A number of the privately owned row houses are open for special tours held annually on the second weekend in October. West of the Dan Ryan Expwy. between 111th and 115th Sts. (phone: 785-8181). For more information, see *Walk 14: Pullman Historic District* in DIRECTIONS.

UNIVERSITY OF CHICAGO Guided walking tours of this illustrious university, founded in 1892 by John D. Rockefeller, include a stop at the *Robie House* (5757 S. Woodlawn Ave.), a fine example of the Prairie School of architecture, designed by Frank Lloyd Wright (as was its furniture) in 1909. The campus also has a marker commemorating the site of the world's first controlled atomic test in 1942 and *Rockefeller Chapel;* anecdotes about the chapel invariably involve famous statesmen, politicians, and celebrities. Free campus tours are conducted Mondays through Saturdays at 10 AM; call in advance for the meeting place. Also on campus is the *Smart Museum of Art,* a permanent collection that spans 5,000 years of Western and Asian art. The campus is in Hyde Park, a neighborhood bounded by Cottage Grove Ave., 55th St., Dorchester Ave., and 61st St. (phone: 702-8374).

WEST SIDE

GARFIELD PARK CONSERVATORY Here are four and a half acres under glass. The *Palm House* alone is 250 feet long, 85 feet wide, and 65 feet high; it looks like the tropics. There's a *Fernery* luxuriant with greenery, mosses, and pools of water lilies. The *Cactus House* has 85 genera, 400 species. At *Christmas,* poinsettias bloom; in February, azaleas and camellias; at *Easter,* lilies and bulb plants; and in November, mums. Open daily. No admission charge. 300 N. Central Park Blvd. (phone: 533-1281).

HALSTED STREET If you have time to get to know only one Chicago street, make it Halsted; locals claim that you could live your entire life perfectly well without ever leaving here. Spanning 20 miles of metropolitan Chicago—from 3766 North to 12961 South and on through West Pullman and Calumet—it boasts hundreds of restaurants, bars, and nightclubs; 30 churches; 50 liquor stores; and offbeat shops you won't find on Michigan Avenue. West of the Loop on Halsted Street is Chicago's Greektown area with restaurants such as the *Neon Greek Village* (310 S. Halsted St.; phone: 648-9800), offering great Greek food—and even belly dancing. Theaters also line some blocks of Halsted Street, as do jazz and blues bars. For more information, see *Walk 11: Halsted—The World on One Street* in DIRECTIONS.

HULL HOUSE Social welfare pioneer Jane Addams founded *Hull House* as a community service organization working for political reform and to improve garbage collection, to end sweatshops, and to protect abused children. Only two of the original *Hull House* buildings still exist, nestled into the modernist *University of Illinois* campus, with exhibits commemorating Addams, who was a peace activist, a humanitarian, and the first North American woman to win the Nobel Peace Prize. There are also exhibits commemorating her associates and the neighborhood they served. Closed Saturdays. No admission charge. 800 S. Halsted St. (phone: 413-5353).

MEXICAN FINE ARTS MUSEUM The first Mexican museum in the Midwest, and the largest in the country, pays tribute to the wide and varied Mexican culture with exhibits, theatrical performances, and workshops. The museum's gift shop specializes in Mexican folk art and multilingual publications. Closed Mondays. No admission charge. 1852 W. 19th St. (phone: 738-1503).

OUTSKIRTS

BROOKFIELD ZOO Some 200 acres divided by moats and natural-looking barriers make this one of the most modern zoos in the country. There is an indoor rain forest, special woods for wolves, a bison prairie, a replica of the Sahara, and a dolphin show. *Tropic World* features South American, Asian, and African birds, primates, and other animals. Open daily. Admission charge except on Tuesdays and Thursdays. 1st Ave. at 31st St. in Brookfield, 15 miles west of the Loop. Take Rte. 290 or I-55 to the 1st Ave. exit (phone: 242-2630 or 708-485-0263).

CHICAGO BOTANIC GARDEN This 300-acre collection of plants, trees, and shrubs from around the world is open year-round—except *Christmas Day.* Its special attractions include a three-island Japanese garden, a rose garden, 10 greenhouses, and a mile-long nature trail. There also is a tram tour of the gardens, an exhibit hall, a library, the *Museum of Floral Arts,* a gift shop, and a café. Admission charge to park your car, only. Half a mile east of the Edens Expwy. at Lake-Cook Rd. in Glencoe (phone: 708-835-5440).

FOX RIVER CASINOS Gambling has come to the Chicago area, if not yet to the city itself: A couple of cities along the Fox River on the Chicago area's western edge have welcomed the arrival of floating casinos—boats that cruise the river for two and a half hours once a group of gamblers is onboard. Sailings are scheduled throughout the day and night. In Aurora, *Hollywood Casino*, which offers slots, blackjack, craps, and poker, is open daily, all day (one of its half-dozen restaurants offers breakfast). There's an admission charge and reservations are necessary for the casino on weekends. The casino is docked in Aurora, 35 miles southwest of the Loop on I-88, along New York Street at the Fox River (phone: 708-801-7000). In the waters off Joliet, the *Empress River Casino* also offers the usual games of chance and numerous places to eat. Its sessions last two hours and departures are throughout the day. The casino is open daily; there's an admission charge. Reservations are necessary on weekend evenings. To get there, take I-55 south of Joliet to the Chanahon exit; the casino is docked along Empress Drive (phone: 815-744-9400).

FRANK LLOYD WRIGHT HOME AND STUDIO In Oak Park, approximately 10 miles west of the city, this home and studio, designed by the master himself, was the birthplace of the so-called Prairie School of architecture and is a fine example of that style. At the center of the home is a fireplace around which the rest of the rooms are spread. Wright, who was self-taught, also designed the furniture—perhaps in his two-story, octagon-shaped, cantilevered drafting room. Open daily. Admission charge. Guided tours are required. 951 Chicago Ave., Oak Park (phone: 708-848-1500). This is also the headquarters of the *Oak Park Tour Center,* which operates architectural walking tours of the town which is home to several other Wright buildings (see *Oak Park,* below).

LIZZADRO MUSEUM OF LAPIDARY ART Located 45 minutes from Chicago, its collection of Oriental jade carvings is one of the most extensive in the US. About 150 exhibits show off cameos, gemstones, minerals, and fossils. Closed Mondays. Admission charge except on Fridays. 220 Cottage Hill Rd., Elmhurst (phone: 708-833-1616).

MORTON ARBORETUM Sterling Morton ran a salt company ("when it rains, it pours"), but he was more fond of trees than salt (his birthday, April 26, is now recognized as Arbor Day), and therefore his niece established an arboretum in his name. A 1,500-acre living museum of roads and trails through an extraordinary array of flora—4,000 species at a recent count—its highlights include a Japanese garden, a prairie fragrance garden, a pinetum of conifers, dwarf shrubs, and every other kind of green that can be coaxed to grow in Illinois's harsh climate and clay soil. Open daily. Admission charge. Located about 25 miles west of downtown, easily accessible on I-88, where it intersects with Rte. 53 (phone: 708-719-2466).

OAK PARK Twenty-five buildings in this suburb, most of them remarkably contemporary looking, show the development of Frank Lloyd Wright's Prairie style of architecture. In addition to the architect's residence/workshop (see above), Wright's *Unity Temple* (875 Lake St., Oak Park; phone: 708-848-6225) is open to the public. There are daily tours (except on holidays); admission charge. The homes of Edgar Rice Burroughs and Ernest Hemingway (see *Museums*) are here, too, along with numerous gingerbread and turreted Queen Anne mansions. The *Oak Park Tour Center,* based in the *Frank Lloyd Wright Home and Studio,* operates most area walking tours as well as a visitors' center, where you can see photo exhibitions and take in an orientation program. At the *Wright Plus Festival,* the third Saturday in May, many private homes are open to the public. For more information, call the *Oak Park Visitor Center* (158 N. Forest St.; phone: 708-848-1500).

O'HARE INTERNATIONAL AIRPORT Opened in 1955, the world's busiest airport was named for Congressional Medal of Honor recipient Edward O'Hare, a navy pilot killed at the Battle of Midway. Nearly 57 million passengers pass through here annually. There are free 90-minute tours of the terminals and taxi-ways daily; for tour information, call the *Chicago Department of Aviation* (phone: 686-2300).

RAVINIA PARK In name, this park is a tribute to the little streams that wend their way through steep cliffs to Lake Michigan. In reputation, it's the place where musical talent, such as the *Chicago Symphony Orchestra* and *Peter, Paul & Mary,* is drawn from around the world for open-air concerts in the summer. Locals relish an evening on the 36-acre lawn to which they bring their own picnics, wine, and candles for one of Chicago's most sybaritic yet spiritual celebrations. There is also a variety of restaurants where visitors can carry out all that's needed for a memorable picnic under the stars or dine in style before taking their seats in the covered pavilion. Open June through *Labor Day.* Admission charge to the park; additional charge for pavilion seats only. Reservations advised for pavilion seats. Located on Green Bay and Lake-Cook Roads in Highland Park, it's about an hour's drive from the city. Take Edens Expwy., then Rte. 41, north to the Ravinia exit; better yet, take the 40-minute ride on *Metra's* Northwestern line, which has a stop right in the park (phone: 728-4642).

SIX FLAGS GREAT AMERICA An extravagant roller coaster and a double-tiered carousel are the highlights of this theme park featuring more than 130 rides, shows, and attractions. Musical shows are performed throughout the season, and there's a giant participatory play area for kids, complete with merry-go-rounds and rides. It also is home to the world's largest *IMAX* movie theater. Open weekends only in May and September; open daily *Memorial Day* through *Labor Day*. Admission charge. Located one hour and fifteen minutes from Chicago, it is off I-94 at Rte. 132 in Gurnee (phone: 708-249-1776).

EXTRA SPECIAL

You don't have to go very far from downtown to reach the North Shore suburbs. Take Sheridan Road north through the lovely old suburbs of Evanston and Winnetka, or follow US 41 or I-94 north. US 41 goes through Lake Forest, an exquisite residential area, and Lake Bluff, site of the *Great Lakes Naval Station.* Along the way, there are several excellent restaurants, especially *Carlos'* (see *Eating Out*) and *Froggy's* (306 Green Bay Rd., Highwood; phone: 708-433-7080). In the working class town of Waukegan, *Mathon's* seafood restaurant has been delighting seafood addicts since before World War II (from Sheridan Rd. turn east on Mathon St., then one block south to Clayton St.; phone: 708-662-3610; closed Mondays). A few miles north on Sheridan Road is the *Illinois Beach State Park,* with a nature refuge offering miles and miles of unspoiled beach (Sheridan and Wadsworth Rds., Zion; phone: 708-662-4811). Heading inland from Waukegan on Route 120 leads directly to lake country. Although the area is not a state park, there are many lakes in the region after Route 120 becomes Route 134. Three large lakes near the Wisconsin border—Fox, Pistakee, and Grass—offer water sports, fishing, golf, and tennis. Right on the Wisconsin border, the 4,900-acre *Chain O'Lakes State Park* has campsites and boat rentals. Pick up Wilson Road north at Long Lake, which is on Route 134, then take Route 132 past Fox Lake. This leads to US 12, which runs to Spring Grove and the state park (phone: 708-587-5512).

Sources and Resources

TOURIST INFORMATION

The *Chicago Visitor Information Center,* in the historic *Water Tower* (N. Michigan Ave. and Pearson St., Chicago, IL 60611; phone: 567-8500), distributes a downtown map that pinpoints major attractions and hotels. You also may get information from the *Chicago Office of Tourism* (310 S. Michigan Ave.; phone: 744-2400). For information on Illinois, contact the state hotline (phone: 800-223-0121). The *Mayor's Office of Special Events* provides information on listings of special events (phone: 744-3315).

LOCAL COVERAGE Chicago's newspapers are the *Sun-Times* and the *Tribune;* both are morning dailies. Other local publications include the *Reader*, a weekly newspaper that has the most complete listing of events and reliable event reviews, and *Chicago* magazine, a monthly whose section of restaurant reviews is the most up-to-date local source on where and what to eat. Also useful are the following *Chicago Transit Authority* brochures, available at El and subway stations: the *Chicago Street Directory,* which locates streets by their distance from State Street or Madison Street; the *CTA Route Map* of bus, subway, and El routes; and the *CTA Downtown Transit Map.*

TELEVISION STATIONS WBBM Channel 2–CBS; WMAQ Channel 5–NBC; WLS Channel 7–ABC; WGN Channel 9–superstation; WTTW Channel 11–PBS; WFLD Channel 32–Fox.

RADIO STATIONS AM: WMAQ 670 (news); WGN 720 (talk/sports); WBBM 780 (news); WLUP 1000 (rock). FM: WBEZ 91.5 (public radio for Chicago); WNUA 95.5 (smooth jazz); WBBM 96.3 (talk/news); WLUP 97.9 (rock); WFMT 98.7 (classical); WKQX 101.1 (classic rock); WGCI 107.5 (pop/rap).
   Chicago also has four 24-hour Spanish language stations: WOJO 105.1 FM and AM stations WIND 560, WOPA 1200, and WTAQ 1300.

TELEPHONE The area code for Chicago is 312. The area code for all of Chicago's suburbs is 708. Unless otherwise indicated, the telephone numbers in this chapter take the 312 area code.

SALES TAX City sales tax is 9%, and there is a 14.9% hotel tax.

GETTING AROUND

BUS, SUBWAY, AND EL *Chicago Transit Authority* operates bus, subway, and El services (phone: 836-7000). The basic fare is $1.50 (there are discounts for off-hour trips and for seniors). Packs of 10 tokens are available at most currency exchanges and cost only $12.50.

CAR RENTAL For information on renting a car, see GETTING READY TO GO.

TAXI Cabs can be hailed in the street or picked up at stands in front of the major hotels. You also can call one of Chicago's taxi services: *American United* (phone: 248-7600); *Flash Cab* (phone: 561-1444); or *Yellow and Checker Cabs* (phone: TAXI-CAB).

TOURS To explore on your own, follow the walking tours in this guide outlined in DIRECTIONS. For an aerial view of Chicago, there are helicopter tours, including sunset flights, run by *Head West Sky Operations* (at *Waukegan Regional Airport;* phone: 708-546-3333). For a river view, *Mercury Cruise Line* (phone: 332-1353), *Odyssey Cruises* (phone: 708-990-0800), and *Wendella Sightseeing Boats* (phone: 337-1446) offer boat trips on the Chicago River and Lake Michigan daily from mid-April through mid-October. A charter craft, *Engine Company #41,* runs sightseeing excursions on a 92-foot fireboat; call the *Chicago Fire Boat Cruise Company* (phone: 579-1988). The *Spirit of Chicago,* at *Navy Pier* (455 E. Illinois St.; phone: 836-7899), has dining, dancing, and moonlight cruises, as well as narrated tours. Other sightseeing cruise lines include *A Admiral's Sight-Seeing Cruise Line* (641-7245), *Chicago from the Lake* (phone: 527-2002), and *Shoreline Sightseeing* (phone: 222-9328).

At street level, try the *Chicago Architecture Foundation*'s bus tour of important architectural sites (phone: 922-3432). The *Historic Pullman Foundation* offers tours of the landmark district where the *Pullman Railroad* built offices and housing for its workers in the 19th century. Several private firms offer bus tours around Chicago; call *American Sightseeing Tours* (phone: 427-3100), the *Chicago Gray Line* (phone: 427-3107), and the *Chicago Motor Coach Company* (phone: 922-8919). There's also a do-it-yourself tour by public bus. The No. 151 bus route starts in the Loop, goes through *Lincoln Park,* past the *Historical Society,* and into New Town. When you've had your fill, get off and catch the same bus going in the opposite direction. *Untouchable Tours* (phone: 881-1195) offers a two-hour bus ride through neighborhoods once frequented by Chicago's notorious gangsters. Tours depart from the *Water Tower Pumping Station* (in winter, tours are held only on Wednesdays and weekends). *Chicago Supernatural Tours* (708-499-0300) offers tours of lurid and legendary sites, including haunted houses, sites of notorious murders, and gangster hideouts.

If a horse and buggy ride strikes your fancy, contact *J. C. Cutters,* which has a carriage stand at the corner of Superior Street and Michigan Avenue (phone: 664-6014); or *Antique Coach and Carriage* (700 N. Michigan Ave.; phone: 735-9400). For a guided tour that highlights Chicago's literary and cultural history, call Leah Axelrod's *My Kind of Tour* (PO Box 924, Ravinia Station, Highland Park, IL 60035; phone: 708-432-7003).

The *Chicago Architecture Foundation (CAF)* conducts about 50 different architectural tours of the city. The *CAF* Saturday bus tours depart from 224 South Michigan Avenue (phone: 922-3432). The four-hour tours may be booked in advance, although walk-in visitors are accepted if space is available. There are also boat tours of the Chicago River from May through October. Days and times vary and some weekday tours are included, so it is best to call for a schedule (phone: 527-1977). The 90-minute tours leave from North Pier (phone: 922-TOUR for recorded information). For self-guided walking tours, see Ira J. Bach's architecturally oriented *Chicago on Foot* (Chicago Review; $16.95), as well as *Chicago Access* (HarperCollins; $18). For ethnic areas, we recommend *Chicago, City of Neighborhoods* by Dominic A. Pacyga and Ellen Skerrett (Loyola University; $22.95).

TRAIN *Metra* (phone: 322-6900) offers commuter service between the city and its suburbs. Trains depart from the *North Western Station* (500 W. Madison St.) to the north and northwest suburbs; from *Union Station* (210 S. Canal St.) to the west and southwest suburbs; and from the *Randolph Street Station* (151 E. Randolph St.) and the *LaSalle Street Station* for the south suburbs (phone: 322-6777). *Amtrak* (phone: 800-872-7245) departs from *Union Station.*

LOCAL SERVICES

AUDIOVISUAL EQUIPMENT *Audio Visual Systems* (phone: 733-3370).

BABY-SITTING Check at your hotel or contact the following: *American Child Care* (505 N. Lake Shore Dr., Suite 203; phone: 644-7300), with licensed and insured baby-sitters who will care for children in a hotel suite or accompany youngsters over the age of 12 to museums and parks; or *Nanny's Sitting Service* (103 Fern St., Island Lake; phone: 708-526-2853), which charges hourly for child care in the northern suburbs.

BARBERS *Frank's Barber Shop* (in the *Monadnock Building* at the corner of Van Buren and Federal Sts.; phone: 922-0904) and *Truefitt & Hill* (*900 North Michigan Avenue,* Sixth Floor; phone: 337-2525).

BUSINESS SERVICES *International Office Centers* (203 N. LaSalle St., Suite 2100; phone: 346-2030).

DRY CLEANERS *Downtown Cleaners* (331 S. LaSalle St.; phone: 939-3718; and 407 S. Peoria St.; phone: 733-8174); *King Cleaners & Tailors* (16 E. Delaware Pl.; phone: 337-3896); *Pronto One-Hour Cleaners* (1700 W. Madison St.; phone: 666-8943); and *Sewing Express Cleaners & Alterations* (803 W. Randolph St.; phone: 226-3110). Most hotels offer dry-cleaning service, too.

EYEGLASS REPAIR/REPLACEMENT *American Vision Center* (10 N. Michigan Ave.; phone: 346-0222; and 540 N. Michigan Ave.; phone: 644-0885); *Eyelines* (300 W. Washington Blvd.; phone: 236-6460); *LensCrafters* (205 N. Michigan Ave.; phone: 819-0205); and *Pearle Vision Center* (134 N. LaSalle St.; phone: 372-3204; and 350 N. Michigan Ave.; phone: 726-8255).

LIMOUSINES *Airport Express Limousine Service* (phone: 227-1000) is available around the clock.

MECHANICS/ROAD SERVICE *B's Brothers Automotive and Towing* (2901 N. Clybourn Ave.; phone: 787-2266) and *Wells Automotive Service* (1317 N. Wells; phone: 944-9388).

MEDICAL EMERGENCY For information on area hospitals and pharmacies, see GETTING READY TO GO.

MESSENGER SERVICES *Cannonball Messenger Service* (phone: 829-1234) and *Chicago Messenger Service* (phone: 666-6800).

PHOTOCOPIES/FACSIMILES *Aims Copy Services* (69 W. Washington Blvd.; phone: 332-2604) and *Modern Impressions* (123 W. Madison St.; phone: 368-8445). In addition, *Kinko's* has many sites in the city, some of which are open 24 hours a day. Check the phone book for exact locations.

PHOTOFINISHING *Fromex One-Hour Photo System* (188 W. Washington Blvd.; phone: 853-0067) and *Magna One-Hour Photo* (540 N. Michigan Ave.; phone: 527-0776).

POST OFFICES For information on local branch offices, see GETTING READY TO GO.

PROFESSIONAL PHOTOGRAPHERS *Photo Ideas* (phone: 666-3100) and *Stuart-Rodgers-Reilly Photographers* (phone: 787-8696).

SECRETARIES/STENOGRAPHERS *International Office Center* (phone: 346-2030). Many hotels have business centers as well.

SHOE REPAIR *Bee Hive Shoe Works* (1 N. Dearborn St.; phone: 236-4837; 11 N. Wells St.; phone: 263-4888; 320 N. Michigan Ave.; phone: 419-8444; and 79 E. Madison St.; phone: 419-1660) and *Sam the Shoe Doctor* (162 W. Van Buren Blvd.; phone: 939-9571; 132 S. Franklin St.; phone: 332-9390; 101 W. Adams St.; phone: 332-8528; and *Sears Tower,* lower level at Franklin St.; phone: 876-9001).

SHOESHINE *Frank's Barber Shop* and *Truefitt & Hill* (see *Barbers*).

TRANSLATORS *Berlitz* (phone: 782-7778); *Chicago-European Language Center* (phone: 276-6683); and *Joan Masters & Sons* (phone: 787-3009).

WESTERN UNION/TELEX Telegrams (phone: 800-325-6000 to find the location nearest you). For information on money transfers, see GETTING READY TO GO.

OTHER *A.S.A.P. Word Processing* (phone: 558-9333); *Business Center* (in the *O'Hare Hilton* phone: 686-0400) for desk space and typewriters, conference rooms, photocopying; and *H.Q. Headquarters Company* (phone: 214-3500) for word processing, telex, facsimile, conference rooms.

SPECIAL EVENTS

Chicago is a city of year-round festivals, and every season brings a variety of shows and celebrations, many with a special ethnic or cultural focus. If no information number is given for a particular event, call the city's *Department of Special Events* (phone: 744-3315) for up-to-the-minute details.

The first ethnic celebration of the year is *Chinese New Year* in late January or early February, when all Chinatown turns out for its dragon parade, fireworks, and other festivities.

February brings the *Chicago Folk Festival,* sponsored by the *University of Chicago* and featuring folk music, arts, crafts, and food (phone: 702-9793). February is also *Black History Month,* which is celebrated with special exhibits at the *DuSable Museum* and other cultural institutions.

In March, the entire city plunges wholeheartedly into *St. Patrick's Day,* even dyeing the river green for the occasion. The official *St. Patrick's Day Parade,* which runs along Dearborn Avenue from Wacker Drive to Van Buren Boulevard, is held on March 17 (phone: 263-6612). On the Saturday closest to March 17, there is the separate *South Side Irish St. Patrick's Day Parade* (phone: 238-1969).

April brings the *Easter Flower Shows,* held at both the *Lincoln Park Conservatory* and the *Garfield Park Conservatory* (phone: 294-4770). In heavily Mexican Pilsen, *Easter* is observed with a reenactment of Christ's walk to Golgotha on *Good Friday.* In May, the same neighborhood holds a *Cinco de Mayo* (Fifth of May) festival celebrating Mexico's successful (if only temporary) repulsion of invading French forces in 1862. Downtown on the first weekend of May, three international art expositions attract dealers from around the world; and the *International Theater Festival,* also in May, draws top international and domestic productions.

In June, the festival season gets into full swing with the two-day *Gospel Festival,* followed a week later by the *Chicago Blues Festival,* both in *Grant Park* (phone: 744-3315). June also brings the *Old Town Art Fair,* which fills block after block of charming Lincoln Park residential streets with artists and craftspeople selling their wares. On *Father's Day,* it's time for the *Printer's Row Book Fair,* when hundreds of new and used book dealers line the streets of the South Loop.

The week-long *Taste of Chicago* begins in June and ends on July 3 with an immense fireworks display. Restaurateurs fill several acres of *Grant Park* with booths offering samples of their wares, and popular radio stations broadcast the nearly continuous music performed on stages up and down the main thoroughfare. The *Chicago Country Music Festival* adds to the festivities, which end with a rousing *Fourth of July* celebration, when the *Grant Park Symphony Orchestra* performs the "1812 Overture" accompanied by a dazzling fireworks display.

Another event during *Fourth of July* weekend is the *Motorola Western Open Golf Tournament* (phone: 708-724-4600) at Cog Hill in suburban Lemont. Mid-July brings the *Air and Water Show,* which features a display of precision flying; the best place to watch it is North Avenue Beach.

In August, lovely old *Oz Park* (so named because *Wizard of Oz* writer Frank Baum lived there) gives a party that's geared toward children. Other August events are the *Gold Coast Art Fair,* now held in the River North gallery district; the *Venetian Night* parade of colorfully lighted boats through Monroe Street Harbor; the *Bud Billiken Day Parade,* a noisy and joyful celebration of the city's African-American community, held on the South Side (phone: 225-2400); and the *Midwest Buddhist Temple Ginza Holiday,* held in Old Town. On the turf course at *Arlington International Racecourse,* the world's top thoroughbreds compete in the prestigious and colorful *Arlington Million* (phone: 708-255-4300).

Highlights of *Labor Day* weekend include the *Chicago Jazz Festival;* performers at the four-day event have included Ray Charles, Miles Davis, and Ella Fitzgerald (phone: 744-3370). Later in September, *"Viva! Chicago,"* a two-day celebration of Latin music, attracts lovers of salsa, merengue, mambo, and samba to *Grant Park* (phone: 744-3315). There's also a celebration modeled after the German *Oktoberfest,* sponsored by the *Berghoff* restaurant (phone: 427-3170) and held on Adams Street from State Street to Dearborn Avenue. During the last weekend of the month, the *Latino Film Festival* runs for 10 days at theaters around the city. Call for locations and film listings (phone: 431-1330 or 935-5744).

October features the last of the year's major parades, on *Columbus Day* in the Loop. This is also the month when the city hosts a two-week *International Film Festival,* an annual tradition since 1965. Various theaters on the North Side screen the long list of films (phone: 644-3400).

November marks the start of the *Michigan Avenue Holiday Lights Festival* (from the Saturday before *Thanksgiving* through December 31); processions of horse-drawn carriages and fireworks add to the festivities along the Magnificent Mile, which glows with holiday lights. During the holiday season, State Street windows get dressed up and the *Goodman Theatre* (phone: 443-3800) presents its now-classic *Christmas Carol.* And, finally, December brings the *Nutcracker* ballet to the *Arie Crown Theater* at *McCormick Place* (phone: 791-6000).

MUSEUMS

In addition to those described in *Special Places,* other museums of interest include the following:

BALZEKAS MUSEUM OF LITHUANIAN CULTURE This unique museum has dolls, textiles, folk art, antique weapons, and a hands-on children's museum. Open daily. Admission charge. 6500 S. Pulaski Rd. (phone: 582-6500).

DUSABLE MUSEUM OF AFRICAN-AMERICAN HISTORY Chicago more than likely is the country's only major city whose first permanent resident was of African descent. Set in the South Side's *Washington Park,* the museum is named after Jean-Baptiste Point duSable, a fur trader from Haiti who settled on the banks of the Chicago River in 1789. Among the museum's major features are a 10-foot-high carved mahogany mural depicting highlights of African-American history; there also is a large display of African artifacts. Among the changing exhibits are depictions of life in the Caribbean. Open daily. Admission charge. 57th St. at S. Cottage Grove (phone: 947-0600).

ERNEST HEMINGWAY MUSEUM Located in suburban Oak Park where the author was born and raised, the museum mounts major exhibitions on Hemingway's life and times and work. Closed Mondays, Tuesdays, Thursdays, and Fridays. Admission charge. 200 N. Oak Park Ave. (phone: 708-848-2222).

MUSEUM OF HOLOGRAPHY More than 150 three-dimensional images created by lasers are displayed. Closed Mondays and Tuesdays. Admission charge. 1134 W. Washington Blvd. (phone: 226-1007).

POLISH MUSEUM OF AMERICA Offers 350 paintings by Polish and Polish-American artists, costumes, and a 30,000-volume library. Closed *Christmas Eve* and *Christmas Day.* No admission charge. 984 N. Milwaukee Ave. (phone: 384-3352).

SPERTUS MUSEUM OF JUDAICA A collection that spans 3,500 years of Jewish history, plus special temporary exhibitions. Closed Saturdays, Jewish holidays, and some federal holidays. Admission charge. 618 S. Michigan Ave. (phone: 922-9012).

SWEDISH-AMERICAN MUSEUM Historic documents plus works of famous Swedish artists, including Carl Larson and Anders Zorn; at *Christmas,* there is a traditional Swedish *Festival of Lights* complete with candles, *Christmas* decorations, and songs. Closed Mondays. Admission charge except for children under 12. 5211 N. Clark St. (phone: 728-8111).

UKRAINIAN NATIONAL MUSEUM A large collection of folk art, including Ukrainian ceramics, *Easter* eggs, and costumes. Closed Mondays through Wednesdays. Admission charge. 2453 W. Chicago Ave. (phone: 276-6565).

In addition, great sculpture and art can be seen in the plazas of downtown skyscrapers: Harry Bertoia's spellbinding *Sounding Sculpture,* at the *Standard Oil Building* (200 E. Randolph St.); *Flamingo,* a stabile by Alexander Calder, at Federal Center Plaza (Adams and Dearborn Sts.); Calder's gaily colored mobile *Universe,* in the *Sears Tower* lobby (Wacker Dr. and Adams St.); sculptor Claes Oldenburg's 101-foot-high baseball bat, *Batcolumn* (600 W. Madison St.); Marc Chagall's *Four Seasons* mosaic, at First National Plaza (Monroe and Dearborn Sts.); and *Chicago's Picasso* (its formal title because no one could agree on a name), a giant sculpture on the Richard J. Daley Plaza (Washington and Clark Sts.). For more information see *Walk 1: The Loop—A Heritage in Stone and Steel* in DIRECTIONS.

And don't miss Chicago's roof art. There are four wind-powered sculptures, each weighing more than a ton, atop the city's *Sporting Club* (211 N. Stetson St. near the *Fairmont* hotel). *Children of the Sun,* by Japanese artist Shingu, is made of stainless-steel pipe and punched metal.

MUSIC TO MUNCH BY

If you're at Richard J. Daley Plaza (on Washington and Clark Sts.) at lunchtime, you might catch a free concert. There are noon music and dance performances under the giant *Chicago's Picasso* sculpture two or three days a week from June through September, weather permitting (phone: FINE-ART or 346-3278 for schedule information).

MAJOR COLLEGES AND UNIVERSITIES

The *University of Chicago,* known for its economics and social science departments, has its main entrance at 5801 South Ellis Avenue (phone: 753-1234). Other institutions of higher education include: *De Paul University* (25 E. Jackson Dr. and in Lincoln Park at 2323 N. Seminary Ave.; phone: 341-8000); *Illinois Institute of Technology* (3300 S. Federal St.; phone: 567-3000); *Loyola University* (820 N. Michigan Ave.; phone: 915-6000; and 6525 Sheridan Rd.; phone: 274-3000); *Northwestern University* (Chicago Ave. and Lake Shore Dr.; phone: 908-8649; and in Evanston; phone: 708-491-3741); *Roosevelt University* (430 S. Michigan

Ave.; phone: 341-3500); and the *University of Illinois at Chicago* (601 S. Morgan St.; phone: 996-3000). In addition, there are dozens of private colleges throughout the city's suburbs.

SHOPPING

Some of Chicago's best sights are indoors, along the aisles of the city's many shops and department stores. While Los Angeles boasts Rodeo Drive and New York has Fifth Avenue, in Chicago the chic shopping district is known as the Magnificent Mile, the blocks along North Michigan Avenue between the Chicago River and Oak Street. Along the Magnificent Mile is *900 North Michigan Avenue,* an enclosed mall of elegant stores; a block away is *Water Tower Place,* another elegant indoor shopping center; and *Chicago Place,* an eight-level enclave of upscale shops, is at 700 North Michigan Avenue. Oak Street, just west of Michigan Avenue, is lined with international designer shops. State Street in the Loop is the setting for *Marshall Field's. T. J. Maxx, Filene's Basement,* and *Toys R Us* are also on this famed shopping street.

North Pier Chicago, a renovated multi-use building that was formerly a shipping terminal, has three floors filled with dozens of unusual shops and restaurants as well as museums and gamerooms. Locals looking for fine jewelry at good prices head for the *Mallers Building* (5 N. Wabash St.), which features 16 floors of retail and wholesale jewelry stores. And Hyde Park, a neighborhood near the *University of Chicago,* is the place for bookworms.

Avid shoppers also trek to the River North district's boutiques (north of the river, west of LaSalle St.); the Armitage Avenue/Halsted Street/Sheffield Avenue shops; the stores along Clark Street (in the Fullerton area); and the *Century Mall* (Diversey Pkwy./Clark St.), which was once a movie theater. The *Merchandise Mart,* between Orleans and Wells Streets and the Chicago River, has stores from many of the national chains. (For a list of the city's top antiques shopping areas, see *Antiques: Chicago's Best Hunting Grounds* in DIVERSIONS.) Here are some of our favorite Windy City shops.

Accent Chicago Every item in stock has "Chicago" imprinted on it—and we mean everything. *Water Tower Place,* Level 7 (phone: 944-1354); *Sears Tower* (phone: 993-0499); and the *Chicago Hilton and Towers* (phone: 360-0115).

Archicenter Although this is actually the museum/office for the *Chicago Architecture Foundation,* it has one of the most complete gift shops for those seeking architecture-theme souvenirs. Its book collection is especially impressive. *Santa Fe Bldg.,* 224 S. Michigan Ave. (phone: 922-3431/2).

Avventura Some of the showiest men's shoes anywhere, plus more traditional footwear, ties, and belts. It's worth a trip here just to see the giant black cowboy boots with the red bull on front and No. 23 on back, custom designed for Michael Jordan. *Water Tower Place,* Level 4 (phone: 337-3700).

Bloomingdale's The Midwest flagship store for this legendary New York retailer has six floors of merchandise plus four spas and two restaurants. The Art Deco touches are a plus. *900 North Michigan Avenue* (phone: 440-4460).

Bogner A branch of the German retailer specializing in high-end ski wear, cashmere, and leather goods. 56 E. Oak St. (phone: 664-6466).

Bottega Veneta Fine Italian leather items, carefully crafted and tastefully displayed. Everything from luggage to desk accessories, plus a small selection of women's shoes and scarves. 107 E. Oak St. (phone: 664-3220).

Branca Elegant home furnishings, from picture frames to linen; many items are hand-painted by the owner. 65 W. Illinois St. (phone: 822-0751).

C. D. Peacock Founded the same year as the city itself, in 1837, this store has purveyed silver, crystal, jewelry, and fine china to Chicagoans ever since. With chandeliers, fine cabinetry, and bronze peacock doors, it's known for its service (and for its expert repair shop). In *Northbrook Court* on Lake-Cook Rd., Northbrook (phone: 708-564-8030).

Carson Pirie Scott and Company You can't get any more Chicago than this department store, whose Windy City tradition stretches back more than 130 years. Even if you aren't in a spending mood, stop by to see the elegant building designed at the turn of the century by architect Louis Sullivan (note the distinctive iron ornamentation on the northwest corner). 1 S. State St. (phone: 641-7000).

Cartier The Midwest outpost of the fine French jeweler. 630 N. Michigan Ave. (phone: 266-7440).

Chanel Classic clothes and accessories from this world-famous name. 940 N. Michigan Ave. (phone: 787-5500).

Chiasso Euro-design (largely Italian and contemporary) in fine home furnishings and gifts. *Chicago Place,* 700 N. Michigan Ave. (phone: 642-2808); 231 S. LaSalle St. (phone: 357-0437); and 303 W. Madison St. (phone: 419-1121).

City of Chicago The place for memorabilia and souvenirs, this store carries everything from tote bags to a Chicago manhole cover to the ever-popular Chicago street signs. Pick up one in stock or special order a custom-made sign. 435 E. Illinois St. (phone: 467-1111).

Crate & Barrel Ten Chicago area stores that purvey everything for the home, from pie plates to pine furniture. The flagship store is a knockout at 646 N. Michigan Ave. (phone: 787-5900).

Elements The last word in designer housewares and jewelry by international artisans. 738 N. Wells St. (phone: 642-6574).

Famous Fido's Just about everything for dogs and cats, including the "Famous Fido's Doggie Deli" with a dining area and carryout of all-natural dog food, pet treats, and cakes. 1533 W. Devon Ave. (phone: 973-3436).

Fannie May Chicago's favorite chocolates for more than seven decades are sold in more than 100 shops around the city. Best-known outlets: *Water Tower Place* (phone: 664-0420) and *North Pier* (phone: 527-9372).

FAO Schwarz Kiddie heaven, with dolls, stuffed animals, and video games galore. Grownups don't have a bad time here, either. *Water Tower Place,* Level 2 (phone: 787-8894) and 840 N. Michigan Ave. (phone: 587-5000).

Feline Inn This is the ultimate cat hotel, where owners board their feline companions. But it also is a celebration of cats, with the feline theme emblazoned on watches, earrings, rings, pins, bracelets, and countless other items. Owner Peg O'Boyle paints figurines and planters devoted to the meow crowd. She also sells pedigree kittens. 1445 N. Wells St. (phone: 943-2230).

Flashback Retro collectibles from television shows of the 1960s and 1970s, including "Lost in Space" and "Rocky and Bullwinkle" lunch boxes, "I Dream of Jeannie" dolls, and the poster that made Farrah Fawcett an overnight pinup girl. 3450 N. Clark St. (phone: 929-5060).

Gianni Versace This Italian designer's two-story boutique is stocked with his latest fashions. 101 E. Oak St. (phone: 337-1111).

Giorgio Armani The noted Milanese designer offers his beautifully tailored *haute* threads to fashion-savvy devotees of both sexes. This is the only source of Armani *couture* collections between the coasts. 113 E. Oak St. (phone: 751-2244).

Godiva Chocolatier For those with a taste for sumptuous sweets. If chocolate is not your fatal attraction, try the rich cappuccino and espresso at this shop in *Water Tower Place,* Level 3 (phone: 280-1133).

The Goldsmith Custom-designed jewelry, plus a great selection of antique gems—and a repair service. *Water Tower Place,* Level 2 (phone: 751-1986).

Gucci The fine Italian leather emporium, with merchandise ranging from men's and women's sportswear and shoes to key rings. *900 North Michigan Avenue* (phone: 664-5504).

Hammacher Schlemmer Everything imaginable in elegant and unique gifts, from heated pet beds to a personalized Wurlitzer to a wide variety of kitchen and electronic gadgets. 618 N. Michigan Ave. (phone: 664-9292).

Illinois Artisans Shop A wide array of items made by the state's top craftspeople. *Thompson Building,* 100 W. Randolph St. (phone: 814-5321).

Isis Unusual fashions for women, all in one-size-fits-all, including hand-painted items, fringed jackets, and parachute-silk skirts. 38 E. Oak St. (phone: 664-7076).

Krivoy Named for her grandmother, Cynthia Hadesman's shop offers dresses, skirts, and hats whose styles run the gamut from contemporary to antique. 1145 W. Webster Ave. (phone: 248-1466).

Mallers Building This 21-story office building has 16 floors of retail and wholesale jewelers. Here shoppers can buy diamonds, get a watch repaired, sell silver and gold, and have a favorite piece engraved. Stop on the third floor to visit a genuine old-time deli with great cheese blintzes and potato pancakes. 5 N. Wabash St.

Marshall Field's The quintessential Chicago retailer (founded in 1853) and a pioneer of American department stores, it purveys all manner of merchandise, from apparel to rare books to Chicago's favorite Frango mints. Services offered here range from wardrobe coordinators to translators who help overseas visitors hurdle any shopping language barriers. In addition to nearly 150 departments aimed at the latter-day equivalent of the carriage trade, the store has a wonderful assortment of food counters on the seventh floor; tucked away on this floor is the *Bowl & Basket,* a good spot for hearty soup and a sandwich carved from a slab of beef or ham. Afternoon tea is a *Field's* tradition—as is the huge, beautifully decorated *Christmas* tree that dominates the store each holiday season. 111 N. State St. (phone: 781-1000). There is a second downtown store at *Water Tower Place* (phone: 781-1234).

Museum Shop of the Art Institute of Chicago Mobiles, stained glass, books, note cards, calendars, and a variety of high-quality gifts, including faithful reproductions of works in the museum's collection, are sold. An extensive stock of jewelry is especially worth inspecting. On *Valentine's Day,* a calligrapher is on hand to personalize cards. N. Michigan Ave. at Adams St. (phone: 443-3534).

NBC Store The *NBC Tower* houses a shop that carries NBC memorabilia, plus T-shirts emblazoned with the names of your favorite TV shows. 455 N. Columbus Dr. (phone: 836-5555).

Nicole Miller Novelty print silk scarves and ties, plus eveningwear for men and women. 62 E. Oak St. (phone: 664-3532).

Nike Town The latest in shoes and sportswear in a visually dramatic setting, surely worth a visit if not a purchase. 669 N. Michigan Ave. (phone: 642-6363).

North Beach Leather Trendy leather fashions for men and women; repair service, too. *Water Tower Place,* Level 3 (phone: 280-9292).

Nuts on Clark Nuts, coffee, wine, exotic teas, fruit, and chocolate are featured at this 30,000-square-foot store, just two blocks north of *Wrigley Field.* 3830 N. Clark St. (phone: 549-6622).

Pavo Real Boutique Sweaters from Peru and Bolivia plus handmade jewelry crafted by local and international artists. *900 North Michigan Avenue* (phone: 944-1390).

Sonia Rykiel Knits, knits, and more knits are featured in this designer's boutique—everything from dressy sportswear to activewear with a Gallic touch. There's a small line of children's wear, too. 106 E. Oak St. (phone: 951-0800).

Sony Gallery of Consumer Electronics For sampling and buying the latest in electronic marvels for business and entertainment. 663 N. Michigan Ave. (phone: 943-3334).

Sugar Magnolia Great jewelry, unique children's clothes, beaded T-shirts, and creations by young designers are among the stock in trade. Upscale vintage reproductions and designer jeans round out the collection. 34 E. Oak St. (phone: 944-0885).

Tiffany & Co. The Midwest branch of the place where Audrey Hepburn breakfasted. 715 N. Michigan Ave. (phone: 944-7500).

Ultimo Men's designer fashions; plus women's apparel, shoes, and jewelry. 114 E. Oak St. (phone: 787-0906).

A Unique Presence Exceptional crafts and gifts in a year-round art fair atmosphere. Unusual items from more than 175 North American artists. 2121 N. Clybourn Ave. (phone: 929-4292).

Waterstone's One of the two US branches of the famous British bookseller specializing in literature, art and travel books, history, and biography. 840 N. Michigan Ave. (phone: 587-8080).

Women & Children First The only truly feminist bookstore in the city offers regular book signings and special events linked to feminism in literature. 5233 N. Clark St. (phone: 769-9299).

PERSONAL SHOPPERS

If you don't want to traipse but still want to take advantage of Chicago's chic stores, call any of the city's major department stores for personal shoppers. The personal shoppers at *Neiman Marcus* even make house (or hotel) calls. *Bloomingdale's* has separate personal shopper services for men and women.

SPORTS AND FITNESS

There's plenty of major-league action in town year-round.

BASEBALL The *White Sox* play at *Comiskey Park* (35th and Shields, off the Dan Ryan Expwy.; phone: 924-1000). Seating 43,500 spectators, this state-of-the-art park is equipped with efficient escalators and elevators, plus numerous services and concessions for the fans. The *Cubs* play at *Wrigley Field* (Addison and Clark Sts.; phone: 404-2827), now also at night.

BASKETBALL The 1993 *NBA* champion *Bulls,* only the third team in history to win three consecutive *NBA* titles, play at the new *United Center* (1800 W. Madison St.; phone: 733-5300).

BICYCLING The city's vast lakefront and extensive forest preserves not only offer wide-open spaces but also a mainly flat terrain; the only hills are gentle ones, and the woods—even those next to busy thoroughfares—are quiet. Serious cyclists should bring their own bikes; those who are just interested in a casual ride can rent bicycles at the *Village Cycle Center* (1337 N. Wells St., just south of North Ave. and close to *Lincoln Park;* phone: 751-2488). Come early, especially on weekends. For more information about cycling, contact the *Chicagoland Bicycle Federation* (PO Box 64396, Chicago, IL 60664; phone: 427-3325). Some favorite cycling circuits are below:

FREEWHEELING ROUTES

Lakefront Bike Path The ride along the lakefront is fairly empty during much of the week. On weekends it can be crowded, particularly along the midsection north of the Loop. The full lakefront bike path runs from 5800 North, at the northern end of *Lincoln Park,* along Oak Street Beach, and out by *Navy Pier;* it crosses the river and continues south through *Grant* and *Burnham* parks to *Jackson Park* on the South Side, a ride of nearly 12 miles. There are places to pick up food and drinks along the way.

Forest Preserves All of Chicago's forest preserves maintain paved or gravel bike paths. For specifics, call individual districts (see the list under *Horsing Around* in DIVERSIONS). One path is the 10-mile North Branch Bicycle Trail, which follows the Chicago River's northern branch from 6400 North at Devon Avenue in the city to the *Chicago Botanical Garden* in Glencoe. The well-marked, paved path is frequently crowded on summer Sunday afternoons, but it's delightful in the evenings and during the rest of the year; there's a restaurant in the garden. For a map, contact the *Cook County Forest Preserve* (phone: 708-366-9420).

Illinois Prairie Path One of the finest trails in the state, this 45-mile stretch winds along an abandoned railroad track through parts of Cook, Kane, and DuPage counties. It begins in west suburban

Maywood and heads either to southwestern Aurora or west to Batavia and the Fox River. The trail goes through suburban towns, farmlands, prairie, and meadowlands. A guidebook is available from the nonprofit *Illinois Prairie Path Association* (Box 1086, Wheaton, IL 60187; phone: 708-752-0120).

BOCCE Remember how good Marlon Brando looked playing this Italian bowling game in *The Godfather*? Nearly 400 members of the *Highland Bocce Club* gather at *Highwood Bocce Court* (440 Bank La.; phone: 708-926-8118), beneath an Italian deli and the train tracks, to play in good weather. There also are *bocce* courts at three city parks: *McGuane* (290 S. Poplar Ave.), *Riis* (6110 W. Fullerton Ave.), and *Smith* (2526 W. Grand Ave.).

BOWLING Turn back the clock 35 years and try *Southport Lanes* (3325 N. Southport Ave.; phone: 472-1601), where boys still set pins for the four alleys. Some Chicagoans rate this as the best of its kind. For 24-hour-a-day bowling, try *Waveland* (3700 N. Western Ave.; phone: 472-5900).

CRICKET Games sponsored by the *United Cricket Conference* are played Sundays at noon from mid-May through mid-September in *Washington Park* (55th St. and King Dr.; phone: 684-6530).

FISHING The most popular pier within the city limits is the largest, at Montrose Harbor (4400 North at Lake Shore Drive, at the north end of *Lincoln Park*). For those who want to take a boat out, try *Chicago Sportfishing Association,* (in Burnham Harbor, on South Lake Shore Dr.; phone: 922-1100), a nonprofit association of licensed charter boat captains organized to promote sportfishing (mostly for trout and salmon). The association also will make arrangements for pleasure cruising. *Midwest Charter Boat Association* (phone: 935-4188) is another coalition of licensed charter boat captains who take parties out for fishing, pleasure cruises, or diving. Boats can accommodate from four to six passengers. Charters set out from all the city's major harbors: Montrose, Belmont, Diversey, and Burnham.

FITNESS CENTERS *Combined Fitness Centre* (1235 N. LaSalle St.; phone: 787-8400) admits non-members for a fee.

FOOTBALL The *NFL Bears* play at *Soldier Field* (Lake Shore Drive, south of Roosevelt Rd.; phone: 708-295-6600).

GOLF Chicago has 18 public golf courses, some along the lakeshore. The most accessible municipal course is *Marowitz,* traditionally known as *Waveland,* a nine-hole course in *Lincoln Park* (3700 N. Waveland Ave.; phone: 753-8670, *Chicago Park District*). The *Chicago Park District* offers golf instruction (phone: 753-8670). For special tee-off places outside the city limits, see *Great Golf Nearby* in DIVERSIONS.

HIKING The *Forest Preserve District* for Cook and Du Page Counties offers numerous places to hike (phone: 708-366-9420). The *Sierra Club* (53 W. Jackson Blvd.; phone: 431-0158) also organizes outings.

HOCKEY The *NHL Blackhawks* play in the new *United Center* (1800 W. Madison St.; phone: 733-5300).

HORSE RACING Thoroughbreds race at four tracks in the Chicago area: *Arlington Park* (Euclid Ave. and Wilke Rd., Arlington Heights; phone: 708-255-4300); *Hawthorne* (3501 S. Laramie Ave., Cicero; phone: 708-780-3700); *Maywood Park* (North and Fifth Aves., Maywood; phone: 708-626-4816); and *Sportsman's Park* (3301 S. Laramie Ave., Cicero; phone: 708-652-2812).

ICE SKATING Once temperatures dip below 45F, ice skating begins at Daley Bicentennial Plaza (337 E. Randolph St.; phone: 294-4790) and Block 37 in the Loop (State and Washington Sts.; phone: 744-2893). There also is ice skating year-round at the indoor rink at *McFetridge Sports Center* (3843 N. California Ave.; phone: 478-0211). Skate rentals are available at all three places.

JOGGING There's a jogging path along the entire lakeshore from *Jackson Park* north to *Lincoln Park,* accessible via numerous pedestrian walkways.

POLO Matches are held in summer at the *Oak Brook Polo Club* (3500 Midwest Ave., Oak Brook; phone: 708-990-POLO).

SAILING Lake Michigan offers superb sailing, but as experienced sailors can tell you, the lake is deceptive. Storms with winds of up to 40 knots can blow in suddenly. Check with the Coast Guard before going out (phone: 708-251-0185).

SKIING There are more than 50 ski clubs in the Chicago area. For information, contact the *Chicago Metro Ski Council* (PO Box 7926, Chicago, IL 60680; phone: 346-1268).

SOCCER Montrose, with four fields, is *the* soccer place. Walk up the 32-foot Cricket Hill for a bird's-eye view of the games. The *International Soccer League* plays on Sundays; the less popular, though equally enthusiastic, *Central American Soccer League* plays Saturdays. Weekend games start in the summer and run through October.

SWIMMING Oak Street Beach (at the top of Michigan Ave.) and North Avenue Beach (1600 North Ave.) afford swimming with skyscrapers as a backdrop; admission to both is free. The most accessible public beach outside the city is in north suburban Wilmette. There's an admission charge.

TENNIS The *Chicago Park District* has 708 outdoor municipal courts, including two downtown tennis facilities. The better of the two (by far) consists of 12 well-lit clay courts at Daley Bicentennial Plaza, in the northern end of *Grant Park*

(337 E. Randolph St.) near several residential high-rises. The courts are open daily. Reservations are necessary; there's a court fee (phone: 294-4790).

TOBOGGANING The *Cook County Forest Preserve District* operates 14 slides at five locations daily when the weather allows. Equipment rentals are available (phone: 708-366-9420).

THEATERS

For schedules and tickets, call the *League of Chicago Theatres's Hot Tix Hotline* (phone: 977-1755), or visit a *Hot Tix* booth (108 N. State St.; in Evanston, at the Sherman Avenue municipal parking garage between Church and Davis Sts.; in Oak Park, at 158 Forest Ave.; in Arlington Heights, at the *Metra* train station at 19 E. Northwest Hwy.; and at many *Rose Records* stores throughout the Chicago area). Full-price, advance-sale tickets are available by phone or at *Hot Tix* booths. Half-price day-of-sale tickets are sold for cash only at the booths on Mondays through Saturdays (Wednesdays through Saturdays at Evanston, Arlington Heights, and Oak Park locations); half-price Sunday tickets are sold at the booths the day before. *Ticketmaster's Chicago Arts Line* (phone: 902-1500) takes phone orders for full-price, advance-sale tickets for an additional surcharge—which varies depending on the specific show.

Chicago's thriving theater scene breaks down into two camps: eclectic showcases for homegrown talent, and Broadway-caliber commercial houses. Listed below are three of our favorite Chicago companies.

CENTER STAGE

Goodman Theatre The second-oldest regional theater in the country, the *Goodman* mounts frequent productions of works by living writers, brings classics up to date in eye-opening ways, and stages that colorful favorite, *A Christmas Carol*, at the end of the year. There are actually two theaters housed here: the *Studio*, which seats 135, and the *Mainstage*, which seats 683. Between the two theaters, eight to 10 plays are produced annually; because the productions are usually well received (and have long runs), the season extends throughout the year. 200 S. Columbus Dr. (phone: 443-3800).

Organic Theater Dedicated to producing world premiere theater such as the science fiction trilogy *Warp!* and the recent adaptation of Clive Barker's horror tale *In the Flesh*, the *Organic Theater* has explored the full range of theatrical expression. David Mamet's *Sexual Perversity in Chicago* started out here, too. 3319 N. Clark St. (phone: 327-5588).

Steppenwolf Theatre Chicago's acclaimed pipeline to both Hollywood and Broadway, this homegrown company launched the careers of

John Malkovich and Emmy-winner Laurie Metcalf (of "Roseanne" fame); Garry Marshall and Steve Martin have developed original plays for the cutting-edge *Steppenwolf* troupe. The company's production of *The Grapes of Wrath* won it a Tony, and its New York production of *The Song of Jacob Zulu* (which featured the South African group *Ladysmith Black Mambazo*) earned raves. In addition to its excellent ensemble, *Steppenwolf* boasts one of the city's finest (and newest) theaters. Each year the company produces five or six main-stage shows and a smattering of smaller workshop performances. 1650 N. Halsted St. (phone 335-1650).

Other Chicago theatrical troupes include: the *Victory Gardens Theater* (2261 N. Lincoln Ave.; phone: 871-3000), dedicated to staging plays by such local playwrights as James Sherman (*Beau Jest*) and John Logan (*Hauptmann*); the funky *Remains Theatre* (phone: 549-7725), known for its talented artists as well as its laid-back attitude; the *Pegasus Players* (1145 W. Wilson Ave.; phone: 271-2638), renowned for their productions of Stephen Sondheim musicals; *Shakespeare Repertory* (1016 N. Dearborn St.; phone: 642-2273), which focuses exclusively on the Bard's works; and *City Lit Theater Company* (3914 N. Clark St.; phone: 271-1100), which specializes in adapting works of literature for the stage. Several local troupes share space in the *Theatre Building* (1225 W. Belmont Ave.; phone: 327-5252); it's worth a quick call to find out what's playing there.

The main commercial theaters are the *Auditorium Theater* (50 E. Congress Pkwy.; phone: 922-4046; 922-2110 for performance information), where both *The Phantom of the Opera* and *Les Misérables* played for years; the *Shubert* (22 W. Monroe St.; phone: 977-1700); the *Apollo Theater Center* (2540 N. Lincoln Ave.; phone: 935-6100); the *Briar Street Theatre* (3133 N. Halsted St.; phone: 348-4000); and the *Wellington Theater* (750 W. Wellington St.; phone: 975-7171). The *Mayfair Theatre* at the *Blackstone* hotel (636 S. Michigan Ave.; phone: 786-9120) presents *Shear Madness,* a comedic mystery involving audience participation, nightly except Tuesdays.

Dinner-theaters include the *Drury Lane South* (2500 W. 95th, Evergreen Park; phone: 779-4000); *Marriott's Lincolnshire Theatre* (10 Marriott Dr., Lincolnshire; phone: 708-634-0200); *Pheasant Run* (*Pheasant Run Lodge,* Rte. 64, St. Charles; phone: 708-584-6300); and the *Candlelight Playhouse,* the nation's first dinner-theater (5620 S. Harlem Ave. in Summit; phone: 708-496-3000).

Chicago's arts and theater community in recent years has given more attention to poets with innovative forums called "Poetry Slams." In the best beat tradition, Chicago's top performance poets listen, read, and compete at the nationally recognized *Uptown Poetry Slam,* held Sundays at the *Green Mill* cocktail lounge (4802 N. Broadway; phone: 878-5552). The *West Side Poetry Slam* is geared toward a more genteel audience, which is encouraged to participate on Tuesdays at *Fitzgerald's* (6615 W. Roosevelt Rd. in Berwyn; phone: 708-788-2118).

Fans of classic, foreign, or art films will find them at *Facets Multimedia* (1517 W. Fullerton Ave.; phone: 281-4114); the *Film Center of the Art Institute* (Columbus Dr. at Jackson Blvd.; phone: 443-3737); and *Fine Arts Theater* (418 S. Michigan Ave.; phone: 939-3700). For a golden-age film experience, try the *Music Box,* with its mammoth screen, sky ceiling with winking stars and moving clouds, dramatic lobby—and great popcorn. Films shown here are Hollywood standards, foreign fare, and some independents (3733 N. Southport Ave.; phone: 871-6604). The *Biograph,* where John Dillinger was gunned down, also still shows films (2433 N. Lincoln Ave.; phone: 348-4123).

MUSIC

Good music (and lots of it) abounds all over the city. The world-renowned *Chicago Symphony Orchestra,* under the baton of Daniel Barenboim, can be heard from late September until early June at *Orchestra Hall,* a National Landmark building (220 S. Michigan Ave.; phone: 435-6666). The orchestra also plays at the *Ravinia Festival* outside the city in Highland Park from late June through August (1575 Oakwood Ave. at Lake-Cook and Green Bay Rds.; phone: 708-433-8800). Don't miss the *Grant Park Symphony Orchestra,* which plays four times weekly in the summer under the stars along Lake Michigan. Concerts are free; audiences usually pack picnic dinners and sit out on the lawn. Another favorite is the *Chicago Sinfonietta,* a professional orchestra that performs classical, romantic, and contemporary music at *Orchestra Hall* on the campus of *Rosary College* (7900 W. Division St. in River Forest; phone: 708-366-1062).

Some of the hottest tickets in town from September through February are for performances of the *Lyric Opera of Chicago,* which stages classics and new productions at the *Civic Opera House* (20 N. Wacker Dr.; phone: 332-2244). *Chamber Music Chicago* (phone: 242-6237) presents classical and avant-garde music concerts at venues throughout the city. From February through May, you can hear the *Chicago Opera Theater* (2936 N. Southport Ave.; phone: 663-0555), which performs operas in English.

As for dance, *Ballet Chicago* presents classical ballet; the *Hubbard Street Dance Company* and the *Joel Hall Dance Company* are known for jazz; modern dance is the forte of the *Joseph Holmes Dance Company;* and the *Chicago Repertory Dance Ensemble* stages classical and modern dance. Each spring the *Civic Theater* (20 N. Wacker Dr.; phone: 346-0270) presents a series of dance performances featuring local troupes and internationally renowned companies, such as the *American Ballet Theater.* The *Dance Center of Columbia College* (4730 N. Sheridan; phone: 271-7928) offers contemporary, modern, and avant-garde dance performances throughout the year. For the current schedule of dance events, call the *Chicago Dance Coalition*'s 24-hour information line (phone: 419-8383).

NIGHTCLUBS AND NIGHTLIFE

Don't leave the Windy City without taking in some of its fine blues, jazz, reggae, and folk music. Or try an offbeat bar, a neighborhood sports pub, or a comedy club in one of the few Midwest cities where nightlife lasts until dawn.

Chicago's blues tradition is revered, and some of the country's finest blues performers can be found in a handful of clubs around the city. *Blue Chicago* (937 N. State St.; phone: 642-6261) books a lot of notable female performers, as does its sister bar, *Blue Chicago on Clark* (536 N. Clark St.; phone: 661-0100). Crowded *B.L.U.E.S.* (2519 N. Halsted St.; phone: 528-1012) is built around solid blues acts and a lively environment; its roomier relative, *B.L.U.E.S. Etcetera* (1124 W. Belmont Ave.; phone: 525-8989), books major acts. At *Buddy Guy's Legends,* in the former home of Chess Records (754 S. Wabash Ave.; phone: 427-0333), bluesman Guy holds court over new and veteran performers. But Chicago's standout blues club is *Kingston Mines* (2548 N. Halsted St.; phone: 477-4646), where local blues musicians—and celebrities—go after other clubs have closed. Blues enthusiasts may also want to venture to the South Side's haven, the *Checkerboard Lounge* (423 E. 43rd St.; phone 624-3240), or to the West Side to check out *Rosa's* (3420 W. Armitage Ave.; phone: 342-0452), Chicago's friendliest blues bar.

As strong as the city's blues legacy is its love of jazz. At *Andy's Lounge* (11 E. Hubbard St.; phone: 642-6805), patrons dressed in anything from T-shirts to pin-stripes enjoy jazz at lunchtime (live music starts at noon) and after work (sets start at 5 PM). The *Cotton Club* (1710 S. Michigan Ave.; phone: 341-9787) is decorated with photos of the stars of the original Harlem club. Joe Segal's *Jazz Showcase* at the *Blackstone* hotel (636 S. Michigan Ave.; phone: 427-4846) draws such top jazz performers as McCoy Tyner and Dorothy Donegan. The *Green Mill* cocktail lounge (4802 N. Broadway; phone: 878-5552) looks like the Al Capone haunt it once was, with an ornate interior and live jazz six nights a week. As its name suggests, the *Gold Star Sardine Bar* (680 N. Lake Shore Dr.; phone: 664-4215) is ultra-tiny, but attracts big names—Liza, Tony, and Frank have all stopped by to give unannounced performances.

Jazz also reigns supreme at *Pops for Champagne* (2934 N. Sheffield Ave.; phone: 472-1000), an upscale jazz club with a formal French garden and a choice of champagnes to sip while you relax and listen. *Yvette* (1206 N. State St.; phone: 280-1700) features enthusiastic twin piano duets, while its sister establishment *Yvette Wintergarden* (311 S. Wacker Dr.; phone 408-1242) offers combos for dancing. The elegant *Inta's* (308 W. Erie St.; phone 664-6880) is the perfect spot for dancing to jazz orchestras, enjoying an evening snack, or savoring a fine cigar in the club's smoking lounge.

North Clark Street is to reggae what North Halsted Street is to blues. A Caribbean pub-crawl might begin at the *Wild Hare* (3530 N. Clark St.; phone: 327-4273). Cross the street to find *Exedus II* (3477 N. Clark St.;

phone 348-3998). Local and international reggae bands perform at both bars seven nights a week.

The *Old Town School of Folk Music* (909 W. Armitage Ave.; phone: 525-7793) is Chicago's premier folk music venue and also sponsors frequent concerts by musicians from South America, Africa, and Europe. The *Abbey Pub* (3420 E. Grace St.; phone: 478-4408) is the place for traditional Irish music, and at *No Exit* (6970 N. Glenwood St.; phone: 743-3355) folk musicians perform while the crowd sips java and plays chess.

Chicago's lively dance spots range from the mega-clubs (huge playhouses with separate rooms for dancing, live music, games and pool, or conversing) housed in warehouses west of the Loop to little neighborhood bars. The most chic of the big clubs is *Shelter* (564 W. Fulton St.; phone: 648-5500); if you go, dress to kill and be prepared to deal with difficult doormen. *Ka-Boom!* (747 N. Green St.; phone: 243-8600) has a two-level dance floor and a kooky cabaret lounge with giant teacup-shape booths. A giant dance floor dominates *Crobar* (1543 N. Kingsbury; phone 587-1313), the newest mega-club in town.

Smaller but equally lively dance clubs abound. The *Lizard Lounge* (1824 W. Augusta Blvd.; phone: 489-0379) is an eclectic little spot known for its funk and K-tel kitsch nights. The DJs at the *Artful Dodger* (1734 W. Wabansia Ave.; phone: 227-6859) spin everything from 1960s British rock to world beat to high-energy dance tracks. *Red Dog* (1958 W. North Ave.; phone: 278-1009) is a spacious second-story dance club that overlooks the funkiest intersection in artsy *Wicker Park*. *Neo* (2350 N. Clark St.; phone: 528-2622) offers a different theme each night. *Berlin* (954 W. Belmont Ave.; phone: 348-4975) draws an especially flamboyant crowd.

More informal pubs and taverns include *Sheffield's Wine and Beer Garden* (3258 N. Sheffield Ave.; phone: 281-4989), which has an extensive selection of exotic and imported and domestic micro-brewed beers; the fireplace in the back café and pool room keeps things cozy in wintertime. Also try *John Barleycorn Memorial Pub* (658 W. Belden St.; phone: 348-8899), where classical music soothes patrons trying any of 30 imported beers against a backdrop of prints of famous paintings and sculptures; in the summer, it has the city's most attractive outdoor beer garden. *Lucky's* (213 W. Institute Pl.; phone: 751-7777) is the trendy hangout of the young and beautiful, most of whom show up in something expensive and black. Sports bars are also plentiful: In the shadow of *Wrigley Field, Hi-Tops* (3551 N. Sheffield Ave.; phone: 348-0009) is the largest in town. There's also *Justin's* (3358 N. Southport Ave.; phone: 929-4844), with two satellite dishes and six TV sets, and *McGee's* (950 W. Webster Ave.; phone: 871-4272), where the folks behind the bar say you can request any game you want on the projection TV set in the back room.

Though the video sing-along craze started in Japan, *karaoke* (which means "empty orchestra") has caught on here in the Midwest. The most popular *karaoke* bars in Chicago are *Who's Next* (711 N. State St.; phone: 943-8780) and *Kerrigan's* (2310 W. Lawrence Ave.; phone: 334-0620).

Two-steppers and line-dancing fans can strut their spurs at several country-and-western clubs about town. The clubs offer free lessons at least one night a week. *Bub City* (901 W. Weed St.; phone: 266-1200) and *Whiskey River* (1997 N. Clybourn Ave.; phone: 528-3400) are the premier country-and-western dance bars in the city; *Cadillac Ranch* (1175 W. Lake St., Bartlett; phone: 708-830-7200) is another fun place.

COMIC RELIEF

Chicago has been a comedy center since the 1959 founding of the *Second City* comedy club, whose graduates include Joan Rivers, David Steinberg, the Belushi brothers, and much of the cast of *Saturday Night Live*. *Second City* and its spin-off, *Second City E.T.C.*, are located at 1608 and 1616 North Wells Street, respectively (phone: 337-3992). Meanwhile, the *Comedy Womb* is a star-making club above the *Pines* restaurant (8030 W. Ogden St. in Lyons; phone: 708-422-0030), and *Zanies* (1548 N. Wells St.; phone: 337-4027) features the best of the locals as well as such national talent as Richard Lewis. The *Improv* (504 N. Wells St.; phone: 782-6387), with 400 seats, and the *Funny Firm* (318 W. Grand Ave.; phone: 321-9500) feature national acts as well as up-and-coming talent. Said to be giving *Second City* stiff competition is the *Annoyance Theater* (3153 N. Broadway; phone: 929-6200), a group of loonies who put on such bizarre productions as *Manson: The Musical* and *Coed Prison Sluts* at their makeshift theater.

Best In Town

CHECKING IN

There are quite a number of interesting hotels in Chicago, varying in style from the intimate clubbiness of the *Tremont* and the *Talbott* to the super-modern elegance of the *Ritz-Carlton* and *Le Meridien*. Unless otherwise noted, all listed here have at least one restaurant; the choice of eating places normally increases with the price of a room and the size of the hotel. Big hotels have shops, meeting places, and nightly entertainment. All hotels have air conditioning, private baths, TV sets, and telephones unless otherwise mentioned. Most of Chicago's major hotels have complete facilities for the business traveler. Those hotels listed below as having "business services" usually offer such conveniences as meeting rooms, photocopiers, computers, translation services, and express checkout, among others. Call the hotel for additional information. Rates in Chicago are higher than in most other Midwestern cities: Expect to pay $180 to $250 per night for a double room in expensive hotels; $100 to $160 in those classified as moderate; and from $50 to $90 in those listed as inexpensive. If money is no object, ask for a room with a view. North Michigan Avenue hotels are close to the Gold Coast, *Lincoln Park,* and *Water Tower Place;* Loop locations (about 10 minutes away by taxi) are convenient to businesses and the fine old downtown department stores.

For B&B accommodations, contact *Bed and Breakfast Chicago* (PO Box 14088, Chicago, IL 60614; phone: 951-0085). They also rent homes and apartments while their owners are away. Units are available in the downtown, Near North, Lakeshore, Lincoln Park, and nearby neighborhoods at prices starting at $55 per person per night.

The city government, in conjunction with dozens of hotels, offers special winter rates from September through March. The *Chicago Office of Tourism* (phone: 744-2400) can provide a list of hotels with reduced rates or special packages for visitors during the winter (or off-season). There are also many hotels in the suburbs, most located near office complexes and major highway interchanges. The major chains have hotels at or near *O'Hare Airport* and along the TriState Tollway; a few are listed below. Rates tend to be lower outside the city limits. All telephone numbers are in the 312 area code unless otherwise indicated.

For an unforgettable experience in the Windy City, we begin with our favorites, all of which fall into the expensive category, followed by our cost and quality choices of accommodations, listed by price category.

ROOMS AT THE TOP

Chicago Hilton and Towers Restored to its 1927 grandeur, this 30-story landmark also boasts lavish, modern amenities. The 1,543 rooms include the Towers, with 120 suites. One of these, the $4,000-per-night Conrad Hilton Suite, has its own heliport, plus four private elevators and the services of a maid and butler. The hotel has a fully equipped fitness center, and a telephone answering machine can be hooked up to guestrooms. Other pluses include a self-service parking garage, and a computerized concierge—just touch the computer screen to find out about personal services, shopping, dining, and entertainment in the area. *Kitty O'Shea's Pub* is a surprisingly authentic Irish saloon staffed by Irish men and women under a government exchange program. *Buckingham's* restaurant offers a fine menu, plus an impressive selection of 120 single-malt Scotch whiskeys. Additional amenities include 24-hour room service and business services. In the South Loop area. 720 S. Michigan Ave. (phone: 922-4400; 800-HILTONS; fax: 922-5240).

Drake A fabulous lobby with an ornate marble fountain, rooms with old-fashioned high ceilings, plus a graciousness rare in hotels these days (the elevators even have velvet-covered benches), set this Hilton property apart. The 535-room property offers the *Cape Cod Room* (see *Eating Out*), a favorite seafood eatery, and the

Oak Terrace with a fine view of the Gold Coast. The hotel has 24-hour room service, a concierge, and business services. In the North Michigan Avenue area. 140 E. Walton St. (phone: 787-2200; 800-HILTONS; fax: 787-1431).

Four Seasons One of the city's most luxurious hotels occupies 19 floors of a stunning high-rise that also is home to the local branch of *Bloomingdale's* and numerous other classy emporia. There are 343 rooms (more than a third boast separate sitting rooms), an opulent Presidential Suite, and 16 residential apartments in this member of what is arguably the best-managed hotel group in the world. *Seasons* restaurant serves exquisitely prepared nouvelle American dishes (see *Eating Out*). Guest facilities include two-line telephones, a spa, a sauna, and an indoor swimming pool. Other amenities are 24-hour room service, a concierge, and business services. In the North Michigan Avenue area. 120 E. Delaware Pl. (phone: 280-8800; 800-332-3442; fax: 280-9184).

Inter-Continental A meticulous restoration has brought this 338-room Art Deco gem, built in 1929 as the *Medinah Athletic Club,* back to its former splendor. Intricate marble, bronze, and brass fixtures; painted ceilings; and sculptured details are among the treasures unearthed here. Guestrooms boast furnishings of inlaid fruitwood, and bedspreads inspired by 19th-century French toile design. Afternoon tea and freshly baked raisin scones served with preserves and thick Devonshire cream are late-day musts. Overlooking the entryway, the *Boulevard* restaurant offers first-rate continental fare. The ornate marble pool on the 14th floor was once used by Johnny Weissmuller, Olympic swimmer and star of *Tarzan.* There's a concierge desk and business services. 505 N. Michigan Ave. (phone: 944-4100; 800-327-0200; fax: 944-3050).

Nikko Chicago This elegant, 425-room hotel overlooking the Chicago River was built by Japan's largest hotel chain. Japanese touches abound, with landscaped indoor gardens and Japanese artwork—some suites even have tatami sleeping rooms. Its *Celebrity Café* offers American food; the *Benkay* is a fine Japanese restaurant. A jazz trio is featured in the *Hana Lounge* nightly (except Sundays). Other pluses are 24-hour room service, a concierge, a health club, and business services. In the Loop. 320 N. Dearborn St. (phone: 744-1900; 800-NIKKO-US; fax: 527-2650).

Omni Ambassador East Located on the residential Gold Coast, convenient to Oak Street and North Michigan Avenue shopping, it's also a short walk to the *Lincoln Park Zoo.* Listed on the National Register of Historic Places, the landmark hotel boasts 275 rooms and 52 suites, all beautifully decorated. The hotel is still home to the famous *Pump Room* restaurant, a Chicago institution. The entryway is lined with photos of famous guests—from Bogie and Bacall to Frank Sinatra and Queen Elizabeth II—all of whom have dined in Booth No. 1. The restaurant also features live entertainment, with dancing to a three-piece band, and standard (but well-prepared) fare (see *Eating Out*). Amenities include 24-hour room service, a concierge, and business services. On the Gold Coast. 1301 N. State Pkwy. (phone: 787-7200; 800-THE-OMNI; fax: 787-4760).

Park Hyatt If you want pampering, this elegant 255-room hostelry across from the historic *Water Tower* is the place to be. Indulgences and little "extras" here include fresh fruit and candy in guestrooms; a suite with an 1898 Steinway piano; three-times-a-day maid service; complimentary car wash (if you've driven here); and a fleet of courtesy cars that includes a 1965 Rolls-Royce Silver Cloud III. Afternoon tea is served in the lobby lounge, and there's elegant dining in the acclaimed *La Tour* restaurant. Other nice extras: a champagne bar, a weekend caviar bar, and a classical guitarist in the lounge. The hotel offers 24-hour room service, a concierge, and business services. 800 N. Michigan Ave. (phone: 280-2222; 800-233-1234; fax: 280-1963).

Ritz-Carlton Contemporary and chic, this beautifully appointed 432-room luxury establishment, a member of the fine Four Seasons chain, rises 20 stories above its 12th-floor lobby; the beautifully proportioned fountain is a signature centerpiece. Housed in the spectacular *Water Tower Place* complex, it has all the accoutrements of elegance, including a fine health club and skylit indoor swimming pool. Its *Café* offers first-rate continental fare in a lush setting, just off the lobby. Amenities include 24-hour room service, a concierge, and business services. In the North Michigan Avenue area. 160 E. Pearson St. (phone: 266-1000; 800-241-3333; fax: 266-1194).

EXPENSIVE

Claridge With 174 rooms and six suites (three with wood-burning fireplaces), this reasonably priced hotel is 10 minutes from the Gold Coast and steps away from Astor Street's elegance and Division Street's bars. Health club facilities are available nearby and *My Neighborhood* restaurant serves Italian, Spanish, and continental fare. Business services are also available. 1244 N. Dearborn St. (phone: 787-4980; fax: 266-0978).

Fairmont Opulent and sophisticated, its 700 rooms and suites overlook the city skyline and Lake Michigan. Located in *Illinois Center* between the Chicago

River and *Grant Park,* it features such appointments as marble bathrooms equipped with TV sets, telephones, and lighted dressing tables. Amenities include 24-hour room service, a concierge, and business services. In the Loop. 200 N. Columbus Dr. (phone: 565-8000; fax: 856-9020).

Hyatt on Printer's Row A National Historical Register building in the Printer's Row District, it has an elegant green-and-black lobby, 161 rooms and suites, lounges, meeting areas, an exercise room and gym, plus the first-rate *Prairie* restaurant (see *Eating Out*). Other amenities include a concierge, complimentary morning newspaper, and business services. In the South Loop area. 500 S. Dearborn St. (phone: 986-1234; 800-233-1234).

Hyatt Regency Chicago With 2,000 rooms in two ultramodern towers, this leading convention hotel is conveniently located between the Loop and N. Michigan Avenue, just south of the Chicago River. There's fine dining at *Truffles,* and the *Big Bar* has the city's most extensive selection of brandies. Amenities include 24-hour room service, a concierge, and business services. 151 E. Wacker Dr. (phone: 565-1234; 800-233-1234; fax: 565-2966).

Hyatt Regency O'Hare Ideal for a comfortable overnight stop between planes. There are 1,100 rooms, a health club, a plant-filled, multistory atrium lobby, and a rotating rooftop restaurant. Amenities include 24-hour room service, a concierge, and business services. 9300 W. Bryn Mawr Ave.; South River Rd. exit off Kennedy Expwy. (phone: 708-696-1234; 800-233-1234; fax: 708-696-1418).

Le Meridien Chicago There are 247 rooms, 35 suites, and six penthouse suites in this elegant hotel. Its *Brasserie Bellevue* restaurant offers unusual interpretations of traditional dishes. Rooms have CD players, VCRs, and remote-control TV sets. Health club facilities are available nearby. On the Gold Coast. 21 E. Bellevue Pl. (phone: 266-2100; 800-543-4300).

Omni Chicago In the heart of downtown, this 347-suite link in the Hyatt chain has luxury amenities offered in an apartment-like setting. Its *Cielo* restaurant offers a superb continental menu with an Italian accent and a fourth-story view of Michigan Avenue. 676 N. Michigan Ave. and Huron St. (phone: 944-6664).

Radisson Plaza Ambassador West This historic hotel on the Gold Coast was built in 1924; its 216 rooms were renovated in 1989. Staying here offers a taste of living in Chicago's most elegant neighborhood; down the street and around the corner are blocks of turn-of-the-century homes; you're also steps away from the nightlife on Division Street and a brisk walk from North Michigan Avenue. Amenities include a restaurant, a concierge, a gift shop, business services, room service, and parking (for an additional fee). Weekend packages are available year-round and include a horse-drawn carriage ride. On the Gold Coast. 1300 N. State Pkwy. (phone: 787-7900; 800-333-3333; fax: 787-2067).

Swissôtel Spectacular views of the Chicago River and Lake Michigan are the pride of this property, along with 625 spacious guestrooms (among the largest in the country at 450 square feet) complete with marble baths. Despite the hotel's distinctly European flavor (more than 20% of the staff and close to half the guests are European), *Land of Plenty,* its signature dining room, emphasizes American cooking. Business services are available. 323 E. Wacker Dr. at Illinois Ctr. (phone: 565-0565; 800-65-GRAND).

Tremont The paneled lobby, with its elaborate moldings and chandeliers, is more like a private sitting room than a public foyer. The 139 rooms offer traditional elegance. The hotel also is the home of *Cricket's,* one of Chicago's best restaurants (see *Eating Out*). Amenities include 24-hour room service, a concierge, and business services. In the North Michigan Avenue area. 100 E. Chestnut St. (phone: 751-1900; 800-621-8133; fax: 280-1304).

MODERATE

Allerton Close to museums and shopping on Michigan Avenue and 10 minutes from the Loop, this 380-room property is an economical but quite pleasant choice—and a steal in this location. There's a new restaurant, called *The Avenue,* which offers moderately priced American dishes. Business services are available. 701 N. Michigan Ave. (phone: 440-1500; fax: 440-1819).

Bismarck There are 525 rooms including some nice suites. The *Chalet* is open for lunch and dinner, and business services are available. 171 W. Randolph St. at LaSalle St. (phone: 236-0123; fax: 236-3177).

Executive House Offering 415 rooms and 60 suites, all with wonderful city views. The *LaSalle* restaurant offers fine continental cooking; and guests can use nearby health club facilities. Catering to members of the international business community, it offers a special telephone system that allows access to dialing and travel instructions in various foreign languages. Other business services are available as well, as is valet parking. 71 E. Wacker Dr. (phone: 346-7100; 800-621-4005).

Holiday Inn City Centre Architecturally more interesting than you might expect, this 500-room establishment has many amenities—swimming pools and a health club, indoor tennis courts, racquetball, and free parking—making it almost a bargain. There's also a concierge desk, and business services are available. 300 E. Ohio St. (phone: 787-6100; 800-HOLIDAY; fax: 787-6259).

Holiday Inn O'Hare Convenient to the airport and the many offices nearby, it has 507 rooms and offers weekend packages. The hotel's "Holidome" has indoor and outdoor pools, a health club, saunas, a tanning salon, and a gameroom. Other amenities include free parking, three restaurants, two bars, and business services. 5440 River Rd., Rosemont (phone: 708-671-6350; 800-HOLIDAY).

Marriott Downtown This convention hotel dates from the 1960s, but its 1,172 rooms were extensively renovated a couple of years ago. Located right on Michigan Avenue, it's within walking distance of the *Water Tower, North Pier,* and both of the city's major gallery districts, and not far from the Loop. Its spacious lobby includes a cocktail area and piano bar where guests can watch each other come and go; its three restaurants offer a choice of seafood, Italian fare, and steaks. It also boasts two lounges, 24-hour room service, an extensive health club and pool, business services, and shopping. Parking is available for a fee. 540 N. Michigan Ave. (phone: 836-0100; 800-228-9290; fax: 836-6139).

INEXPENSIVE

Best Western Grant Park Near the funky art life of the south Loop, this modest 172-room property is also within walking distance of the downtown museums, shopping, and offices. It has a Mexican restaurant, and room service is available. There's also a fitness center and an outdoor pool. 1100 S. Michigan Ave. (phone: 922-2900; 800-528-1234).

Days Inn Lake Shore Drive Convenient to North Michigan Avenue and Lake Shore Drive, this 33-story, 578-room hotel offers marvelous views, an outdoor pool, standard business services, on-premise parking, and all laundry services, plus a revolving banquet hall on the top floor. Its *Gold Star Sardine Bar* is one of the city's popular after-hours spots, offering cabaret singers nightly. 644 N. Lake Shore Dr. (phone: 943-9200; 800-325-2525).

HoJo Inn This 70-room motel is in the River North gallery district, a formerly seedy neighborhood that has become quite fashionable. Its coffee shop is popular with neighboring office workers, and there's free parking—right in front of each room. 720 N. LaSalle St. (phone: 664-8100).

Quality Inn Downtown Located just west of the Loop in the midst of Greektown's lively nightlife and restaurant scene, it's also right next to the Kennedy Expressway. There are 406 rooms, plus a restaurant, a lounge, and an outdoor pool. Parking and room service are available. 1 S. Halsted St. (phone: 829-5000).

EATING OUT

The city's restaurant business is booming, and some of the finest cooking in America can be found here. Expect to pay $70 or more for a meal for two at those restaurants we've described as expensive; between $50 and $70 at places in the moderate category; and less than $40 at our inexpensive choices. Prices do not include drinks and wine, tips, or taxes. Unless otherwise noted, all restaurants are open for lunch and dinner, and all telephone numbers are in the 312 area code.

For an unforgettable dining experience, we begin with our culinary favorites, all of which fall into the expensive range, followed by our cost and quality choices, listed by price category.

INCREDIBLE EDIBLES

Ambria Everything about this place charms, from the comfortable setting to the menu's sophisticated variations on nouvelle cuisine. Dinner might begin with a salad of sliced duck, pine nuts, and fresh pears with red currant dressing, or a tropical lobster salad. Desserts are simply remarkable. There's also a *dégustation* dinner for four or more with samplings of many dishes. Closed Sundays. Reservations necessary. Major credit cards accepted. 2300 N. Lincoln Park W. (phone: 472-5959).

Carlos' Yes, it's worth the drive. Ever since it opened a decade ago, this elegantly appointed dining room, located about 35 miles north of the city in Highland Park, has been one of the Chicago area's top-rated restaurants. While owners Carlos and Debbie Nieto keep the front of the house running smoothly, chef Gabriel Viti creates such dishes as squab ravioli with garlic sauce, veal medallions and wild mushrooms in a rosemary-scented sauce, and roast lobster with couscous. Desserts are equally enticing; the chocolate quintet should satisfy even the most discriminating chocoholic. Though it tends to get a bit crowded, service doesn't suffer—nor does the food. Closed Tuesday. Reservations advised. Major credit cards accepted. 429 Temple St., Highland Park; take Eden Expy. to Rte. 22, Green Bay Rd. exit (phone: 708-432-0770).

Charlie Trotter's A recipient of the James Beard award for Best Midwest Chef, Charlie Trotter produces first-rate fare in elegant surroundings. A converted townhouse in residential Lincoln Park with a dramatic two-level atrium, the place has an ambience that sets the mood for the meal to come. And *Trotter's* innovative cuisine—which might include such unusual dishes as seared foie gras with roasted Forelle pear and squab consommé, Casco cod with truffled leeks and roasted shiitake mushrooms, or potato and *chèvre* terrine served with a crispy potato and sauerkraut napoleon in a caraway seed vinaigrette—doesn't disappoint. The vegetarian option is surprisingly popular and often wins kudos even from committed carnivores. The menu changes daily. If you want to sit at the chef's table in the kitchen—one of Chicago's hottest dining tickets—be sure to call ahead (way ahead); there is a six-month waiting list for Saturday nights. Closed Sundays and Mondays.

Reservations necessary. Major credit cards accepted. 816 W. Armitage Ave. (phone: 248-6228).

Frontera Grill and Topolobampo A pair of upscale Mexican dining rooms. *Frontera* specializes in tempting appetizer platters of guacamole, deep-fried chicken taquitos, and ceviche. *Topolobampo* offers, among other treats, roast pork loin with red-chili apricot sauce and pumpkin purée. Closed Sundays and Mondays. Reservations advised. Major credit cards accepted. 445 N. Clark St. (phone: 661-1434).

Gordon Owner Gordon Sinclair is a real presence on the American dining scene, and his eponymous restaurant in trendy River North is as avant-garde as its proprietor. To say that the swank, tongue-in-cheek decor—mismatched chairs and lush paintings juxtaposed with faux marble and fine linen—is unique is an understatement. Typical dishes include beef tenderloin served with oven-roasted potatoes and a gorgonzola/arugula pesto; seared *ahi* tuna and jumbo prawns prepared with lobster oil and citrus vinaigrette; and roasted shrimp and duck ravioli with mushroom sauce. Open daily. Reservations advised. Major credit cards accepted. 500 N. Clark St. (phone: 467-9780).

Le Mikado Posh is the first word that comes to mind for this dining room set in a luxury apartment building in Chicago's Gold Coast neighborhood. Chef Daniel Kelch bows to his mother's heritage with Japanese accents in the decor and the menu, turning out a stellar array of Eurasian dishes such as tempura fried oysters; saffron risotto topped with crisp-skinned quail, cooked Chinese style; and roasted free-range chicken with honey and herbs and topped with a warm hazelnut/lemon/bacon vinaigrette. The three-course prix fixe dinner is an outstanding value. Open daily for dinner only. Reservations advised. Major credit cards accepted. 21 W. Goethe St. (phone: 280-8611).

Prairie Quite possibly where the term "Midwestern cooking" was coined, this intimate spot offers fine regional fare. The decor is elegant and uncluttered à la Frank Lloyd Wright, and the open kitchen is a fine place to pick up new cooking techniques as you watch your food being prepared. Whitefish smothered with onions, crisp bacon, puréed squash, and smoked whitefish caviar is just one of the thoughtfully prepared entrées, and those willing to chance an extra pound should try the warm carrot raisin cake with bourbon glaze and sugarplums. Closed Sundays. Reservations advised. Major credit cards accepted. 500 S. Dearborn St. (phone: 663-1143).

Arun's One of the city's most elegant Thai dining spots, it offers such daily specials as quilted shrimp with fried rice cracker and curry sauce, prawns with garlic-lime sauce, and catfish curry. End the meal with fragrant layered rice custard and Thai iced coffee. Open for dinner only; closed Mondays. Reservations advised. Major credit cards accepted. 4156 N. Kedzie Ave. (phone: 539-1909).

Bice The people watching here may be even more of a draw than the food; in summer, diners can sit outdoors and observe Chicago street life as it passes by. The menu features fancy preparations of Italian dishes, and the three-level dining room is decorated in a contemporary style, with dark wood paneling and tablecloths of imported Italian linen. Closed Sunday lunch. Reservations advised. Major credit cards accepted. 158 E. Ontario St. (phone: 664-1474).

Cape Cod Room An institution, this seafood spot serves reliable fresh pompano, lobster, and other finny fare. Closed *Christmas*. Reservations advised. Major credit cards accepted. *Drake Hotel,* 140 E. Walton St. (phone: 787-2200).

Cricket's Styled after the *"21" Club* in New York, the decor here features red-checkered tablecloths, bare floors, low ceilings, walls festooned with corporate memorabilia, and a menu that includes chicken hash Mornay and various daily specials. A very good choice for Sunday brunch, and popular for people watching any time. Open daily. Reservations necessary. Major credit cards accepted. *Tremont Hotel,* 100 E. Chestnut St. (phone: 280-2100).

Eli's the Place for Steak Founder Eli Schulman wanted to establish a place where his friends in business and real estate could enjoy a fine steak, prime roast, or liver and onions, as well as each others' company. Now run by his son Mark, the establishment maintains its clubby atmosphere. Be sure to save room for Eli's now nationally renowned cheesecake. You can start your diet tomorrow. Open daily. Reservations advised. Major credit cards accepted. 215 E. Chicago Ave. (phone: 642-1393).

Everest Room An elegant French restaurant, it has a commanding view from atop the *Chicago Stock Exchange Building* in Chicago's financial center. The cornucopia of original dishes reflects the chef's Alsatian roots. Try roast filet of sea bass wrapped in crisp shredded potatoes, black squid risotto, salmon soufflé, oxtail terrine with horseradish sauce, or venison with elderberries. Apple strudel is a recommended dessert. There is a special pre-theater menu and a seven-course *dégustation* menu that provides a good sampling of the superb fare. Closed Sundays and Mondays. Reservations necessary. Major credit cards accepted. 440 S. LaSalle St. (phone: 663-8920).

Le Français For years, Jean Banchet made this one of America's finest French restaurants. Today the kitchen is in the hands of Roland and Mary Beth Liccioni, and the still-excellent fare has a somewhat lighter touch. Standouts include rack of lamb served with tiny fresh vegetables and couscous, stuffed Dover sole, Lyonnaise sausage served *en croûte* with port wine sauce, and crayfish bisque. The pastries are superb. Closed Sundays. Reservations necessary. Major credit cards accepted. 269 S. Milwaukee Ave., Wheeling; take Kennedy Expwy. to Rte. 294 north, Willow exit (phone: 708-541-7470).

Gene and Georgetti In an old, wood-frame building near the *Merchandise Mart,* hearty sirloin, T-bone steaks, and animated conversation mingle. This eatery also dishes up popular Italian dishes and huge salads. Closed Sundays. Reservations unnecessary. Major credit cards accepted. 500 N. Franklin St. (phone: 527-3718).

Jackie's In this intimate 50-seat neighborhood spot serving some of the finest nouvelle cuisine in the city, French food with Oriental highlights is featured: Consider delicate orange-honey-glazed squab served with Chinese vermicelli and cabbage garnished with cashews and cloud-ear mushrooms. Lobster salad is served with rock shrimp and smoked mussels over fettuccine flavored with saffron and squid ink. Mousse-filled "chocolate sack" is owner/chef Jackie Shen's signature dessert. Closed Sundays and Mondays. Reservations necessary. Major credit cards accepted. 2478 N. Lincoln Ave. (phone: 880-0003).

Jimmy's Place Owner Jimmy Rohr has a passion for grand opera, and he uses it to provide a backdrop for his truly unique restaurant. Chef/partner Kevin Shikami's food is the equal of the arias that accompany it. Typical of the offerings (culinary, that is) are tuna tartare; rack of lamb baked in phyllo and finished with a light white wine curry sauce; steamed fluke with lobster medallions, steamed spinach, and lobster sauce with caviar; and Tosca's kiss, a chocolate *ganache* strewn with pecans and topped with warm caramel sauce. Bravo! Closed Sundays. Reservations advised. Major credit cards accepted. 3420 N. Elston Ave. (phone: 539-2999).

Morton's of Chicago Another fine steak-and-potatoes establishment whose loyal fans gulp down everything from kosher hot dogs to chicken in the pot to fabulous cheesecake. Open daily. Reservations advised. Major credit cards accepted. 1050 N. State St. (phone: 266-4820). There are more moderately priced versions in suburban Westchester (1 Westbrook Corporate Center; phone: 708-562-7000) and in Rosemont (9525 W. Bryn Mawr Ave.; phone: 708-678-5155).

Nick's Fishmarket The number of choices on the menu is bewildering, but it's tough to make the wrong decision here. The cold appetizer assortment of shellfish is always a good bet, and try the pan-fried whole baby salmon or an abalone dish as an entrée. First National Plaza location closed Sundays. Reservations necessary. Major credit cards accepted. First National Plaza, Monroe St. (phone: 621-0200) and 10275 Higgins Rd., Rosemont (phone: 708-298-8200).

Palm Owned by the same people who run the well-known New York restaurants called *Palm* and *Palm, Too,* this eatery has a similar decor of sawdust-covered floors and walls hung with drawings of regular patrons. Also like its East Coast counterparts, the kitchen here specializes in producing great steaks and lobsters. Closed Sundays. Reservations necessary. Major credit cards accepted. 181 E. Lake Shore Dr. (phone: 944-0135).

Le Perroquet Recently reopened by innovative Michael Foley of *Printer's Row,* this sumptuous spot is as elegant as before, with grilled seafood, creative presentations of game birds, and heavenly desserts prepared in the famed Foley style (although he is not the chef here). Closed Sundays. Reservations advised. Major credit cards accepted. 70 E. Walton St. (phone: 944-7990).

Pump Room A winning formula of fine food, diligent service, and lovely decor have made this a legend among Chicago restaurants. Continental dishes are the mainstays, but there are some nouvelle cuisine specialties; both are complemented by the restaurant's good wine list. Open daily. Reservations necessary. Major credit cards accepted. *Omni Ambassador East Hotel,* 1301 N. State Pkwy. (phone: 266-0360).

Seasons This opulent, urbane room features some of the most inventive nouvelle preparations in the city, all with an American accent. Try the quail with game-sausage stuffing or the venison. Open daily. Reservations necessary. Major credit cards accepted. *Four Seasons Hotel,* 120 E. Delaware Pl. (phone: 280-8800).

Spiaggia With picture windows overlooking the Magnificent Mile, this is one of Chicago's most stylish Italian dining places. There's subdued Art Deco lighting and a piano tinkling in the background, and the menu features ambitious pasta dishes, grilled fish, roast chicken, and specialties such as grilled veal chop with fresh sage. Its little sister café across the hall is more casual—yet still stylish and very romantic—and is a good spot to share a thin, blistery pizza or perhaps enjoy an excellent rendition of osso buco. Closed Sunday lunch. Reservations advised. Major credit cards accepted. 980 N. Michigan Ave. (phone: 280-2750).

Yoshi's Café French technique and Japanese mastery combine to produce a menu featuring such inventive dishes as striped sea bass stuffed with herbs and served with lobster cream sauce, sautéed veal medallions on homemade buckwheat pasta, and tuna tartare on a bed of guacamole. Open for dinner only; closed Mondays. Reservations advised. Major credit cards accepted. 3257 N. Halsted St. (phone: 248-6160).

Art Institute Restaurant in the Park Even many long-time Chicagoans think this elegant spot overlooking *Grant Park* is for members only: not so. Designed by the late Norman DeHaan, the stylish yet comfortable dining room offers first-rate service and a continental menu with magnificent desserts. Open for lunch only; closed Sundays. Reservations advised. Major credit cards accepted. Columbus Dr. between Monroe St. and Jackson Blvd. (phone: 443-3543).

Bella Vista This vast place was once a bank and the restaurant's owners (who are also responsible for *Bacino's* popular pizza places) took full advantage of the space with lush trompe l'oeil murals on all the walls; the tableware picks up both the color and floral motifs of the murals. The menu is contemporary Italian; diners can walk through the glassed-in wine rooms. Reservations advised. Major credit cards accepted. Somewhat out of the way, but convenient to *Wrigley Field* and *Lincoln Park;* also a block away from an elevated stop on the Howard Line. 1001 W. Belmont Ave. (phone: 404-0111).

Bistro 110 Everything about this place really clicks: an energetic ambience mixed with inventive yet casual cooking. The food—most notably items prepared in the wood-burning oven—is everything bistro fare should be. Meals begin with a lovely roasted garlic served with a crusty baguette. Especially popular entrées are cassoulet, oven-roasted chicken, and steak *au poivre.* Their Sunday brunch features live jazz. Open daily. Reservations advised. Major credit cards accepted. 110 E. Pearson St. (phone: 266-3110).

Blackhawk Lodge Many years ago, co-owner Doug Roth's father ran the *Blackhawk Inn,* a stylish and hearty favorite in the Loop. Now Roth *fils* has teamed with first-generation restaurateur Larry Levy to create a version of a Wisconsin summer camp for grown-ups. The concept works at this lively and popular place. The contemporary American fare, which is heavy on light foods like fish and salads, may have been inspired by summers at the lake, but it's far more interesting. Crowds move out to a screened-in porch in the summer. Open daily. Reservations advised. Major credit cards accepted. 41 E. Superior St. (phone: 280-4080).

Blue Mesa Southwestern cooking is one of this city's latest dining crazes, and Santa Fe style reigns in this comfortable room of whitewashed adobe and bleached pine. Lovers of wonderfully pulpy guacamole and steaks smothered in green chilies and onions will be quite content. Reservations necessary for parties of eight or more. Open daily. Major credit cards accepted. 1729 N. Halsted St. (phone: 944-5990).

Bub City A rollicking, mammoth, down-home Texas eating house, featuring shrimp and crab barbecue and "Big Easy" (read, New Orleans) bayou music to wash it all down. This is one loud, entertaining joint. Wear denim. Open daily. Reservations advised. Major credit cards accepted. There's lots of parking near this out-of-the-way spot, where Halsted Street and North Avenue meet. 901 W. Weed St. (phone: 266-1200).

Bukhara This Indian place claims its recipes go back 1,000 years. The focus is on marinated fresh seafood, poultry, beef, and lamb roasted in tandoori (hollow clay ovens). Try the tandoori chicken in pomegranate juice or the shish kebab with cumin-flavored lamb. Finish with a pudding of dates, almonds, and milk. Open daily. Reservations advised. Major credit cards accepted. 2 E. Ontario St. (phone: 943-0188).

Café Ba-ba-Reeba! Everything about this place is festive and upbeat. The emphasis on *tapas* (Spanish appetizers) gives diners an opportunity to sample lots of dishes, although entrée-size options are also available. Selections change, but the menu usually includes such specialties as octopus in vinaigrette, grilled sausage, paella, and flan for dessert. Closed for lunch Mondays and in January and February. Reservations unnecessary. Major credit cards accepted. 2024 N. Halsted St. (phone: 935-5000).

Carson's Probably the best spareribs in the city. Salads with a creamy, anchovy-flavored dressing and tangy au gratin potatoes are the other lures. Don't dress up because bibs (supplied) are essential. No reservations, so expect to wait. Open daily. Major credit cards accepted. 612 N. Wells St. (phone: 280-9200); 5970 N. Ridge Rd. (phone: 271-4000); 400 E. Roosevelt Rd., Lombard (708-627-4300); and 8617 Niles Center Rd., Skokie, for carryout only (phone: 708-675-6800).

The Eccentric This is Oprah Winfrey's baby, and it lives up to its name: lots of wild colors, paintings by local artists, an amalgam of French, English, American, and Italian cooking styles, and such dishes as cold fruit soup with chili peppers. Don't pass up Oprah's lumpy mashed potatoes with horseradish. Open daily. Reservations advised. Major credit cards accepted. 159 W. Erie St. (phone: 787-8390).

Emilio's Iberian and inventive, from the man who introduced *tapas* to Chicago at *Café Ba-ba-Reeba!* Open daily. Reservations unnecessary. Major credit cards accepted. 4100 W. Roosevelt Rd., Hillside (phone: 708-547-7177).

Geja's Café This restaurant has good food—from fondue to seafood—and a romantic atmosphere, with flamenco and classical guitar played every night of the week. There's a superb wine list. Reservations advised. Major credit cards accepted. 340 W. Armitage Ave. (phone: 281-9101).

Hat Dance Kicky, as the name suggests: Aztec decor, Mexican food with a Japanese accent. Closed at lunch weekends. Reservations advised. Major credit cards accepted. 325 W. Huron St. (phone: 649-0066).

Hatsuhana Delicious sushi and sashimi; tables as well as counter seating is available. Open daily. Reservations advised. Major credit cards accepted. 160 E. Ontario St. (phone: 280-8287).

Italian Village Visitors to Chicago may wonder why there are so few restaurants in the Loop; likely because executives go to private clubs and office workers do fast food or company cafeterias. But the *Italian Village* offers three, right in the middle of the downtown area. Downstairs is the clubby and casual *La Cantina;* on the second floor is a country restaurant called the *Village Room;* both are reasonably priced and offer a standard selection of Italian fare. Main floor *Vivere* is a recent addition, offering far more sophisticated, and pricey, regional Italian dishes in a dramatic setting. *La Cantina* and the *Village Room* are closed Sunday lunch; *Vivere* is closed Saturday lunch and Sundays. Reservations advised. Major credit cards accepted. 71 W. Monroe St. (phone: 332-7005, *La Cantina* and *Village Room;* 332-4040, *Vivere*).

Maggiano's A Chicago hot spot, it packs them in nightly. The menu features hearty Italian fare served on heaping platters meant to be shared. Breads from the *Corner Bakery* (right next door) are not to be missed. Open daily. Reservations advised. Major credit cards accepted. 516 N. Clark St. (phone: 644-7700).

Printer's Row Chef Michael Foley awakens sluggish palates with his delicious fare. Choose to dine in either the snug wine library, an intimate room lined with bookcases (including Michael's cookbooks); a cozy room decorated with a hunting motif; or the main dining area. Like *Prairie, Printer's Row* specializes in innovative Midwestern fare, which Foley helped define. The roast pheasant with *jus au natural* and five kinds of onions and the grilled salmon with basil cream sauce and sun-dried-tomato pasta are true standouts. Chocoholics should dive into the chocolate terrine studded with fresh raspberries or the white and dark chocolate cheesecake with amaretto sauce. Closed Sundays. Reservations advised. Major credit cards accepted. 550 S. Dearborn St. (phone: 461-0780).

Santorini's The elegant decor draws the elite of Chicago's Greek community; the menu, featuring lamb chops wrapped in phyllo and several seafood dishes, is equally classy. Open daily. Reservations advised. Major credit cards accepted. 138 S. Halsted St. (phone: 829-8820).

Scoozi A cavernous former garage that's been turned into a smashing gathering place with evocative period decor. Besides the chef's daily specials, the unusually large menu includes provincial Italian specialties such as a three-foot-long pizza served on a wooden plank (calorie counters, fear not; they do come smaller); osso buco (braised veal shanks); and pheasant that is smoked on the premises and served with a choice of soft, baked, or sautéed polenta (the Italian version of grits). Closed at lunch weekends. Reservations advised. Major credit cards accepted. 410 W. Huron St. (phone: 943-5900).

Shaw's Crab House This is a mammoth, immensely popular pre-World War II–style seafood house. Don't miss the stone or soft-shell crabs if they're in-season. The pecan pie may be Chicago's best. Open daily. Reservations advised.

Major credit cards accepted. 21 E. Hubbard St. (phone: 527-2722). *Shaw's Blue Crab Lounge* (660 Lake Cook Rd., Deerfield; phone: 708-948-1020) is a similar, but more casual, enterprise under the same ownership.

St. Germain Bakery-Café If this lively bistro makes you wonder whether you are on the Gold Coast or the Left Bank, no wonder; that's the intention. Particularly popular for Sunday brunching, it specializes in breads and croissants. The ambience is terrific. There are pastries, pâtés, and cheese to go as well. Open daily. Reservations advised for Sunday brunch only. Major credit cards accepted. 1210 N. State Pkwy. (phone: 266-9900).

Szechwan House The hot-and-sour soup and the crispy duck are just as appetizing as the chef's more unusual dishes—snails in spicy sauce and deep-fried ground shrimp wrapped in seaweed. Open daily. Reservations advised. Major credit cards accepted. 600 N. Michigan Ave. (phone: 642-3900).

Tucci Milan Offering elegantly prepared Italian dishes, it's very popular at lunch with the advertising set. The vast array of antipasti (try the goat cheese or eggplant) leads to entreés such as meatless lasagna, rosemary-seasoned chicken cooked on a spit, and thin-crust pizza. Closed Sunday lunch. Reservations advised. Major credit cards accepted. 6 W. Hubbard St. (phone: 222-0044).

Tuscany A newcomer drawing crowds to Little Italy west of the Loop, this stylish northern Italian trattoria offers innovative pasta dishes and an extensive wine list. Rack of lamb, rotisserie chicken, and risotto are specialties. Open daily. Reservations advised. Major credit cards accepted. 1014 W. Taylor St. (phone: 829-1990).

INEXPENSIVE

Ann Sather's There actually are three, but the original (on West Belmont Ave.) may be the world's only Swedish restaurant housed in a former funeral home. The menu varies from time-honored Swedish dishes to hearty American fare: pork sausage patties and rich country gravy, and beefsteak and eggs with cinnamon rolls. Brunch is particularly good. Open daily. Reservations unnecessary. MasterCard and Visa accepted. 929 W. Belmont Ave. (phone: 348-2378); 5207 N. Clark St. (phone: 271-6677); and 1329 E. 57th St., Hyde Park (phone: 947-9323).

Army & Lou's This hangout for Chicago aldermen serves the best soul food in the city. Try the greens and neck bones, the Northern beans with ham hocks, the smothered chicken and corn bread dressing, or better yet, the "Taste of Soul," which includes everything from chicken to catfish to chitlins and ham hocks. Closed Tuesdays. Reservations unnecessary. Major credit cards accepted. 422 E. 75th St.(phone: 483-3100).

Beau Thai One of Lincoln Park's fine collection of Southeast Asian eateries. Specialties include *pad thai,* a warm noodle dish; duck Beau Thai, cooked with cashews and vegetables; and sweet, creamy cold Thai coffee for dessert. Closed Mondays. Reservations accepted on weekends only. Major credit cards accepted. 2527 N. Clark St. (phone: 348-6938).

Berghoff Another Chicago tradition—and one sometimes thinks it's the only local restaurant visitors have ever heard of. Although the service is rushed, the meals are bountiful and the selection wide-ranging: ragout, Wiener schnitzel, steaks, and seafood. Closed Sundays. Reservations accepted for five or more. Major credit cards accepted. 17 W. Adams St. (phone: 427-3170).

Billy Goat Tavern Every newspaper town has to have a bar where reporters and editors congregate for inexpensive drinks and greasy fries. For Chicagoans, this home of juicy thick burgers is the place. The walls of the underground bar are decorated with clippings from some of the city's journalistic legends; and though its decor won't win any awards, it's a lively lunchtime spot with newspaper people, local sports fans, and tourists. It's worth a stop for a taste of gritty old Chicago. Open daily. No reservations. No credit cards accepted. 430 N. Michigan Ave. (phone: 222-1525).

Ed Debevic's The creation of Rich Melman, king of Chicago restaurateurs, this is a 1950s diner that has crowds lining up outside. Burgers, chili, malts, fries, and a rollicking *American Graffiti* atmosphere. Wear crinolines and chew bubble gum—just like the waitresses! Open daily. No reservations. No credit cards accepted. 640 N. Wells St. (phone: 664-1707).

Greek Islands You can find thoughtfully prepared dishes such as gyros, squid, lamb, and fresh broiled red snapper at this simple eatery. The decor is pleasant, with blue-and-white–checkered cloths, and it's particularly popular with faculty at the nearby *University of Illinois.* Open daily. Reservations unnecessary. Major credit cards accepted. 200 S. Halsted St. (phone: 782-9855).

Hard Rock Café Yes, Chicago has one, too. The walls of this hip hamburger emporium are covered with an assortment of rock music artifacts and declarations of world peace. Chili and grilled burgers lead the menu. Wash it all down with a fruit and honey "health shake." At the very least, it's the place to pick up an essential addition to any trendy T-shirt collection. Open daily. No reservations. Major credit cards accepted. 63 W. Ontario St. (phone: 943-2252).

Helmand Come here for savory Afghan baby pumpkin and lamb Kabuli in an exotic, attractive setting. Top off the meal with cheese-like *burfee* or baklava baked with ground pistachios. The service is as good as the food. Open for dinner only; closed Sundays. Reservations advised. Major credit cards accepted. 3201 N. Halsted St. (phone: 935-2447).

Ina's Kitchen Ever since Ina Pinckey opened this cozy spot in Lincoln Park a few years back, there have been lines out the door. Breakfast is served until 3

PM, when the kitchen closes. Lunch is added to the menu at 11:30 AM. Specials include a noodle and vegetable frittata, corn and black-bean scrapple, whole-wheat oatmeal pancakes, and a full range of pastries. Open for breakfast and lunch only. Closed Sunday. No reservations. No credit cards. 934 W. Webster Ave. (phone: 525-1116).

Lou Mitchell's For those who consider the idea of awakening before noon a barbaric proposal, make an exception and head for this outstanding breakfast spot. Freshly squeezed orange juice is followed by perfectly prepared pancakes, omelettes served in the pan, biscuits baked that morning, and fantastic coffee. Formica tabletops, eccentric waitresses, and a low-key clientele complete the picture. Lunch is served here, too, but breakfast has made this place a landmark on the city's restaurant scene. The doors open at 5:30 AM. Closed Sundays. No reservations. Major credit cards accepted. 563 W. Jackson Blvd. (phone: 939-3111).

Parthenon This eatery, a Greektown institution for more than two decades, offers good food in comfortable surroundings. The extensive menu runs from chicken shish kebabs to Greek sausage to baked lamb's head. Juicy gyros and wine-marinated octopus are among the bite-size appetizers; for dessert, try the moist almond-honey cake. Open daily. Reservations advised for groups of six or more. Major credit cards accepted. 314 S. Halsted St. (phone: 726-2407).

Pasteur This attractive corner storefront is among the best of some two dozen Vietnamese restaurants in the city. Recommended entrées are whole fried red snapper topped with sweet-salty sauce with scallions and lime or the charming nest of crispy fried egg noodles filled with seafood and vegetables. Closed Monday lunch. Reservations advised on weekends. Major credit cards accepted. 4759 N. Sheridan Rd. (phone: 271-6673).

Three Happiness Get a group together and head out early to avoid a wait at Chinatown's favorite dim sum spot. It's big, crowded, noisy, and dirty, but you'll feast for about $10 per person. Skip the regular menu; wait for the carts laden with steamed dumplings and buns, deep-fried pastries, plates of cold meat, scrumptious sweets, and other exotic fare that comprises the traditional Cantonese tea lunch. Open daily. No reservations. Major credit cards accepted. 2130 S. Wentworth Ave. (phone: 791-1228).

Tulpe This Lithuanian haven with only eight tables exemplifies the best in neighborhood restaurants, offering hearty, honest cooking at low prices in unpretentious surroundings. Among the specials are meat-filled dumplings, juicy pork chops, roast chicken, and homemade sausage. The staff is cheerful and friendly. During warm weather, there is outdoor dining on weekends. No liquor is served. Open daily for breakfast, lunch, and early dinner (until 8 PM). No reservations. No credit cards accepted. 2447 W. 69th St. (phone: 925-1123).

Wishbone A fun spot that serves up some terrific down-home Southern cooking. Chicken is the thing here: Grilled until juicy, Southern-fried, or Louisiana-blackened in a salad. Don't miss dessert, either: marble cheesecake, pecan pie served plain or oozing chocolate, and custard like Mom used to make. Open for breakfast, lunch, and dinner; closed Saturday lunch and Sunday lunch and dinner. No reservations. Credit cards accepted at Washington Street location only. 1001 W. Washington St. (phone: 850-2663) and 1800 W. Grand Ave. (phone: 829-3597).

HOT DOG! (AND PIZZA, TOO)

If all of the above fails to appeal to your culinary sensibilities, *Michael's* (1946 N. Clark St.; phone: 787-DOGS) is a terrific alternative. It's also just the spot for those with the I-can't-get-a-good-hot-dog blues. The special here is the "chardog," a half pound of spicy beef on a soft bun with onions, tomatoes, cucumbers, pickles, mustard, relish, and perhaps the kitchen sink. (If you're not in the mood for a hot dog, *Michael's* also offers an incredible salad bar, stuffed baked potatoes, grilled sandwiches, and world-famous cheddar fries.)

Hamburger and hot dog fans would be remiss to miss *Gold Coast Dogs* (2100 N. Clark St.; phone: 327-8887; 418 N. State St.; phone: 527-1222; and 325 S. Franklin St.; phone: 939-2624), where they can sample a real Chicago hot dog (it comes with fresh onions and peppers, not soggy sauerkraut). For funky 1950s fare, *Byron's* (850 W. North Ave.; phone: 266-3355) will take you back to the days of the drive-in, as will *Portillo* in the suburbs (806 W. Dundee Rd., Arlington Heights; phone: 708-870-0870; 611 E. Golf Rd., Schaumburg; phone: 708-884-9020; and 950 S. Barrington Rd., Streamwood; phone: 708-213-6656).

Finally, a visit to this city's eating establishments wouldn't be complete without a taste of Chicago's famous deep-dish pizza—layer upon layer of toppings baked in a deep pan. The pioneer of this pizza fit for Goliath is *Pizzeria Uno* (29 E. Ohio St.; phone: 321-1000), a place whose food more than makes up for its lack of atmosphere. Also in the area is *Pizzeria Due* (619 N. Wabash Ave.; phone: 943-2400), under the same ownership and serving the same hearty fare. *Gino's East* (160 E. Superior St.; phone: 943-1124) uses cornmeal crusts to vary the flavor. Other places to try this local delicacy are *Giordano's of Lincoln Park* (1840 N. Clark St.; phone: 944-6100); *Bacino's* (75 E. Wacker Dr.; phone: 263-0070; and 2204 N. Lincoln; phone: 472-7400); and *Edwardo's Natural Pizza* (1321 E. 57th St.; phone 312-241-7960; and 9300 Skokie Blvd., Skokie; phone: 708-674-0008). The latter also serves another local favorite, stuffed pizza—a thick, gooey, pie-like creation. All of the above eateries are open daily; reservations are unnecessary and major credit cards are accepted.

Diversions

Exceptional Pleasures and Treasures

Quintessential Chicago

Proud Chicagoans not only can readily point to their "city that works" as home to the skyscraper, but also as home of one of the country's first golf courses, deep-dish pizza, the flaming Greek cheese dish *saganaki*, jazz and blues, and celebrated writers who captured the city's spirit and the world's imagination. Chicago boasts an impressive list of native sons and daughters who shaped the development of the nation, invented new social and educational institutions, or left their imprint on the city's cultural scene.

A city of superlatives, Chicago is home to the world's tallest buildings, the widest range of ethnic communities, and the greatest concentration of Nobel Prize winners. Past and present, the city has spawned merchants and mobsters, lawyers and longshoremen, musicians and politicians, moguls of commerce and visionary thinkers—and is proud of them all.

JAZZ AND BLUES Say "blues" and you have to say Chicago—the city brought the world such musical legends as Muddy Waters, Bo Diddley, and Alberta Hunter. Starting with the Depression, Chicago was a magnet, attracting hundreds of thousands of blacks from the Deep South who migrated northward in search of jobs. They brought the blues of the Mississippi Delta to the funky, run-down bars and nightclubs of Chicago's black ghettos; it was here that the music of the Deep South—gritty, rhythmic, and elemental in its imagery—was transformed by the addition of the electric guitar into what became known as the Chicago blues. By the 1960s, a generation of white kids had discovered and fallen in love with the sound. Today, the blues is still an integral part of Chicago's musical signature, and the city is a place where only the best blues musicians survive and flourish.

One of the city's most respected "sweet home Chicago" joints is the tiny *B.L.U.E.S.*, across the street from the somewhat more grungy *Kingston Mines*. Both offer live music seven nights a week, along the strip affectionately known as "the street" to the blues musicians who come here—and jam until dawn once the clubs have closed for the night. Not to be forgotten is *Buddy Guy's Legends*, the club owned and operated by the blues guitarist who influenced dozens of major musicians, from Eric Clapton to Jimi Hendrix. Also see *Nightclubs and Nightlife* in THE CITY for all three. In June, the *Petrillo Band Shell* in *Grant Park* is the setting for a three-day Chicago blues festival featuring headliners from across the country.

Jazz, one of the other great American popular musical forms, also has a long history here. The seeds of Chicago's colorful musical legacy were sown in 1893 at the *World's Columbian Exposition*, which drew 26 million visitors to the city, including a large number of black musicians who came to see and play at the event. Jazz may have originated in New Orleans, but Chicago was one of the principal conduits for spreading it throughout the country and eventually the world. There are some who even claim that the term "jazz" came from turn-of-the-century Chicago musician Jasbo Brown, whose improvisational music style prompted his audiences to yell, "More, Jas!"

In the 1930s, the *Savoy Ballroom* was where Louis Armstrong belted out high Cs on his trumpet; Duke Ellington, Ella Fitzgerald, Dizzy Gillespie, and Benny Goodman also were regulars. Chicago clubs hosted a veritable "Who's Who" of jazz: Pianist Dorothy Donegan, drummers Buddy Rich and Gene Krupa, Billie Holiday, Earl "Fatha" Hines, master clarinetist Jimmy Noone, Tommy Dorsey, and other legendary greats regularly appeared in the city's nightclubs and ballrooms. And for many years, clubs such as *London House* and the *Blue Note Club* helped keep jazz flourishing in Chicago.

Another Chicago phenomenon is the so-called Austin High Gang—jazz musicians who went to school at, or who were associated with, *Austin High School*. Cornet player Jimmy McPartland and top sax stylist Bud Freeman attended Austin, and Benny Goodman was an acknowledged member of the gang, even though he wasn't an Austin alum.

The *Savoy* is gone now, as are many of Chicago's jazz and blues pioneers, but their musical tradition remains. In the city's nightclubs and concert halls today, fans can hear everything from wrenching blues to swing, from Dixieland to bebop to avant-garde jazz. For visitors eager to hear why Chicago is a toddlin' town, see *Music* in THE CITY.

CHICAGO LEGENDS Chicago isn't known as the "Windy City" because of the stiff breezes that whip off the lake (although they'll definitely chill you in February). The nickname was bestowed by East Coast journalists in honor of the blowhards and boosters who convinced the US Congress that Chicago, not New York City, was the most appropriate site for the 1893 *World's Columbian Exposition*, which celebrated the 400th anniversary of Europe's discovery of the Americas. Chicago was a year late getting the exposition off the ground, but once it did, the city put on quite a big show; in numbers, one of every three Americans visited here.

The lake aside, Windy City residents have plenty to be proud about: poets (Carl Sandburg, Eugene Field); architects (Frank Lloyd Wright, Louis Sullivan); Nobel Prize winners (Milton Friedman, James Cronin); educational innovators (John Dewey, William Rainey Harper); legal minds (Clarence Darrow); social reformers (Jane Addams, Ida B. Wells, Frances Willard); merchants (Marshall Field); mail-order kings (A. Montgomery Ward, Richard

Sears); butchers for the masses (Philip Armour, Gustavus Swift); and writers (Theodore Dreiser, Finley Peter Dunne, George Ade, Ben Hecht).

At the turn of the century, Chicago further distinguished itself by producing such writers as Sherwood Anderson (*Winesburg, Ohio*), Edgar Lee Masters (*Spoon River Anthology*), Hamlin Garland (*Son of the Middle Border*), and L. Frank Baum (*The Wizard of Oz*). There also were writers and muckrakers like Upton Sinclair, whose *The Jungle* created a national sensation and galvanized efforts to regulate the meat-packing industry. Thanks to James T. Farrell, Studs Lonigan was born in Chicago. And Nobel Prize winner Saul Bellow established his reputation writing about people from Chicago and those who have passed through it.

Those who more recently have distilled Chicago and made art of it operate in different media. The crusty and quick-witted columnist Mike Royko has made himself rich poking fun at Chicago's politicos. In the performing arts, David Mamet served his apprenticeship in the city's small experimental theaters, then went on to become a Pulitzer Prize–winning playwright; in film, John Hughes has brought his version of Chicago's suburbs to the movies. The mystery novel, too, is a burgeoning local art form, exemplified by novelist Sara Paretsky, who uses the city and its haunts as the backdrop for her crime stories.

Chicago's architects have also made their mark: Helmut Jahn the most controversial, Stanley Tigerman the most cerebral, and the various members of the firm of Skidmore, Owings & Merrill the most celebrated. But it is for its politicians that Chicago is most widely known, most particularly in the person of the late Richard J. Daley, one of the last of the old-style big-city power brokers. "Boss" of the city for more than 20 years, he let few things happen without his approval. Through a vast network of personal contacts, he made sure the streets were swept and the garbage picked up (at least in the precincts that voted for him); what money changed hands in the process he didn't want to know about. Today, the Boss's son, Richard M. Daley, wears the mayor's mantle.

And then there's Oprah: television personality, movie actress, shrewd business manager—and magnate. And she has ignored the lure of Hollywood, demonstrating a commitment to Chicago with investments like her popular restaurant, the *Eccentric* (see *Eating Out* in THE CITY), and Harpo Studios, where she tapes her show and produces others.

But no discussion of Chicago legends can begin or end without mentioning Al Capone, who started in Chicago as a bodyguard to the mobster-owner of a nightclub and rapidly moved up the ranks in an infamous reign of terror. One of the flashiest gang rulers, "Scarface" defied the law and outwitted fellow mobsters until he was nailed by the federal government on, of all things, tax evasion. A battle for supremacy between bootleggers, the Irish group on the North Side and the Italian one, led by Capone, on the South Side, resulted in the 1929 St. Valentine's Day Massacre, in which members of Bugsy Moran's North Side gang were gunned down by Capone's men posing as police officers. Even though Capone was sent to prison in 1931, mob fighting continued, some of it still under his control.

It is possible to relive those "good old days"—and get to see some of Chicago's less well-known neighborhoods—by taking a trip with *Untouchable Tours* (phone: 312-881-1195). Guides dressed as mobsters and wielding harmless Tommy guns pile their audience into a black, bullet-riddled bus and drive them past defunct breweries, the site of the nightclub where Capone got his start; the tottering *Lexington* hotel, from which Scarface ran his empire; and the grassy lot where the St. Valentine's Day Massacre took place.

PIZZA AND RIBS On *Christmas Day* in 1865, the *Union Stock Yard* opened on Chicago's South Side. During its heyday it was the world's largest meat-packing district, a complex that included a bank, a hotel, and a daily newspaper devoted to the meat-packing industry. Although the stockyard and its famous restaurant, the *Stockyard Inn,* closed in 1971, Chicago's tradition as a meat town remains—there's not much that can beat a thick Chicago cut of prime aged beef or a rack of the city's famous finger-licking ribs saturated in barbecue sauce. But this also is the place to test authentic deep-dish pizza, which Chicagoans claim as one of their city's major contributions to American gastronomy. The Windy City version is a piece of pie at least an inch thick, loaded with cheese and combinations of sausage, green peppers, onions, mushrooms, ground beef, bacon, anchovies, and almost any other topping imaginable. Deep-dish (or "Chicago-style") pizza traces its roots to the landmark pizza parlor *Pizzeria Uno,* which opened in Chicago in 1943. The word spread almost as fast as the cheese, and 12 years later a sister restaurant, *Pizzeria Due,* opened; both still do a rousing business. See *Eating Out* in THE CITY. Part of the fun is standing in line with hungry Chicagoans and tourists, waiting to see if the pizza lives up to its reputation. It does.

MAGNIFICENT MILE In the mid-1960s, real estate developer Arthur Rubloff began turning the area along Michigan Avenue between Oak Street and the Chicago River, an elegant stretch of unusual and predominantly exclusive shops and restaurants known mainly to natives, into the Magnificent Mile, one of the world's classiest shopping centers. At its head, Oak Street now rivals Rodeo Drive with its list of luxury emporia: *Ultimo* and *Marilyn Miglin,* plus imports like *Hermés, Bottega Veneta, Giorgio Armani,* and *Gianni Versace,* to name a few. Although a hefty budget is necessary to shop here, browsing among the elegant fittings is free, and who knows? Maybe that dress of your dreams has been marked down. But regardless of whether you shop or just stop, don't miss this elegant, extravagant expanse.

LAKE MICHIGAN Chicago owes its existence to Lake Michigan and the Chicago River, the link between the Great Lakes and the Mississippi River. The city's first permanent resident, Jean Baptiste Point duSable, opened a trading post here in 1781 (Marquette and Joliet came in 1679 but didn't stay). By the 1880s, Chicago had grown to become the nation's busiest port.

But when the course of the river was reversed in the 1890s and the Port of Chicago moved south to Lake Calumet, a farsighted group of businessmen commissioned architect Daniel Burnham to draw up a Plan of Chicago. Burnham envisioned an unobstructed waterfront as part of a citywide system of parks and boulevards that began at the lakeshore in *Jackson Park*, on the South Side, ran through the city's core, and ended in *Lincoln Park*, on the North Side. Burnham's legacy lives on in Chicago's waterfront today; 29 miles of publicly owned and accessible shoreline, with 31 public beaches and a number of harbors, lagoons, and parks—a place for sunbathing, golfing, jogging, tennis, sailing, fishing. "Make no small plans," Burnham advised, "they have no magic to stir men's souls." His generation of Chicagoans, at least, heeded his advice.

SUMMERS IN THE CITY Summer in Chicago means different things to different people.

Baseball fans (or fanatics) flock to *Wrigley Field* or *Comiskey Park* to watch either the *Cubs* or the *White Sox. Comiskey Park,* home to the *White Sox*, is a $150-million high-tech environment for a determinedly low-tech game ("refreshingly antiseptic," says a critic) that is drawing new fans to an old team. Over on the north side of town, the ever-hopeful *Cubs* try to swing their way into the *World Series* at *Wrigley Field.* "The Cubbies, they love to break your heart," says a fan (the last time the team won a *World Series* was in 1908), but the scoreboard is not neon yet, the ivy is real, and you needn't know anything about the game to relish an afternoon here.

Music lovers head for *Grant Park* concerts and other summer music festivals, held nearly every weekend from June to September. If Chopin and champagne are more your style, pack a picnic and head for the expanse of lawn at *Ravinia,* summer home to the *Chicago Symphony Orchestra* and venue for all manner of pop, classical, and jazz concerts (audience members sit on the grass, many of them with lavish picnics spread out on white linen tablecloths, china, silverware, and crystal). All you need is the admission fee and a blanket. Located in suburban Highland Park 25 miles north of the Loop, *Ravinia* can be reached by train from *North Western Station* (phone: 312-RAVINIA).

Gourmands gravitate to *Grant Park* (along Columbus Drive, one block east of Michigan Ave.) to celebrate *Taste of Chicago,* the city's annual picnic—except no one brings their own food. Instead, dozens of Chicago restaurants offer their varied specialties—ribs from *Arnie's,* cheeseburgers from the *Billy Goat Tavern, Gino's* pizza, *Harry Caray's* fried calamari, hot dogs from *Fluky's,* and *Eli's* famous cheesecake—all to the strains of everything from swing to Strauss offered continuously in the *Petrillo Band Shell.* It all begins the last weekend in June and lasts through the *Fourth of July;* on the night of July 3 it draws the biggest crowds, when the *Grant Park Symphony Orchestra* performs the *1812 Overture* and the city puts on what it contends is the nation's most spectacular fireworks display out over the lake. Summer never felt so good.

A Few of Our Favorite Things

Though Chicago abounds with many treasures, we've singled a few of our favorites. Unwind in hotels that are guaranteed to delight visitors in search of the finest accommodations and savor the best gustatory experiences that the city offers. Follow our lead; we promise you won't be disappointed.

Each place listed below is described in detail in THE CITY chapter.

ROOMS AT THE TOP

The following are some of our special favorites. Each offers the highest caliber of service, food, and big-city ambience. Complete information about our choices can be found on pages 65 to 70 in THE CITY chapter.

Chicago Hilton and Towers
Drake
Four Seasons
Inter-Continental
Nikko Chicago
Omni Ambassador East
Park Hyatt
Ritz-Carlton

INCREDIBLE EDIBLES

There are myriad dining possibilities in Chicago. The places below get our vote for providing a topnotch dining experience—fine service, a rich atmosphere, and, of course, fantastic food. Complete information about our choices can be found on pages 71 to 82 in THE CITY chapter.

Ambria
Carlos'
Charlie Trotter's
Frontera Grill and Topolobampo
Gordon
Le Mikado
Prairie

Antiques: Chicago's Best Hunting Grounds

Antiquing is not reserved for weekends in Chicago—any day of the week will do just fine. The city and its suburbs are filled with shops offering antiquarian treasures—from all manner of Americana to centuries-old European china and clocks to Oriental and Art Deco treasures.

WHERE TO BROWSE

The largest concentration of shops within the city limits is along Belmont Avenue, between Southport (1400 West) and Western (2400 West) Avenues. Other hunting grounds include:

BENKENDORF COLLECTION Fine 17th-and 19th-century clocks from England and France are featured here. *900 North Michigan Avenue,* Level 1 (phone: 312-951-1903).

CARTEAUX JEWELERS Tucked among the modern jewelry here is an impressive selection of antique pieces from estate sales and other sources. 31 N. Wabash St. (phone: 312-782-5375).

CHICAGO RIVERFRONT ANTIQUE MART Five floors of imported and early American furniture and antiques plus an auction hall. 2929 N. Western Ave. (phone: 312-252-2500).

CRETE-BEECHER ANTIQUE DEALERS A clutch of fine antiques shops line Main Street and Route 1, which go through both Crete and Beecher, two of Chicago's far-south suburbs. Spend a few pleasant hours tracking down treasures, then head about 5 miles farther south to the tiny village of Grant Park and have dinner at the *Bennett-Curtis House* (302 W. Taylor St., Grant Park; phone: 815-465-2288), an antiques-filled private home.

FOX RIVER VALLEY The favorite antiquing destination for Chicagoans is a series of charming 19th-century villages 30 miles west of the city. In Geneva, about 15 shops are centered along Third Street; in St. Charles, dozens of dealers fill three malls along Main Street just west of the river (phone: 708-377-6161 for the *Chamber of Commerce*). All are open daily and there are many delightful places to eat nearby. Take I-88 to Route 31 and head north through Batavia to Geneva and St. Charles, or take I-90 northwest to Route 31 and head south 10 miles to St. Charles. Also don't miss the *Kane County Flea Market,* where 1,500 dealers draw crowds the first Sunday each month. It's at Randall Road and Route 38, 2 miles west of Geneva; there's an admission charge (phone: 708-377-2252).

THE GOLDSMITH Mixed in with this shop's custom jewelry designs is a selection of antique pieces. *Water Tower Place,* Level 2 (phone: 312-751-1986).

LONG GROVE Located in a woodsy area 30 miles northwest of Chicago, this is a charmingly restored late-19th century village that was turned into a shoppers paradise some decades back. There are dozens of shops, some specializing in antiques, others in jewelry, cut glass, and crafts. It's located a half mile west of the intersection of Routes 83 and 53 (both major roads) on Old McHenry Road in Long Grove (phone: 708-634-0888).

NEW YORK JEWELERS This century-old diamond and jewelry wholesaler carries a large selection of estate jewelry, including antiques. 3 S. Wabash Ave. (phone: 312-855-0145).

Historic Churches and Synagogues

Chicago boasts some of the nation's most magnificent churches and temples, many filled with fine art and statuary, stained glass windows, and exquisitely carved altars. These houses of worship initially served ethnic groups that emigrated here, many from predominantly Catholic countries. Unfortunately, despite the fact that some of these structures are architectural treasures, the neighborhoods surrounding them have changed, and many no longer have a sizeable enough parish to support and maintain them. One, *Holy Family Church* (on W. Roosevelt Rd.), was saved from demolition and has been magnificently restored by a massive fund-raising effort. Both the *Chicago Architecture Foundation* (phone: 312-922-3432) and the *Illinois Landmarks Preservation Council* (phone: 312-922-1742) give tours of the city's churches and temples. Below are a few of Chicago's most beautiful spiritual settings.

BAHA'I HOUSE OF WORSHIP This nine-sided, domed structure, listed on the National Register of Historic Places, has delicate concrete filigree, resembling a three-tiered wedding cake, and is surrounded by nine flower gardens and almost as many fountains. The Baha'i faith, which originated in 19th-century Iran, emphasizes the spiritual unity of humanity, and the temple's nine sides represent the world's nine major religions. The interior is equally striking—sun-filled and stark, but restful. The structure took four decades (1920 to 1960) to build, while money slowly was raised for its construction. There also is a visitors' center on the lower level. Services are held every day. The church is open to the public. Information: *Baha'i House of Worship,* 100 Linden Ave., Wilmette (phone: 708-256-4400).

HOLY NAME CATHEDRAL Though architecturally undistinguished, this Victorian Gothic building (1874) of lemon-colored limestone is the principal church of the *Roman Catholic Archdiocese of Chicago.* The building, however, is more widely known for its connection with gangland massacres: In 1924, North Sider Dion O'Banion was murdered in his flower shop across the street by Al Capone's South Side gang; two years later, another mob did in Hymie Weiss (a good Catholic boy), missed three of his compatriots, and nicked the church's front steps. (The bullet holes remained there for decades, until they were discreetly repaired.) Information: *Holy Name Cathedral,* Chicago Ave. and N. State St. (phone: 312-787-8040).

NORTH SHORE CONGREGATION ISRAEL Home of one of the city's oldest and largest Jewish congregations, this imposing building—on a bluff high above Lake Michigan—was designed in 1964 by Minoru Yamasaki, who referred to it as "the architecture of light." Its vaults have amber-tinted skylights, and the side windows open on a vista of trees, lawn, and lake. In 1982, Chicago architect Thomas Beeby added a more intimate chapel, classical in design and cylindrical in shape. Though the addition pays no heed to the original design, it won Beeby an award from the *American Institute of Architects.* Visitors are welcome Mondays through Thursdays. Information: *North Shore Congregation Israel,* Sheridan Rd. in north suburban Glencoe (phone: 708-835-0724).

OLD ST. PATRICK'S CHURCH The city's oldest church building (built between 1852 and 1856), *St. Patrick's* survived the Great Chicago Fire (an early parishioner may well have been Mrs. O'Leary, owner of the infamous cow). It also survived the 1959 construction of the Kennedy Expressway, just behind it, which dealt a final blow to the neighborhood. Today, as new housing in the area expands the church's congregation, its pews are once again full on Sundays. On the last weekend in July, the church also sponsors "the world's largest block party," with music, dancing, and enough food and drink to bring out the Irish in anyone who partakes. Information: *Old St. Patrick's,* corner of Desplaines and Adams Sts., just west of the Loop (phone: 312-782-6171).

ROCKEFELLER MEMORIAL CHAPEL This massive Gothic edifice serves the *University of Chicago* and is named for John D. Rockefeller, its chief benefactor. (John D. Rockefeller IV was married here in 1969.) It has lovely stained glass windows and a 72-bell carillon that is noted for its exquisite tone. The chapel's high, vaulted ceiling is richly decorated with tiles; banners from the Vatican Pavilion of the 1964 *New York World's Fair* hang in the nave; and the church is also a venue for numerous concerts. The chapel is open daily to visitors. Information: *Rockefeller Memorial Chapel,* 59th St. and Woodlawn Ave. (phone: 312-702-2100).

ST. CHRYSOSTOM'S For a look at where the Protestant elite lived and worshiped during the early years of this century, visit this Episcopalian church (1894), the courtyard it surrounds, and the elegant turn-of-the-century homes along Dearborn Parkway and on State Parkway and Astor Street, just east of it. The interior houses a replica (on canvas) of the 10th-century mosaic of St. John from a church in Constantinople. Information: *St. Chrysostom's,* 1424 N. Dearborn Pkwy. (phone: 312-944-1083).

ST. JOHN CANTIUS Once home to the city's largest Polish congregation, this 2,000-seat church now offers the city's only mass in Latin; services frequently include Gregorian chants and orchestral music. Built in 1893, its massive altar of cherry and oak is said to have been made for the *World's Columbian Exposition,* held the same year. The rest is Baroque in every way: faux marble columns, gilt, and paintings and tiles on every surface. Information: *St. John Cantius,* 825 N. Carpenter St. at the intersection of Chicago and Milwaukee Aves., a mile west of the *Water Tower* (phone: 312-243-7373).

UNITY TEMPLE Designed by Frank Lloyd Wright in 1905 as a Universalist church, this was the architect's first public building, and the one he called a "little jewel." Considered one of the nation's great architectural showpieces, it is on the National Register of Historic Places. Made of poured concrete because it was an inexpensive material, the temple contrasted sharply with most other church buildings—and much of Oak Park—at the time. Rather than a traditional steeple pointing heavenward, Unity, with its strong horizontal lines, is very solidly earthbound. Its interior is equally striking: all squares, cubes, and rectangles, with a center pulpit and low-hanging balcony and high windows that flood it with light. In recent years, the church has been restored inside and out, the interior to its original colors of cream, brown, and sea green. Included in the architectural tours of Oak Park, it also is open to the public weekday afternoons and on some weekends (call ahead for a schedule); there's an admission charge for tours. Information: *Unity Temple,* 875 Lake St., Oak Park (phone: 708-848-6225 or 708-383-8873 for tour information).

Good Golf Nearby

Home of one of the nation's first 18-hole courses (the *Chicago Golf Club* opened in the western suburb of Wheaton in 1892), Chicago considers its golf courses to be among the best in the country. The city's rolling prairies, woods, and streams adapted well to the design and construction of stunning courses, and the game caught on with the city's elite. By the turn of the century, there were more than a dozen courses in the area, frequented by industrialists, merchants, and professionals. Exclusive golf club membership is still a ticket into Chicago's inner circle; many deals are made on courses like *Bob-O-Link* on the North Shore (which accepts only male members). Early on, the city became the headquarters of the *Western Golf Association;* for years the *Western Open* was played on Oak Brook's *Butler International,* until it moved to the larger *Cog Hill* course in Lemont in 1991. No less an authority than *Golf Digest* claims that Chicago has eight of the country's best golf courses; several of the leading ones open to the public are listed below.

CANTIGNY Located on the estate of the late Robert McCormick, controversial editor and publisher of the *Chicago Tribune,* this club offers a public course in a pampered country-club setting. The course is closed Mondays. Reservations are accepted seven days in advance; greens fees include a golf cart. Information: *Cantigny Golf and Tennis Club,* 27 W. 270 Mack Rd., Wheaton (phone: 708-668-3323).

COG HILL One of the nation's best-known courses (it now hosts the *Motorola Western Open*), it also is the nation's largest public golf facility. The four 18-holers vary in difficulty; the most challenging is *Dubsdread,* the championship course. Near the *Palos Forest Preserve,* its ample clubhouse serves three full meals a day; the links also have a halfway house. Open 365 days a year. Greens fees are lower for the less challenging courses than for the daunting *Dubsdread;* a golf cart for two is an additional charge. Information: *Cog Hill,* 12294 S. Archer Ave., Lemont (phone: 708-257-5872).

FOREST PRESERVE NATIONAL Early in this century, city planners began acquiring undeveloped lands in Cook County for a forest preserve system. Many of the area's golf courses are near these preserves of open meadow, woods, and streams; 18-hole *Forest Preserve National* is actually *in* one of them. The *Western Golf Association* lists it as one of the top 25 courses in the world—the lines that form here long before dawn testify to that fact. Open daily during the season; no telephone reservations. Greens fees are reasonable; golf carts are additional. Information: *Forest Preserve National,* 163rd St. and Central Ave., Oak Forest (phone: 708-429-6886).

KEMPER LAKES Opened in 1979, this well-manicured 18-hole course with bent-grass fairways and large, undulating greens hosted the *PGA Championship* in 1989 and the *Grand Slam of Golf* for several years. Built around several artificial lakes, water comes into play on nine of its holes. Open daily from the beginning of April through the beginning of November. Reservations must be made two weeks in advance; greens fees are high, but include a golf cart. Information: *Kemper Lakes,* Old McHenry Rd., Long Grove (phone: 708-320-3450).

PINE MEADOW Listed as the best public course in 1986 by *Golf Digest,* it has remained among the country's 25 top public courses since that time. With 18 holes spread out over 200 acres, it offers a fair test of all golfing abilities; it also includes an illuminated practice range. Open daily from April through November. Reservations, accepted in advance, must be prepaid with a major credit card. Greens fees do not include a golf cart. Information: *Pine Meadow,* in far north suburban Mundelein (take I-94), 1 mile north of Rte. 176 on Butterfield Rd. (phone: 708-566-4653).

OTHER NEARBY GREENS

The north suburban villages of Wilmette and Glencoe also maintain good 18-hole courses on the edge of the Forest Preserves. They are open daily, April to November, from dawn to dark. The *Wilmette* golf course (near the Lake Street exit on I-94 and Harms Rd.; phone: 708-256-9777) takes reservations one day in advance for weekdays, six days in advance for weekends. The greens fees vary for weekdays and on weekends; a golf cart is additional. *Glencoe* (a few miles farther north) accepts no phone reservations, but will take them in person for weekday games; on weekends, it's first come, first served. Greens fees vary for weekdays and weekends, as well as for nine or 18 holes. Golf carts are an additional charge. To get there, take I-94 (the Edens Expwy.), then Route 41 north to Dundee Road, head east to the second stoplight, and turn left. The country club is a half-mile north, where the road ends, at 621 Westly Road (phone: 708-835-0981).

Horsing Around

There is nowhere within the city's limits to ride horseback (the last stable with access to *Lincoln Park* was closed in the 1960s, when Sandburg Village was constructed). Happily, there are numerous trails in the Forest Preserve Districts in the six-county metropolitan area, Chicago's magnificent system of greenways that surround the city, mainly along the course of the Skokie, Des Plaines, and Fox Rivers.

In Cook County, all riders must be guided, and frequently on weekends there are long waits for mounts. (The city still offers carriage rides, most of which leave from the *Water Tower* on North Michigan Avenue.) Some of the larger and more accessible public stables are listed below; for information on dozens of others, call the Forest Preserve offices: for Cook County, 312-261-8400; for Lake County (north), 708-367-6640; for DuPage County (west), 708-790-4900; for Will County (southwest), 815-727-8700; for Kane County (far west), 708-232-5980.

HAPPY TRAILS Located in the *Lake County Forest Preserve,* this place offers 6 miles of gravel horse tracks. Experienced riders can go without a guide; patrolled trails are marked with appropriate gait, and riders must follow these guidelines or risk being ticketed. Children must be at least 12 years of age. The cost includes the permit fee. Reservations are required a day in advance. Information: *Happy Trails,* on Rand Rd. (Rte. 12) in far northwest suburban Wauconda, one and one-half hours north of the city (phone: 708-526-0055).

WEDGEWOOD For experienced riders, *Wedgewood* offers more than 100 miles of trails that wind through the *Cook* and *Lake County Forest Preserves.* Riders must purchase a license for a nominal fee in addition to the rental fee. Information: *Wedgewood Riding Center,* 699 N. Milwaukee Rd. in north suburban Wheeling, accessible from I-94 (phone: 708-537-9610).

WILLOW BROOK ACRES Riders at all levels are welcome here, but they must be guided on the trails. Horses and guides are available. Riders also must pay a licensing fee (it's good all year). There's a pleasant jaunt over quaint wooden bridges and through quiet woods frequented by deer and other animals. A special treat here is the 90-minute Sunday ride, which includes breakfast. Information: *Willow Brook,* 9501 Austin Ave., in north suburban Morton Grove, accessible from Edens Expwy. (phone: 708-967-9800).

Sailing Chicago's Waterways

With that huge lake out there, you'd think that Chicagoans would do a lot of sailing, and they do—although powerboats are popular as well. Among sailors, *the* event is the annual mid-July *Chicago to Mackinaw,* the nation's longest and oldest freshwater regatta. On weekends from May through

September, there are races from a variety of classes—Stars, J-24s, and Solings are favored choices. Races start from several harbors each weekend: the *Chicago* and *Columbian* yacht clubs at Monroe Street, the *Chicago Yacht Club* branch at Belmont Harbor (3200 North), and *Sheridan Shore* in Wilmette. If you're a sailor, you might try to make friends with a boat owner to get a spot on a crew. For more casual sailing, craft are available for rent from three places in the city and one in suburban Wilmette (see below). Note: The lake is tricky; you should know heading up from jibbing before heading out.

BILL GLADSTONE'S CHICAGO SAILING CLUB For a more challenging time on the water, experienced sailors might want to try a J-22, a 22-foot version of the popular J-24, often raced out of Chicago's harbors. The craft can accommodate up to five people. To be sure you can get a boat (these are popular with regulars), call a week in advance. In addition to the hourly rental fee, there is an additional check-out charge for new customers. They also have a Newport 31 for charter. At the north end of Belmont Harbor, Lake Shore Dr. at 3200 North (phone: 312-871-SAIL).

CHARLOTTE ANN Sailing on this 100-year old, 90-foot, two-masted schooner might be more for the soul than for the body, since a five-member crew does most of the work, but the air is fresh and the view superb. It offers brunch cruises on Sundays; groups receive a discount over the per-person charge. The *Charlotte Ann* sails out of Burnham Harbor, south of the *Adler Planetarium* (phone: 312-643-3400).

CHICAGO PARK DISTRICT Sailboats can be rented from three *Chicago Park District* locations. At Burnham Harbor (between the *Adler Planetarium* and McCormick Place), renters must stay within the spacious harbor; closed Sundays (phone: 312-294-2270). At the *South Side Cultural Center* (6100 South), sailors can venture farther into the lake; closed Mondays through Wednesdays (phone: 312-288-1223). From Farwell Avenue (6900 North, near *Loyola University*), sailors also can go farther out into the lake; closed on Mondays; make reservations a day or two in advance (phone: 312-262-7377).

WILMETTE PARK DISTRICT North suburban Wilmette supports one of the loveliest beaches on the North Shore; you can walk along it for nearly a mile. It also is accessible by public transportation; take the Howard Street line as far as it goes, then switch to the Linden Avenue train and ride to the end of the line. The beach is only four blocks away; the *Baha'i House of Worship* is a lakefront landmark. Windsurfers, 14-foot Barnetts, and HobieCats are available. A deposit is required for all rentals; major credit cards are accepted. Reservations are required, and they can be made up to 48 hours in advance. If you are driving, take Lake Shore Drive north to Sheridan Road and follow it to the *Baha'i House of Worship* (you can't miss it) and start looking for a parking place (phone: 708-256-9662).

A Shutterbug's Chicago

If you can get it to hold still long enough, Chicago is an exceptionally photogenic city. There is architectural variety: Old is juxtaposed with new, ornate with ordinary; there is a skyline bristling with the temples of modern commerce and graced with a 19th-century church spire; and there is the ever-present—and often-photographed—El. There is also natural variety: A column of trees embroiders a park footpath, ivy inches up a colonial red brick building, and a summer sunset sparks the river ablaze. In all, the thriving city, the shimmering lake, the park, the people, and traces of rich history make Chicago a fertile stomping ground for shutterbugs. Even a beginner can achieve remarkable results with a surprisingly basic set of lenses and filters. Equipment is, in fact, only as valuable as the imagination that puts it to use.

LANDSCAPES, WATERSCAPES, AND CITYSCAPES Chicago's bustling byways and historic buildings most often are visiting photographers' favorite subjects. But the city's green spaces and waterways provide numerous photo possibilities as well. In addition to the lions in front of the *Art Institute,* the *Sears Tower,* and the *Fourth Presbyterian Church* on Michigan Avenue, be sure to look for natural beauty: the *Grant Park* elm trees lining South Michigan Avenue, the well-manicured plots of flowers in the *Lincoln Park Conservatory,* and the sailboats and motorcraft that ply Monroe Street Harbor are just a few examples.

Although a standard 50mm to 55mm lens may work well in some landscape situations, most will benefit from using a 20mm to 28mm wide-angle lens. *Shedd Aquarium,* with city skyscrapers looming in the distance, for example, is the type of panorama that fits beautifully into a wide-angle format. Use a detail as a focal point for your shot: A flower, for instance, can be used to set off a view of the Lincoln Park Conservatory area, or people can provide a sense of perspective in a shot of the *Art Institute.* To isolate specific elements of any scene, use a telephoto lens. Perhaps there's a particular carving in a historic church that would make a lovely shot, or it might be the interplay of light and shadow on the Picasso sculpture in Daley Plaza. The successful use of a telephoto lens means developing an eye for detail.

PEOPLE As with taking pictures of people anywhere, there are going to be times in Chicago when a camera is an intrusion. Consider your own reaction under similar circumstances and you get an idea of what would make others comfortable enough to be willing subjects. People often are sensitive to having a camera suddenly pointed at them, and a polite request, while getting you a share of refusals, also will provide a chance to shoot some wonderful portraits that capture the spirit of the city as surely as the scenery does. For candids, an excellent lens is a zoom telephoto in the 70mm-to-210mm range; it allows you to remain unobtrusive while the telephoto lens draws the subject closer. And for portraits, a telephoto can be used effectively as close as two or three feet.

For authenticity and variety, select a place likely to produce interesting subjects. The *Water Tower* is an obvious spot for visitors, but if it's local color you're after, visit Little Saigon or one of the Lincoln Park festivals in mid-July, or the *Bud Billiken Day* parade. The area around *Buckingham Fountain* is a good place for people shots. Aim for shots that tell what's different about Chicago. In portraiture, there are several factors to keep in mind. Morning or afternoon light will add richness to skin tones, emphasizing tans. To avoid the harsh facial shadows cast by direct sunlight, shoot in the shade or in an area where the light is diffused.

SUNSETS When shooting sunsets, keep in mind that the brightness will distort meter readings. When composing a shot directly into the sun, frame the picture in the viewfinder so that only half of the sun is included. Read the meter, set, and shoot. Whenever there is this kind of unusual lighting, shoot a few frames in half-step increments, both over and under the meter reading. Bracketing, as this is called, can provide a range of images, the best of which may well be other than the one shot at the meter's recommended setting.

Use any lens for sunsets. A wide-angle is good when the sky is filled with color-streaked clouds, when the sun is partially hidden, or when you're close to an object dramatically silhouetted against the sky.

Telephotos also produce wonderful silhouettes, either with the sun as a backdrop or against the palette of a brilliant sunset sky. Bracket again here. For the best silhouettes, wait 10 to 15 minutes after sunset. Unless using a very fast film, a tripod is recommended.

Red and orange filters often are used to accentuate a sunset's picture potential. Orange will help turn even a gray sky into something approaching a photogenic finale to the day, and can provide particularly beautiful shots linking the sky with the sun reflected on the ocean. If the sunset is already bold in hue, however, the orange will overwhelm the natural colors. A red filter will produce dramatic, highly unrealistic results.

NIGHT If you think that picture possibilities end at sunset, you're presuming that night photography is the exclusive domain of the professional. If you've got a tripod, all you'll need is a cable release to attach to your camera to ensure a steady exposure (which often is timed in minutes rather than fractions of a second).

For situations such as evening concerts at *Ravinia* or nighttime river cruises, a strobe does the trick, but beware: Flash units often are used improperly. You can't take a view of the skyline with a flash. It may reach out as far as 30 feet, but that's about it. On the other hand, a flash used too close to a subject can cause overexposure, resulting in a "blown out" effect. With most cameras, strobes will work with a maximum shutter speed of 1/125 or 1/250 of a second. If you set the exposure properly and shoot within range, you should come up with pretty sharp results.

CLOSE-UPS Whether of people or of objects, close-ups can add another dimension to your photography. There are a number of shooting options, one of which is to use a 70mm or a 210mm lens at its closest focusable distance. Unless you're working in bright sunlight, a tripod will be worthwhile. If you are very near your subject and there is a good deal of reflective light, it may pay to underexpose a bit in relation to the meter reading.

If you do not have a telephoto lens, you still can shoot close-ups using a set of magnification filters. Filter packs of one-, two-, and three-time magnification are available, converting your lens into a close-up lens. Even better is a special macro lens designed for close-up photography.

A SHORT PHOTOGRAPHIC TOUR

Here are some of Chicago's truly special photograph opportunities.

SEARS TOWER Day or night, the view from the 103rd-floor *Skydeck Observatory* is breathtaking—a wonderful aerial vista for photos. On a clear day, the view from the *Skydeck* encompasses four states (Illinois, Wisconsin, Indiana, and Michigan). The lake looks almost benign, and the city appears lilliputian, colorful, and orderly; watch the tiny El as it winds its way north. For the best photos, use the slowest color film available for your camera (such as ASA 25) and a tripod. If you haven't got one, steady the camera on a railing or use slightly faster film. Don't use a flash, because it will reflect on the *Skydeck* window.

JOHN HANCOCK CENTER It's not as tall as the *Sears Tower,* but the view is just as spectacular. Take your camera up to *Hancock Center*'s 94th-floor observatory and check out the view—on clear days, it stretches 80 miles in every direction. (The same rules for film speed and a tripod apply here as at the *Sears Tower.*)

MONTROSE HARBOR For a fabulous view of the Chicago skyline, walk to the end of this harbor at *Lincoln Park*'s northern end. Here a finger of land stretches far out into the lake, affording shots of high-rises and fisherfolk. Head north on Lake Shore Drive to the Montrose exit and keep bearing right; parking is available.

LINCOLN PARK CONSERVATORY Thousands of varieties of trees, flowers, and vegetation from around the world are on display in this glass-domed indoor facility, also one of the city's most photogenic places. Wander through the three acres of carefully tended gardens. In *Lincoln Park* at 2200 North, just south of Fullerton Ave.

MICHIGAN AVENUE BRIDGE This historic 1919 bridge across the Chicago River offers an excellent vantage point for capturing the vibrant essence of Chicago's powerful urban landscape on film. Sunset lends a stunning play of color to the city's skyscrapers along the river's banks. One of the city's most popular thoroughfares for people and for vehicles, this bridge (and others) is frequently raised and lowered to let passing boats through. If you're lucky enough to be there when it happens, it can make for a super shot.

NAVY PIER Several mayors and numerous civic groups have debated for decades about a real purpose for this delightful relic of the pre-automobile era—when people boarded boats here to spend a day at the dunes. Now being substantially overhauled to serve as a new exposition space, *Navy Pier* remains accessible along all its half-mile length, making it another lakeside spot offering an excellent view of the city's skyline and a perfect spot for photographing boats coming and going on the lake. East of Lake Shore Dr. at the end of Grand St.

OLIVE PARK Just east of *Navy Pier,* this is where you can shoot swimsuit-clad bathers with a city skyscraper as a backdrop. This spit of land was built 25 years ago to house a water filtration plant; across the water are apartment buildings along Lake Shore Drive.

SOLIDARITY DRIVE Named in honor of Chicago's Polish community, this road, which leads out to the *Adler Planetarium,* is one of Chicago's favorite spots for picture taking (visiting morning TV shows choose this as their outdoor location). And indeed, it's quite a view, with the Loop spread out to the north and the boat-studded Burnham Harbor to the south. To get here, take Lake Shore Drive south to McFetridge Street (it will be on the left and comes up quickly) behind the *Field Museum.* Solidarity Drive is just a block north, on the right. During the winter, there are lots of places to park.

THE EL For the least expensive ($1.50) photographic tour of Chicago, take a train. The Ravenswood El winds north from the Loop through what's called Near North, then into upscale Lincoln Park; at Belmont (3200 North), it heads west through Lake View and Ravenswood, old ethnic neighborhoods surrounding former manufacturing districts; then ends where you can get on another train to return. The Howard Street Line comes out of the subway tunnel at Fullerton (2400 North) and heads north to the city's border, through neighborhoods called Uptown, New Town, and Rogers Park. You can get off the train at any stop that's appealing, then aim and shoot. We recommend the Sedgwick, Armitage, and Paulina stops on the Ravenswood line; Addison (*Wrigley Field*), Sheridan, Argyle (Little Saigon), and Morse (Rogers Park) on the Howard line. Pick up either train in the Loop.

Directions

Directions

Introduction

The Second City, City of the Big Shoulders, The Windy City, The City That Works—Chicago seems to have a nickname for every occasion. The only thing it lacks is a nickname that does it justice.

But then, it's hard to sum up a city of such varied appeal. Its skyline is visually stunning, a match for any in the world, and yet it's the city's neighborhoods that give it a flavor all its own. Chicago's culture is sophisticated without being snooty, it has opera and symphony, some of the best, but it also has peerless blues and jazz. People here are accessible, downright friendly for city-dwellers, but they're also shrewd, sharp, and skilled at the art of the deal. And what about that lakefront? It's more playground than working port, but somehow you get the sense that it's the source of the city's wealth. Chicago is the City of. . . who needs another nickname, Chicago is Chicago.

This is a *big* city; it has nearly three million residents within the city limits, and another eight million live in its outskirts, including nearby parts of Indiana and Wisconsin. It stretches 15 miles inland from the lake and 29 miles north to south. Despite those figures, it is astonishingly easy to get around. Not only is it possible to drive to most of the city's major sites, there's often a parking place on the street nearby. If you prefer public transportation, Chicago's efficient *CTA* (a.k.a. the El) zips from Chinatown on the South Side to Little Saigon on the North Side without changing trains, from *Comiskey Park* to *Wrigley Field* in 20 minutes, from *Field's* on State Street to *Field's* at *Water Tower Place* in just five.

As if ease of access were not enough, Chicago's grid plan and street numbering system even make it hard to get lost here. State Street is the north-south axis, Madison Street the east-west axis: 1200 North on any street is at Division Street; 800 West is at Halsted Street. It's like having a built-in compass. Train stations and highway exits all say what hundred east, west, north, or south they are.

One thing visitors quickly discover is that Chicago is a city of neighborhoods. Traditionally, those enclaves have grown up around a common cultural background, but increasingly, the social cement holding them together is a shared lifestyle. Some of the walks that follow immerse the visitor in the city's cultural stew pot of Chinese, German, Greek, Italian, Swedish, and Vietnamese peoples. Other walks cover such commercial highlights as the Loop and the Magnificent Mile, but residential and historical neighborhoods like Lincoln Park, the Gold Coast, and Pullman are also included. Here, too, are strolls that appeal to distinct interests like sculpture and architecture.

As with any big city, there is a dark underbelly to Chicago. But by taking the usual reasonable precautions (don't carry lots of cash, stay out of dark alleys, etc.), you can avoid any unpleasantness during your visit.

There are many more ways to see Chicago than there is room for here, and many more sites than can conveniently be included in these walks. In some cases, it's possible to split a walk up into two parts or more, allowing you to sample smaller bits of the city in a leisurely manner. If time is at a premium, however, *Walk 3: Wacker Drive* offers the best overview of the city and its history. Afterwards, hop on the El and ride around the Loop or head north to prowl the neighborhoods around Argyle Street, stopping for dinner at a Southeast Asian restaurant. For a more leisurely view of the city, take *Walk 11: Halsted Street,* getting off the bus (or out of the car) frequently along this city sampler.

Whatever route you choose will offer something to delight the mind, the senses, or both. There is history here as well as culture. There also is great food, greater architecture, and the greatest people. Norman Mailer called Chicago "the last great American city," and that may be as close as words can come to identifying this manageable metropolis.

Walk 1: The Loop
A Heritage in Stone and Steel

Long Chicago's vibrant business center, the Loop is still the left ventricle of the heartland, pumping goods and services to the Midwest, the nation, and the world. Though the main shopping district has moved from State Street to North Michigan Avenue, just outside the Loop, the towering buildings within the lariat of elevated track from which the area takes its name still house corporate headquarters of *Fortune* 500 companies, high-powered law firms, and international financial services institutions. These imposing structures are not only a symbol of Chicago's business brawn; they are also a reminder that the talents of architects William Le Baron Jenney, Daniel H. Burnham, John Wellborn Root, and Louis Sullivan made Chicago the birthplace of the modern skyscraper.

Though the city's first skyscraper, Jenney's Home Insurance Building, no longer exists, some of the landmarks of modern structural engineering still stand in downtown Chicago. Throughout this century, the Loop's architectural tradition has continued, providing a showcase for the work of such modern giants as Miës van der Rohe, Helmut Jahn, and the firm of Skidmore, Owings & Merrill. Three of the world's five tallest skyscrapers are in this city; two, the *Sears Tower* and the *Amoco Building,* are in the Loop (the third, the *John Hancock Building* is on N. Michigan Ave.). The Loop also is dotted with open-air plazas (many of them settings for sculptures or mosaics by celebrated artists) that add a humanizing touch to the steel-and-glass spires.

This is very much a city of public art, and dozens of murals and sculptures enhance its buildings and plazas, particularly in and around the Loop. Since 1978 the *Department of Cultural Affairs* and the *Department of Public Works* have commissioned some 30 new pieces, which does not include the many works that have been privately sponsored. The *Department of Cultural Affairs* even publishes a *Loop Sculpture Guide.* (Available for a nominal fee at several bookstores or at the *Department of Cultural Affairs,* 78 E. Washington St.; phone: 312-744-6630.)

The mingling of art and commerce here reflects the spirit of a city that takes pride in its tradition of architectural innovation, and in its growing reputation as a cultural center. Indeed, these ideas come together in two structures, the *Auditorium Building* on South Michigan Avenue and the *Civic Opera House* on Wacker Drive, both of which were designed with commercial space that would subsidize theaters or performance spaces, a notion that was unheard of in 1890 when the *Auditorium* was built.

The elevated train, or El, enters the downtown area from the west along Lake Street, then heads east several blocks before it curves south on Wabash

The Loop—
A Heritage in Stone and Steel

N

Monroe Harbor

Grant Park

LAKE SHORE DRIVE

Standard Oil Building

RANDOLPH DR.

COLUMBUS DRIVE

STETSON ST.

Prudential Plaza

BEAUBIEN CT.

MICHIGAN AVENUE

Chicago Cultural Center

Maller Building

Carson Pirie Scott

Inland Steel Building

Art Institute

JACKSON DRIVE

Fine Arts Building

Orchestra Hall

Harold Washington Library Center

Auditorium Bldg.

CONGRESS PARKWAY

LAKE STREET

Marshall Field's

Richard J. Daley Plaza

Chicago Bldg.

LOOP

Palmer House

WABASH AVENUE

STATE STREET

PLYMOUTH COURT

Federal Plaza

DEARBORN ST.

FEDERAL STREET

CLARK STREET

LA SALLE STREET

SHERMAN STREET

WELLS STREET

FRANKLIN STREET

F

S

James R. Thompson Center

First National Bank Bldg.

Marquette Bldg.

Dirksen and Kluczynski

Rookery

Monadnock Building

Chicago Board of Trade

RANDOLPH STREET

WASHINGTON STEET

MADISON STREET

MONROE STREET

ADAMS STREET

QUINCY COURT

JACKSON BOULEVARD

VAN BUREN STREET

WACKER DRIVE

0   mile   1/4

Street, swings west at Van Buren Boulevard, and heads north again and out of downtown along Wells Street. The area now officially known as the Loop generally includes an additional block or two falling just outside of the circumscribing tracks. For those with the energy and sturdy shoes, the best way to see downtown is to hike up and down its streets (the Loop is less than a mile across on the diagonal), looking at the assortment of building designs that represents a century-and-a-quarter of architectural history. (The entire area was burned to the ground in the Great Chicago Fire of 1871.) This walk hits the highlights of the Loop, beginning and ending at the *James R. Thompson* (formerly *State of Illinois*) *Center.*

Before going into Helmut Jahn's blue-glass *Thompson Center* at the corner of Clark and Randolph Streets, notice the abstract sculpture with graffiti-like designs in front of the building; called *Monument with Standing Beast* (1984), it is by French artist Jean Dubuffet. The artwork is meant to be walked through. Its four fiberglass elements seem to represent an animal, a tree, a gateway, and a tower, no doubt a reference to the skyscraper city. The artist had a genuine affection for Chicago, and this is one of only three commissions he completed in the United States.

The dazzling atrium of the *Thompson Center* (100 W. Randolph St.) is worth seeing for itself, as well as for an interesting untitled sculpture by John Henry at the entrance. The gallery and a shop with items by Illinois artisans are both good places to browse. On the lower level concourse are numerous eateries as well as shops specializing in Chicago souvenirs.

When you leave the center, walk a half block south on Clark Street to Richard J. Daley Plaza, facing Washington Street between Clark and Dearborn Streets. In 1964, when the 31-story *Civic Center* that dominates this plaza was completed, few words of praise were heard for its ugly, rust-colored Cor-Ten steel cladding. And in 1967, when a 50-foot-tall sculpture made of the same steel was plunked down in the plaza in front of the building, indifference grew to downright disdain. For all of its sophistication, Chicago also is known to look with low-brow skepticism on highfalutin' ideas of art and architecture. Sure the sculpture was a Picasso, but what was it? And why was it made out of rusty metal? As time passed, the self-weathering Cor-Ten assumed a handsome reddish-brown patina and the unnamed sculpture (it's referred to as *Chicago's Picasso*) became a truly civic center, attracting noonday crowds and serving as a landmark for casual meetings. After Richard J. Daley, Chicago's four-term mayor, died in 1976, the building, which housed offices and courtrooms, and its plaza were renamed in his honor. The Loop's first outdoor modern artwork, now a source of pride and an unofficial symbol for the city, went on to precipitate an avalanche of sculpture in the downtown area.

During the summer, Daley Plaza is a center for outdoor activity, featuring a popular lunchtime concert series called *Under the Picasso.* From June through September the music (or dance) begins at noon, two or three days a week. Arrive early, it's standing room only by 11:45 AM (phone: 312-

FINE ART for schedule information). On other days the plaza hosts a farmers' market and crafts fair. For information about the market and fair, call the *Mayor's Office of Special Events* (phone: 312-744-3370).

Across the street in a small plaza (69 Washington St.) is a work by Picasso's friend, rival, and fellow countryman, Joan Miró. Miró's *Chicago* (1981) is a figure of a woman that recalls ancient sculptures of goddesses. Look for the star that is embedded in one of the ceramic tile insets and for the miniature of the figure depicted in braille. Miró, like Picasso, gave his design to the city as a gift; money to construct the work was raised locally.

From this plaza, stroll east along Washington Street to *Marshall Field's* (111 N. State St.). This landmark emporium, determined to "give the lady what she wants," has defined service for generations of American retailers and their clients. Before entering the store note the large circular sculpture, *Being Born*, by Virginio Ferrari. Surrounded by a reflecting pool, the sculpture, with its two stainless-steel elements that fit together with precision, symbolizes the exacting standards of the tool-and-die industry that commissioned it. During the summer, this is a favorite lunch spot.

Also note the vacant lot across the street, the site of a stalled development project. Ironically, this block once held the office building where, according to legend, Louis Sullivan met his partner, engineer Dankmar Adler, and began one of the most fruitful collaborations in American architectural history. This also is hallowed ground for the legal profession: Another building that once stood on this block housed the law office of Clarence Darrow. In 1894, long before the famed Scopes trial (in which he argued for the right to teach evolution in schools), Darrow made his reputation locally by defending socialist leader Eugene V. Debs following the bitter Pullman strike. Here, too, were the offices of John Peter Altgeld, the populist Governor of Illinois who was driven from office in 1896 for saving three Haymarket rioters from the gallows. Several organizations have combined efforts to give the block new life, with a summer art school for city children and, in winter, a public ice rink.

Now walk inside the famed *Marshall Field's* to see the gold-topped columns on the main floor and the recently added central atrium. The *Walnut Room*, where generations of elegant young Chicago ladies had their first "lunch" (in white gloves with grandmother), is still serving on the seventh floor. (Also see *Special Places* in THE CITY.)

Exit *Field's* by the Wabash Street side and go south. Look around at the city under the El tracks; what was once a dark, grubby street shunned by shopkeepers is today a cozy retailing area. Among the stores along here are a branch of *Crate & Barrel* (101 N. Wabash St.; phone: 312-372-0100), purveyors of china and glassware, and the main store of bookseller *Kroch's & Brentano's* (29 S. Wabash Ave.; phone: 312-332-7500). This stretch of Wabash Avenue also is called Jewelers Row, and the *Maller Building* (5 S. Wabash Ave.; see *Shopping* in THE CITY) is the jewelry district's center.

At Madison Street (the dividing line between north and south), turn right and walk toward State Street, site of the city's other landmark department store, *Carson Pirie Scott and Company* (1 S. State St.; phone: 312-641-7000). Louis Sullivan's last great commission in Chicago, the 106-year-old store features rectilinear upper floors with characteristic "Chicago windows" (with a fixed center pane and side panes that open), elaborate cast-iron decorations, an elegant rotunda, and canopied entrances.

Across the street is the *Chicago Building* (7 W. Madison St.). This 1905 gem by Holabird & Roche, one of the city's leading architectural firms, provides a brief course in the defining characteristics of Chicago School architecture as it was developed by Sullivan and his followers: A building should have a bottom or base, a shaft or series of similar stories defining its height, and a distinct top; the exterior of the building should reveal its underlying structure; and the interior should be airy and well lit—hence the Chicago window. Unlike others of its vintage, the *Chicago Building* also has its cornice, or top, intact. (The building is now largely vacant and threatened by the wrecker's ball, but city and state landmark commissions are seeking a purchaser who will rescue it from oblivion.)

Continue west on Madison Street to Dearborn Street and the towering, tapered skyscraper of the *First National Bank Building.* The 60-story *First National* is reputed to be the world's tallest bank. On the opposite side of the building (Monroe St.), between Dearborn and Clark Streets, is a plaza where hundreds of office workers lunch during the summer in the shadow of Marc Chagall's glass-and-stone mosaic *Les Quatre Saisons* (The Four Seasons). Perhaps the city's best loved artwork, *The Four Seasons* (1974) is made from hand-chipped stone and glass fragments, as well as bits of Chicago brick. Depicting the seasons of the year as well as the human seasons, from infancy to old age, the colorful work also includes scenes of Chicago's skyline and sailboats on Lake Michigan. The sunken plaza below the mosaic is in the exact center of the Loop and is one of the city's most popular gathering spots.

From this vantage point, look up at the stepped-back top of *33 West Monroe Street.* This building was designed by Skidmore, Owings & Merrill, the renowned architectural firm that has spread Miës van der Rohe's steel-and-glass construction style throughout the world. On the west side of Monroe at this corner is the *Xerox Centre,* recognizable by its distinctive rounded façade.

When you leave the plaza, cross Dearborn Street to the lobby of the *Inland Steel Building* (30 W. Monroe St.) at the corner of Dearborn and Monroe Streets. Inside is *Radiant I* (1958), a gold, stainless steel, and copper sculpture set above a triangular reflecting pool. Created by Richard Lippold, it celebrates the aesthetic possibilities of steel technology.

After leaving the *Inland Steel Building,* backtrack to Madison Street and turn left. About mid-block on Madison Street in the atrium of *3 First National Plaza* is Henry Moore's *Large Upright Internal/External Form* (1983). Since the artist is best known for his reclining figures, the verticality of this piece comes as a surprise, but its humanity does not. The form suggests the sheltering protectiveness of one human being for another. There is also separate cast of the interior form of this work in the north garden of the *Art Institute of Chicago.*

Continue walking west on Madison Street for two and one-half blocks to the intersection at Wells Street to Louise Nevelson's *Dawn Shadows* (1983), a black steel work that the artist claimed was inspired by the area's nickname, the Loop. It is necessary to see this 30-foot-high piece from all sides to fully appreciate it. The nearby El platform provides a marvelous view of *Dawn Shadows* and its reflections in the mirrored façade of the building behind it. Diagonally across the street from the Nevelson sculpture is the *Paine Weber Tower* (181 W. Madison St.); in the Madison Street lobby are two vividly colored metal wall hangings by Frank Stella.

Backtrack one block east to the corner of Madison and LaSalle Streets; look south (right). At the end of LaSalle Street atop the *Chicago Board of Trade,* where grain futures are traded, is a shiny aluminum sculpture of *Ceres* (1903) by Chicago-born John Storrs. The Art Deco figure depicts the Greek goddess of grain and harvest; the artist's maquette (model) of the statue is on view at the *Art Institute of Chicago* (as is the model for *Chicago's Picasso*).

One block south along LaSalle Street, where Monroe and LaSalle Streets intersect, is the city's financial center and headquarters for three of its banks: Northern Trust, Harris Bank, and LaSalle National Bank. Cross LaSalle Street and walk south to 190 South LaSalle Street, a post-modern office building of pink granite with extruded bronze framing the tall glass entryways. This product of New York architects Philip Johnson and John Burgee has a stunning five-story lobby sheathed in marble. Amble through it to the Adams Street entrance, pausing to look at the tapestry created by Helena Hernmarck. The hanging depicts one of the most famous illustrations from visionary architect Daniel Burnham's 1909 Plan of Chicago. Burnham, who had created the much-admired master plan for the *World's Columbian Exposition,* was given the task of planning the entire city. His ambitious work laid out principles of urban planning still followed here.

Go one block south on LaSalle Street to Quincy Court; stop in the middle of the block and turn to the west. The El station visible from here has been refurbished to look as it did a century ago when the train system was still in its infancy. At the corner is the *Federal Reserve Bank* (230 S. LaSalle St.), the government bank that serves the center of the country.

Return to LaSalle Street and walk half a block to its end (at Jackson Blvd.), to the *Chicago Board of Trade Building* (141 W. Jackson Blvd.). This masterpiece of Art Deco architecture was designed by Holabird & Root. Step inside for a look at the lobby's sleek curves, styled with machined precision in nickel and polished granite. If you arrive in the morning, go into the visitors' gallery and watch the frenzied activity on the floor of the world's largest commodities futures trading market. The trading here, in grains, timber, pork bellies, silver, and gold, is largely conducted in a unique sign language. Free tours are offered weekday mornings (phone: 312-435-3590).

Leaving the *Board of Trade,* head north on LaSalle Street, passing by the *Continental Bank Building* (231 S. LaSalle St.), where a lobby of tellers' windows has been turned into retail shops. A plaque on the Jackson Boulevard side of the building commemorates one of the great achievements of the 19th century. On this spot in 1883 the nation was officially divided into four standard time zones, part of an international agreement to standardize time. Before 1883, local time was determined by the whims of the residents, and wreaked havoc with railroad timetables.

Continue on LaSalle Street to Adams Street. On the corner of Adams Street (the street names are carved in the side of the building) is the *Rookery* (209 S. LaSalle St.), an elegant office building designed in 1886 by Burnham & Root. Taking its name from the pigeons that roosted in an earlier building on the site, the terra cotta and brick *Rookery,* with its richly ornamented façade, is a city and a national landmark. Inside is a light-filled atrium that was redesigned by Frank Lloyd Wright in 1905 and a circular stairway that is a must-see.

Walk east on Adams Street to Clark Street, turn right and go to Jackson Boulevard, then walk east (left) to the *Monadnock Building* (53 W. Jackson Blvd.). Dubbed the world's tallest office building at the time of its construction in 1892, the 16-story stone structure is still one of the world's tallest, with massive load-bearing walls (they are six feet thick at their base). This engineering marvel was produced by Burnham & Root, one of the city's most distinguished firms (the south half, completed by Holabird & Roche in 1893, is slightly different from the north half). A thorough restoration begun more than a decade ago is bringing the building back to its former glory. This is a pleasant place to stop for a bagel or a cold drink or to shop for flowers or a fountain pen in one of the elegant stores. Among the most attractive details of the restoration are the mosaic floors and the doors and windows. Take a stairway up a flight or two for a sense of what office life was like a century ago.

Exit the *Monadnock Building* on the Van Buren Street side, turn left and walk a half block to Dearborn Street. Across the street is the *Fisher Building* (343 S. Dearborn St.). This 1896 Daniel Burnham-designed building is notable mainly for its Gothic details and ornamentation incorporating fish and fanciful sea creatures.

Continue north on Dearborn Street past Federal Plaza and the *Dirksen* and *Kluczynski* office buildings (to the right and left, respectively), designed by Miës van der Rohe shortly before his death. It's appropriate to pause here a moment and learn something about this admired and influential architect. Ludwig Miës van der Rohe was one of the many talented émigrés from Hitler's Germany. He came to Chicago in 1938 to teach architecture at the *Illinois Institute of Technology* (then called the *Armour Institute of Technology*). It was from here that he elaborated and refined the notions of design simplicity that revolutionized urban architecture. His familiar dictum "less is more" is stamped indelibly on Chicago's skyline.

In the center of Federal Plaza is a post office and Alexander Calder's *Flamingo* (1974), painted a red he used so often that it is nicknamed Calder red. The giant red loops of the bird-like figure add color and vibrancy to the three federal buildings that form its cage. This sculpture, like the Dubuffet and the Nevelson described earlier, should be explored from every angle.

Walk around the *Dirksen Building* (the federal building to your right) to the other side, where a painted aluminum relief sculpture nearly eight stories tall graces a wall of a building across from the *Dirksen.* This Sol Lewitt wall project is formally titled *Four Directions* (1985). Throughout the day, sunlight plays off its white slats, creating patterns of light that change as the sun runs its course.

From the intersection of Dearborn and Adams Streets, two distinctly patterned buildings are visible: Ahead to the left, at Clark Street, are the *Commonwealth Edison* offices; to the right is the *Marquette Building* (140 S. Dearborn St.), an 1894 Chicago School masterpiece by Holabird & Roche. Over the Dearborn Street entrance to the *Marquette* is a bronze plaque depicting the 1637 discovery of the Chicago River by the Jesuit missionary-explorer for whom the building is named. Louis Comfort Tiffany mosaics illustrating scenes from Father Marquette's travels decorate the lobby.

From the *Marquette,* return to Adams Street and head east. The *Berghoff* (17 W. Adams St.), serving beer and bratwurst since the turn of the century, is a good lunch or refreshment stop. At State Street, turn left, cross the street, and walk a half block north to the *Palmer House* (17 E. Monroe St.). Potter Palmer was one of Chicago's more audacious 19th-century businessmen. After building up a multimillion dollar fortune in the dry-goods trade, he sold out to Marshall Field and bought a large parcel of land along State Street, intending to make it the grandest thoroughfare in the city. To seed his investment he built the original *Palmer House,* the most opulent hotel in the city. Unfortunately, only days after it opened in 1871 it burned to the ground in the Great Fire. The current hotel, the third on this site, was built in 1925 and has an exquisite lobby on the second floor.

Exit the *Palmer House* on the State Street side and walk three blocks south to the *Harold Washington Library Center* (400 S. State St., between Van Buren St. and Congress Pkwy.; phone: 312-747-4999), named in fond remembrance of Chicago's first black mayor, who died in 1987. The nation's largest municipal library building features a stunning piece of floor art that incorporates a quotation from Washington's first inaugural address. It's closed Sundays (also see *Special Places* in THE CITY).

Exit the library at Van Buren and State Streets; go two blocks east to Michigan Avenue. Walk south to the *Fine Arts Building* (410 S. Michigan Ave.; phone: 312-427-7602). Built in 1885 to serve as a showroom for

Studebaker carriages, today it is home to a movie theater (usually showing arty imports) and a bookstore on the ground level; artists' studios, a design school, and recital halls are upstairs. This building has been a refuge for creative people throughout much of its history. One of its most famous residents was Margaret Anderson, who published *The Little Review* here. This literary journal was a forum for many great writers—among the contributors were Sherwood Anderson, Hart Crane, T. S. Eliot, Ernest Hemingway, Aldous Huxley, and Gertrude Stein. Most notorious, however, Anderson dared to print episodes from James Joyce's *Ulysses,* triggering a censorship battle that lasted three years. If it's time for a repast, stop at the *Artist's Café,* where there's outdoor dining in the summer and Greek-inspired dishes all year long.

Next door is the *Auditorium Building* (430 S. Michigan Ave.), a stunning combination of Louis Sullivan's visionary architecture and Dankmar Adler's engineering genius. Conceived as a combination office building, hotel, and opera house, it was once one of the greatest symbols of Chicago's power. Stand in the lobby and admire its marble walls and mosaic floor, or sweep up the grand stairway to the landing that looks out over *Grant Park,* and imagine what it might have been like to check in here in the hotel's heyday. (The building now belongs to *Roosevelt University.*)

The crowning achievement of the Adler-Sullivan collaboration is the *Auditorium Theater* on the Wabash Avenue side of the building. Frank Lloyd Wright considered this 3,661-seat theater (2,412 for a Broadway production) acoustically superb, calling it "the greatest room for music and opera in the world." All seats have unobstructed views. For a theater experience of a lifetime, try to get tickets to whatever is playing here (also see *Special Places* in THE CITY).

Cross Michigan Avenue and walk between the *Bowman* and the *Spearman,* the monumental bronzes at the entrance to *Grant Park;* Yugoslavian artist Ivan Mestrovic felt his works not only honored Native Americans, but celebrated the energy of the "Chicago spirit."

If the weather is nice you might opt at this point to take a short side trip down Columbus Drive to *Buckingham Fountain* and *Grant Park*'s formal gardens. The fountain, a prominent feature of the lakefront, was given to the city in 1927 by Kate Buckingham in honor of her brother, a former director of the *Art Institute.* It is modeled after the *Neptune Fountain* at *Versailles,* but is twice its size; a million and a half gallons of water (monitored by computer) is pumped through it each day; once an hour the central geyser erupts 135 feet into the air.

After viewing the fountain, walk back (north) along Michigan Avenue to the corner of East Jackson Drive and North Michigan Avenue. At this corner is the *Art Institute*'s south garden where Lorado Taft's *Spirit of the Great Lakes* (1913) stands. The fountain's five classically draped female figures hold up giant shells and pour water from one to another in an allegorical imitation of the five Great Lakes. Taft, a Chicago native, supervised the installation of all the sculptural works during the 1893 *World's Columbian Exposition.*

The *Art Institute of Chicago* (Michigan Ave. at Adams St.; phone: 312-443-3600 or 443-3500 for recorded information) is one of the world's great museums. Plan to see it—for its armor collection, its Chagalls and O'Keeffes, the exhibition of textiles and design objects, and most of all for its renowned collection of Impressionist paintings. It's a day trip by itself. The institute is open daily; there's no admission charge on Tuesdays (also see *Special Places* in THE CITY).

There are a few noteworthy works outside the institute building as well. The bronze lions flanking the doorway were sculpted by Edward Kemeys, one of the many artists who participated in the 1893 fair. They are just two members of Kemeys's leonine family: Among his many animal figures are the pair of lions now guarding the entrance to the *Museum of Science and Industry.* On the far side of the museum is the north garden, the site of three important contemporary works. Henry Moore liked his sculptures to be seen outdoors against the sky and trees; here in the garden is the *Large Interior Form* (1975) he gave to the *Art Institute* in 1983. Across from Moore's bronze is Calder's *Flying Dragon;* another of the artist's red stabiles, this one is a depiction of a dragonfly. A recent addition to the garden is David Smith's *Cubi VII,* a stainless steel sculpture of welded geometric forms.

Walk east to the *Art Institute*'s Columbus Drive side. There, in the east garden, is an architectural fragment posing as sculpture: Dankmar Adler and Louis Sullivan's terra cotta arched entrance to the former *Chicago Stock Exchange* was saved from the wrecker's ball and installed here in 1977.

South of the Columbus Drive museum entrance is Isamu Noguchi's *Celebration of the 200th Anniversary of the Founding of the Republic.* The tall, columnar form with 50 panels, one for each of the states, is made of stainless steel and rainbow granite.

Return to the institute's Michigan Avenue entrance; directly across from the museum is *Orchestra Hall,* home of the celebrated *Chicago Symphony.* Next to *Orchestra Hall* (on the corner of E. Jackson Dr. and N. Michigan Ave.) is the *Santa Fe Building,* a classical D. H. Burnham design, now home to the *ArchiCenter* (342 S. Dearborn St.), the Loop center of the *Chicago Architecture Foundation.* Whether you are a casual explorer of the city's wonders or a serious student, this is the place to indulge a craving for more information about Chicago's buildings. In addition to books, periodicals, and posters, the *ArchiCenter* offers architectural tours of the Loop and other parts of the city (phone: 312-782-1776 for recorded tour information).

Now head north along Michigan Avenue four blocks to get to the *Chicago Cultural Center* (78 E. Washington St.; phone: 312-744-6630 or 312-346-3278 for a recorded message), a gem of granite and limestone on the outside, marble and mosaic inside. This fine example of Italian Renaissance architecture was built in 1897 as the main public library and was the height of architectural fashion. Walk up the elegant main stairway to *Preston Bradley Hall;* its Tiffany dome is a splendid setting for the free concerts given here every Wednesday at noon. Occupying much of the *Cultural Center's* main floor is the *Museum of Broadcast Communications,* a fascinating collection of artifacts and audiovisual exhibitions celebrating radio and television history. The center also hosts changing exhibitions of photography, art, and artifacts, most by Chicago artists. The center and the museum are open daily; there's no admission charge (also see *Special Places* in THE CITY).

From the corner of Randolph Street and Michigan Avenue head east on Randolph Drive (it changes from Street to Drive at Michigan Avenue) toward Lake Michigan and the *Standard Oil Building* (200 E. Randolph Dr.). In the building's plaza, one wall of which is a waterfall, is a lovely reflecting pool. The 11 rods that rise out of the pool constitute Harry Bertoia's untitled abstract "musical" sculpture (1975). Bertoia, who died in 1991, was an Italian-born metalworking artist who designed furniture as well as sculpture. The reed-like forms of copper-beryllium and brass sit in a granite base. When the wind blows—which is less often than the appellation "The Windy City" would lead one to expect—the sculpture chimes.

Just west of the plaza is Stetson Street, one of the Loop's quieter venues. Turn right and cross to the west side. Just ahead, atop the turrets of the *Sporting Club* (211 North Stetson St.), are four Japanese wind sculptures. The *Children of the Sun,* as they are called, turn and twist in the shifting breeze.

At Stetson and Lake Streets, turn left past Prudential Plaza to Beaubien Court, named for Mark Beaubien, one of Chicago's earliest settlers and founder of the city's first hotel. Beaubien was an enterprising innkeeper; according to legend he would give his guests a blanket to bed down on only to snatch it back when they were asleep and give it to the next customer. (Not surprisingly, there was always a bed available at his hotel.) Cross Beaubien to Boulevard Towers Plaza at Michigan Avenue and Lake Street. Here Jerry Peart's *Splash* (1986), a brightly colored 21-foot sculpture, enlivens a plaza framed by buildings designed by associates of Miës van der Rohe. The sculpture suggests breaking waves and is a vivid counterpoint to the severe lines of its surroundings.

Exit the plaza on Michigan Avenue, cross to the west side, and turn left, walking one block south to Randolph Street. Here is Israeli artist Yaacov Agam's column *Communication X9* (1983); 360 statues in one that are all a matter of perspective. As you walk around this op-art piece, forms and colors shift and change in an almost dizzying fashion.

Turn right on Randolph Street and walk four blocks (crossing Wabash, State, and Dearborn Streets) to the blue-glass *Thompson Center* at Clark and Randolph Streets, where the route began. If some refreshments are in order after this tour of the Loop, remember there is a food court on the lower concourse level of the building.

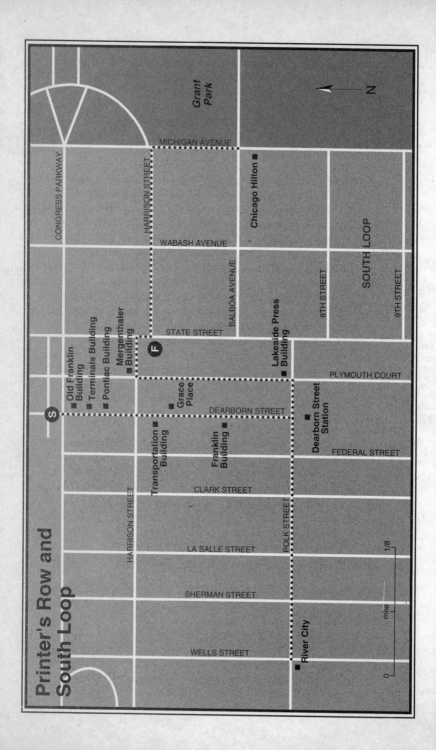

Printer's Row and South Loop

Grant Park

N

CONGRESS PARKWAY

MICHIGAN AVENUE

HARRISON STREET

WABASH AVENUE

Chicago Hilton ■

BALBOA AVENUE

SOUTH LOOP

8TH STREET

9TH STREET

Old Franklin Building ■
Terminals Building ■
Pontiac Building ■
Mergenthaler Building ■

STATE STREET

Lakeside Press Building ■

F

PLYMOUTH COURT

S

Grace Place ■

DEARBORN STREET

Dearborn Street Station ■

Transportation Building ■

FEDERAL STREET

Franklin Building ■

CLARK STREET

HARRISON STREET

POLK STREET

LA SALLE STREET

SHERMAN STREET

0   mile   1/8

River City ■

WELLS STREET

Walk 2: Printer's Row and South Loop

Variously known as the South Loop, Printer's Row, Burnham, or Dearborn Park, the area immediately south of Congress Parkway has been transformed in the past decade. After many years as a derelict and dangerous area, the aging manufacturing district has been reinvigorated with luxurious loft apartments, architects' offices, bookstores, taverns, and coffeehouses.

At the turn of the century Printer's Row was as much a center of the nation's publishing business as New York was. The buildings that now house upscale residences were sturdy enough to withstand the steady pounding of big printing presses, and nearby *Dearborn Street Station,* now a struggling mall, was one of the nation's major rail terminals.

Start this walk from the Loop, heading south on Dearborn Street. Along this block are *Prairie* (500 S. Dearborn St.) and *Printer's Row* (550 S. Dearborn St.), both estimable restaurants featuring distinctly Midwestern cooking (see *Eating Out* in THE CITY for details on both). Other, less expensive eateries are abundant in this neighborhood, among them *Edwardo's* pizza (Congress Pkwy. at Dearborn St.; phone: 312-939-3366); *Lindas Margaritas* (*Dearborn Street Station* at Polk St.; phone: 312-939-6600); and *Taste of Siam* (across from *Dearborn Street Station* ; phone: 312-939-1179).

This district is almost as architecturally rich as the Loop, and since most of the old buildings are still standing, it offers an even better picture of what Chicago looked like while it was inventing American architecture. Particularly notable are the *Old Franklin Building* (525 S. Dearborn St.), the oldest on this block; the *Terminals Building* (537 S. Dearborn St.), with a heavy limestone base and arched entrance; and the *Pontiac Building* (542 S. Dearborn St.), with projecting bays and tripartite Chicago windows. These buildings were some of the earliest skyscrapers in Chicago.

Cross Harrison Street to the *Transportation Building* (600 S. Dearborn St.). This shallow, 22-story structure, dating from 1911, offers great views of the area. Across the street is *Grace Place* (637 S. Dearborn St.), a church in a loft. (If it's open, check out the sanctuary's rough-hewn timbers and sheet-metal cross.) The façade of the 1912 *Franklin Building* (720 S. Dearborn St.) is decorated with colorful tiles depicting scenes of the printer's trade as it existed before the advent of computerized typesetting. *Sandmeyer's Bookstore* (714 S. Dearborn St; phone: 312-922-2104) is worth a visit for its strong collection of books on art and the region. Across the street is the *Prairie Avenue Bookshop* (711 S. Dearborn St.; phone: 312-922-8311), which boasts the nation's largest collection of books on architecture.

Thirsty? Stop in at *Kasey's Tavern* (701 S. Dearborn St.; phone: 312-427-7992), and if it's lunchtime, drop in at *Moonraker,* an outdoor café a few doors south (733 S. Dearborn St.; phone: 312-922-2019). At Polk Street is *Dearborn Street Station.* Dating from 1885, the imposing Romanesque-revival red brick depot is the oldest railroad station in the city. It was exquisitely restored in the late 1980s and set up to be a retail center to serve the neighborhood's growing residential population.

Behind *Dearborn Station* is Dearborn Park, a pleasant and growing residential community of apartments and townhouses built where railroad tracks once led out of the city. Two decades ago, none of this existed; now it's expanding southward to include more single-family houses. The community includes a grade school, as well as housing for senior citizens.

From *Dearborn Station,* detour five blocks west on Polk Street to *River City* (800 S. Wells St.), a futuristic creation of architect Bertrand Goldberg, who also designed *Marina City;* both face the Chicago River. Walk inside to see the unusual serpentine atrium.

Return to Polk and Dearborn Streets in front of the station and go one very short block east to Plymouth Court. At the corner is the *Lakeside Press Building* (731 S. Plymouth Court), built by R. R. Donnelley in 1897 to house part of Lakeside Press's growing operations. Now it's a residence for students at nearby *Columbia College.*

Walk back to Harrison Street along the narrow Plymouth Court. On the corner is the *Mergenthaler Building* (531 S. Plymouth Court), an 1886 structure that's been cleverly adapted for office and residential use. Wedge-shape bays on the south wall extend the space, there's a neon address sign above the door, and at the northeast corner are the remnants of *Tom's Grill*—ivy now grows where hamburgers once fried.

To extend this walk, head east along Harrison Street, first to State Street, where the *Pacific Garden Mission* (646 S. State St.), a homeless shelter, stands. Continue two more blocks east to Michigan Avenue. At Harrison and Michigan are the *Spertus Museum of Judaica* (618 S. Michigan Ave.; phone: 312-922-9012; see *Museums* in THE CITY) and the *Museum for Contemporary Photography at Columbia College* (phone: 312-663-1600). The *Spertus Museum of Judaica* is closed Saturdays, Jewish holidays, and some federal holidays; there's an admission charge. The *Museum for Contemporary Photography* is open daily; there's no admission charge.

The totally renovated *Chicago Hilton Hotel and Towers* also is at this intersection (see *Checking In* in THE CITY). It was in front of the *Hilton* and in *Grant Park* beyond that Chicago police, perhaps antagonized by the flamboyant antics of hippies, yippies, and other radicals, attacked a large group of student protesters during the 1968 Democratic convention. The ensuing "police riot," as it has come to be called, overshadowed the events at the convention that nominated Hubert Humphrey and, according to some, diminished Mayor Richard J. Daley's power.

Head north on Michigan Avenue to return to the Loop.

Walk 3: Wacker Drive

Wacker Drive runs along the south bank of the Chicago River from Lake Michigan to where the river splits into north and south branches, then follows the south branch to the *Sears Tower.* Because the city first grew along the banks of the river, this is one of the oldest parts of Chicago. A century ago, this thoroughfare was called South Water Street and it was lined with a jumble of street vendors and stalls clustered around the city's busy docks. Marshall Field got his start in retailing near here, and it's where Potter Palmer began acquiring real estate.

The riverbank began to change after 1910. It was then that silver-haired civic-improver Charles H. Wacker was appointed head of the *Chicago Plan Commission.* The group was responsible for implementing the 1909 Plan of Chicago, an elegant and innovative attempt to bring reason and order to a city that had grown too fast, and Wacker did it with gusto. As a result of the 1909 Plan, two major railroad stations were moved west of the river, sending traffic away from the city's core, and taking the market with it to Randolph Street. The road along the river, formerly lined with a motley collection of warehouses and aging docks (the Port of Chicago had already moved south to Lake Calumet), was renamed in his honor.

Like many other cities, Chicago has recently rediscovered the river in its own backyard. While the city effectively turned its back on the Chicago River when the buildings along Wacker Drive were constructed, it now wants to incorporate the waterway again, making it a new center of activity.

Though the planned "riverwalk" has yet to be fully realized, a stroll along Wacker Drive goes close to the water and high enough to appreciate the city's majesty. It's easy to get to the starting point of this route; Wacker Drive begins at *Illinois Center,* one block east of Michigan Avenue. Our tour follows the direction of the river's flow, from Columbus Drive west. What's wrong with this picture? The river should flow west to east into the lake, not the other way around. It is another of Chicago's engineering marvels that the city was able to reverse the flow of the river in 1889 to better serve its sanitation needs.

Stand on the narrow pedestrian strip on the upper level of Wacker Drive across from the *Hyatt Regency* hotel at *Illinois Center.* To the east, on the opposite bank of the river, is a fountain that shoots a jet of water across the river once an hour on the hour. The fountain was erected in 1989 by the Metropolitan Water Reclamation District in celebration of its 100th anniversary. It was this agency that built the lock at the mouth of the river to reverse its flow. By doing so, they were able to send water-borne diseases out of the city via a sanitary canal rather than sending them into the lake.

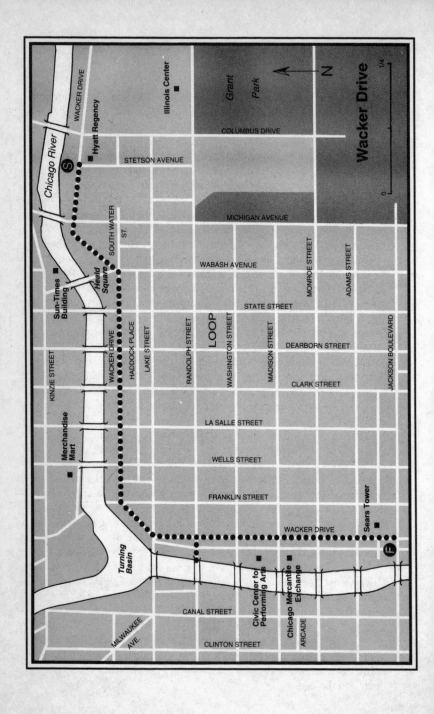

Wacker Drive

Illinois Center was begun nearly 30 years ago as an effort to redevelop the area occupied by the abandoned, century-old *Illinois Central Railroad Terminal.* Miës van der Rohe created a master plan that included many of the buildings on the site shortly before his death in 1969. (The plan, which violates the city's grid system, is now criticized by planners, but it was state of the art at the time.) Three hotels, an apartment building, and four office towers now stand on the site.

Walk west to Michigan Avenue, where there's a quartet of impressive buildings. The two on the other side of the river are the *Tribune Tower,* home of the *Chicago Tribune,* and the *Wrigley Building,* home of the chewing gum. On this side, the one east of Michigan Avenue (333 Michigan Ave.) is in the 1920s style called Moderne, the building on the west side of the street with the curved entrance (360 Michigan Ave.) is neoclassical. All four are particularly striking because they can be seen full-length.

Cross Michigan Avenue, staying on the river side of Wacker Drive, and continue west, passing the *Heald Square Monument* in the middle of the intersection with Wabash Street. The last work by Lorado Taft, one of Chicago's favorite sculptors, this 1941 statue shows George Washington with Robert Morris and Hyam Solomon, two men who helped finance the Revolutionary War. Funds for the construction of the monument were raised by Barnet Hodes, a lawyer and alderman whose Polish-Jewish background was similar to that of Solomon. The low-profile *Sun-Times Building,* headquarters for the city's other daily paper, is visible across the river from here, as are Miës van der Rohe's *IBM Building* and *Marina City.* The latter building, a pioneering concept for urban living, was designed by Bertrand Goldberg, who worked in Miës's studio as a young man. Built in a non-residential area, the round building is given its scalloped effect by the individual decks of each unit.

Along Wacker Drive, 17 bridges cross the Chicago River and its south branch. In the early days of the city, each bridge had a bridge tender whose job it was to raise the bridge for river traffic. Since the river is a critical link between the Great Lakes and the Mississippi River (via the Illinois River), that meant considerable work. Today, boat owners cooperate by coming down the river in groups. When a batch is scheduled to go through, two pairs of bridge tenders man the bridges. They work on consecutive spans, opening and closing one bridge at a time. When a team finishes one bridge, the tenders get into their cars and drive up or down the river (they have special parking privileges) and prepare to open the next bridge in the sequence.

The wall of towers that lines Wacker Drive between Michigan Avenue and Lake Street includes set-back skyscrapers of the 1920s building boom and examples of postmodern classicism from the even bigger boom of the 1980s. As you walk west, notice in particular the rich terra cotta ornament of 35 East Wacker Drive (1926), where Helmut Jahn, Chicago's most famous architect of the moment, has his office; Leo Burnett's gray granite tower at 35 West Wacker Drive (1989), designed by New Yorkers Roche-Dinkeloo; and the first Midwestern building by the Spanish architect Ricardo Bofill at 77 West Wacker Drive. Bofill designed his half, built in 1989, to echo the earlier half built in 1930.

At the Clark Street intersection is a plaque memorializing Chicago's worst maritime disaster. On July 24, 1915, nearly 4,000 employees of the Western Electric Company's Hawthorne Works in Cicero were boarding the *Eastland* when the ship capsized. Eight hundred and twelve people who had been headed for a day's outing at the dunes met their deaths instead. Whole families were wiped out; children who stayed home were orphaned; the firm was decimated. (In 1989, students at the *Illinois Math and Science Academy* in Aurora, thinking this sad episode of Chicago history was nearly forgotten, organized an effort to have this plaque installed.)

Between LaSalle and Wells Streets is the *LaSalle-Wacker Building,* built in 1930. Note its H-shape, unique at that time. It was designed this way to meet the new building codes of 1917. The *Merchandise Mart,* across the river on Wells Street, is the world's largest wholesaling complex. Plans for this massive headquarters for *Marshall Field's* wholesale division began in 1923; the building finally opened in 1931, two years after the stock market crash. *Field's* gave up its wholesale business in the mid-1930s, and the *Mart* was bought at a bargain price by Joseph Kennedy, patriarch of Boston's Kennedy clan. Still a source of the family's wealth, it houses showrooms for the interior design trade and has a shopping mall on its lower two floors. Just beyond the *Merchandise Mart*'s façade is the *Apparel Center,* which provides showrooms for clothing designers.

Cross Wells Street, passing under the El tracks, and pause to look at the handsome curving sheet of green glass ahead on the east side of Wacker Drive. This dramatic 1983 building, designed by New York's Kohn Pederson Fox and executed by Chicago's Perkins & Will, takes its shape from the curve of the river. If the building is open, walk into its lobby; the *Chicago Athenaeum* has a gallery here that features exhibitions on design topics.

As Wacker Drive curves south, it becomes a landscaped boulevard, lined by major office buildings, a project envisioned in Burnham's 1909 plan for the city. At Randolph Street, walk to the bridge over the river. To the west is the *Morton International Building,* headquarters for the firm that mines salt and makes rubber rings for space shuttle engines, among other things. Rather than having its back to the river, as do the older buildings along here, this structure embraces the waterfront; it also boasts the world's tallest clock.

Return to Wacker Drive and walk along its western side to get a better view of the *Civic Opera House* (20 N. Wacker Dr.; see *Music* in THE CITY). Behind this complex of theaters lies another of Chicago's remarkable tales of big business. Samuel Insull, who had been a secretary to Thomas Edison, came to Chicago to run one of the city's many electric companies and eventually established himself as the only electric company in town. He used the wealth from that enterprise to buy up railroads and further enhance his power. When he commissioned the *Civic Opera House* and the skyscraper above it, perhaps as a gift for his wife (a former actress who wanted to return to the stage), he was at the pinnacle of his career. Unfortunately, the building, for which Insull had heavily mortgaged his business, opened shortly before the stock market crash of 1929. Though Insull's Commonwealth Edison company survived on loans for several years, his tottering empire eventually collapsed. The power mogul fled Chicago and died of a heart attack on a subway platform in Paris. He was penniless but well dressed; he was identified by the "SI" embroidered on his shirt cuffs.

At Madison Street look to the west side of Wacker Drive again. The building at 10 South Wacker Drive is headquarters for the *Chicago Mercantile Exchange,* where boisterous traders buy and sell options on all manner of futures, from pork bellies to interest rates. The building is open to the public on weekdays; there's no admission charge. Free tours must be scheduled in advance (phone: 312-930-8249; also see *Special Places* in THE CITY).

The final stop on this tour is the *Sears Tower* (233 S. Wacker Dr.), between Adams Street and Jackson Boulevard. The 110-story tower is 1,454 feet tall. Take a trip to the *Skydeck* (after all, it is the world's tallest building) and get a bird's-eye view of the City that Works. It's open daily and there is an admission charge (phone: 312-875-9696; also see *Seeing the City* in THE CITY).

River North

0   mile   1/4

OAK STREET

WALTON STREET

LOCUST STREET

CHESTNUT STREET

INSTITUTE PLACE

SEDGWICK STREET

Moody Bible Institute

S **F**

CHICAGO AVENUE

Abraham Lincoln Bookshop

River North Concourse

Aquariums by Design

Carl Hammer Gallery

SUPERIOR STREET

FRANKLIN ST.

Brett's Kitchen

LA SALLE STREET

HURON STREET

ERIE STREET

STATE STREET

ONTARIO STREET

WELLS STREET

Rock 'n' Roll MacDonald's

Hard Rock Cafe

Capone's Chicago

OHIO STREET

GRAND AVENUE

CLARK STREET

DEARBORN STREET

WABASH AVENUE

ORLEANS STREET

RIVER NORTH

ILLINOIS STREET

Michael Jordan's

HUBBARD STREET

Criminal Courts Building

KINZIE STREET

KINGSBURY STREET

Merchandise Mart

Harry Caray's

M. M. PLAZA

Wolf Point

Chicago River

Turning Basin

WACKER DRIVE

HADDOCK PLACE

LAKE STREET

N

Walk 4: River North

Originally a manufacturing and warehouse district, River North began to decline after the Second World War, when factories moved out and urban blight moved in. In the mid 1970s, gallery owners discovered the large loft spaces and bargain rents and began trekking over from North Michigan Avenue. Today, the neighborhood not only has been reborn, it has become so populated with trendy restaurants, pricey shops, and designers' studios that some of the art galleries have crossed the Chicago River into a new district called River West. River North now boasts the nation's largest concentration of galleries outside New York City's SoHo, along with a museum of Capone-era Chicago, Oprah Winfrey's restaurant, and lots of other classy dining spots.

It's easy to reach this area; several buses run on State and LaSalle Streets; others, going south only, run on Clark Street. Both the El (at Chicago Ave. and Franklin St., and at the *Merchandise Mart* at Wells St. and the river) and the subway (at Chicago Ave. and State St., and at Grand Ave. and State St.) stop in the neighborhood. If you have a car, there are several parking lots in the area, and on-street parking is available in the evenings. Start this walk at LaSalle Street and Chicago Avenue, and note the *Moody Bible Institute* (742 E. 87th St; phone: 312-783-2707) on the northwest corner. There's a bookstore here and a lovely interior courtyard behind the institute (accessible from LaSalle Street).

Go west one block to Wells Street, then south one block to Superior Street and you'll be at the beginning of Chicago's art gallery district. Start at *Carl Hammer Gallery* (200 W. Superior St.; phone: 312-266-8512) on the corner of Superior and Wells Streets; walk in (browsers are always welcome) and pick up a copy of the *Gallery Guide* (it's free, and it's available in all the area's galleries). Many of the River North galleries are on street level, but some are upstairs (banners hang from their windows). Either consult the guide for what's where or just walk west for the next two blocks, stopping where the spirit moves you. Most galleries are closed Sundays. Many have openings on Friday evenings (except in the summer); wine and munchies are served, the streets are crowded, and anyone can come. Again, the *Gallery Guide* is your source for what's happening when.

The heaviest concentration of galleries is on Superior Street between Wells and Orleans Streets. You might want to make a circle tour, or hop back and forth across the street. For refreshments, *Brett's Kitchen,* a charming hole-in-the-wall with good food, is at the southeast corner of Franklin and Superior Streets (phone: 312-664-6354).

Continue west on Superior Street to Orleans Street. Cross Orleans, turn right and go one block toward Chicago Avenue. *River North Concourse* (750

N. Orleans St.) is a warehouse-turned-emporium featuring several galleries and shops. Most offer art, but *Brandwine* has a fantastic assortment of posters, books, and trivia for science fiction buffs.

Also visit the *Abraham Lincoln Book Shop* (around the corner at 357 Chicago Ave.; phone: 312-944-3085); ring the bell to enter. This warm and inviting store, lined floor to ceiling with glass-doored bookcases, is more like a museum, displaying Lincoln-related art, books, and documents, and attracting Civil War and Lincoln history buffs from around the country. Proprietor Daniel Weinberg is frequently called upon to authenticate Lincoln memorabilia. He is glad to discuss his interests, even if you are only browsing. There is parking near the bookstore.

Across the street and one block west, the Cabrini-Green housing project begins. Along Chicago Avenue, some of these buildings are well-tended; however, the upper floors of the high-rises beyond are empty, burned out, or boarded up. From the south side of Chicago Avenue, look west, where a large red sign announces the headquarters of *Montgomery Ward*. From its warehouse on the river, goods used to be moved by boat to the railroads and then around the nation.

Walk back to Orleans Street and head south. At Superior Street is *Café Lago;* once a working class diner, it is now frequented by artists and art dealers. At Huron and Orleans Streets is the *The Green Door Tavern* (678 N. Orleans St.; phone: 312-664-5496), a popular bar and restaurant in a somewhat rickety looking structure that was one of the first buildings to go up after the Chicago Fire; the food here is good and the ambience terrific. Between these two establishments is a block-long parking lot. Until a disastrous fire in April 1989, the block contained an 1880s building that was the center of the River North gallery district.

Continue one block south to Erie Street, turn right, and walk down a block to Franklin Street. At this intersection is former Chicago *Bear* Walter Payton's *America's Bar* (219 W. Erie St.; phone: 312-915-5986). Across the street is *Flair House,* a restored dairyman's home that is now the office of an advertising agency. Across Erie Street is Oprah Winfrey's *Eccentric,* a restaurant and watering hole. Continue east one block, turn right on Wells Street, and walk one block south to *Ed Debevic's,* which faces Ontario Street. It's the quintessential diner, complete with wisecracking waitresses in saddle shoes and bobby socks. (For more information on *Eccentric* and *Ed Debevic's,* see *Eating Out* in THE CITY.) Right across Wells Street from *Ed Debevic's* is one of the city's newest attractions, *Planet Hollywood* (633 N. Wells St.; phone: 312-266-7827), a multifaceted restaurant decorated with all manner of movie star memorabilia and serving, according to the proprietor, "wholesome American" fare—pizza, hamburgers, sandwiches, and grill items.

Continue south along Wells Street, past three blocks of elegant shops between Ohio and Hubbard Streets. Among the stores here are *Rita Bucheit Limited,* featuring Austrian antiques and artifacts; *Mario Villa* for decorative items; *Arrelle Fine Linens and Down* (445 N. Wells St.; phone: 312-321-3696) for the ultimate in bedding; and *Table of Contents* (444 N. Wells St.; phone: 312-644-9004) for everything to eat with.

On Wells Street between Hubbard Street and the Chicago River is the 1929 *Merchandise Mart,* the world's largest commercial building. The showrooms (featuring interiors and furnishings) are open mainly to dealers and decorators; the first two floors are a retail mall. Walk around to the building's riverfront side to see the restored façade. The *Merchandise Mart* has mounted several large bronze busts of prominent American businessmen, including F. W. Woolworth and Edward Filene, on the outer walls, in a display that it likes to refer to as a "Merchandising Hall of Fame." Enjoy the panoramic view east and south across the river, and west toward the *Apparel Center* (wholesale clothing) at Wolf Point, where the Chicago River divides into north and south branches.

Retrace your steps along Wells Street back to Hubbard Street, then walk one block east to LaSalle Street. At that corner, look north one block to Illinois Street, where an immense basketball on the top of the red brick building announces *Michael Jordan's,* a popular new restaurant (500 N. LaSalle St.; phone: 312-644-3865). Long lines indicate how many people want to eat here, and it doesn't take reservations. Continue two more blocks east along Hubbard Street to Dearborn Street. The massive stone building on the northwest corner is the old *Criminal Court,* where the famed movie about Chicago newspaper reporters, *The Front Page,* was set. At Dearborn Street, go south one block to Kinzie Street and *Harry Caray's,* a restaurant in a Dutch-inspired commercial building (33 W. Kinzie St.; phone: 312-828-0966). This popular local Italian-American spot is named after the *Cubs*'s beloved announcer; you can see its huge "Holy cow!" banner (Caray's favorite expression) from blocks away.

Head one block back to Clark Street and walk north along several blocks of late 19th-century buildings that now house elegant restaurants like *Gordon's, Frontera Grill* and *Topolobambo,* and *Maggiano's* (see *Eating Out* in THE CITY) as well as shops and offices above. Even if you're not in the mood for a meal, you might want to sample the extraordinary selection of breads at *The Corner Bakery,* part of *Maggiano's;* it's at the corner of Clark Street and Grand Avenue. At Ohio Street is a trio of treats, including the *Rock 'n' Roll McDonald's* (600 N. Clark St. at Ohio St.), a must-see: Its funky decor includes life-size *Beatles,* Archie and Betty in a red Corvette, and a wondrous collection of wacky artifacts. It has the usual reliable menu and is one of the busiest *McDonald's* in the world. Right across the street is another new attraction, *Capone's Chicago* (605 N. Clark St.; phone: 312-654-1919), a light-hearted celebration of an aspect of the city's past some local boosters would like to forget. The outside is a movie-set version of numerous storefronts associated with that era; inside, a dramatic show runs every 30 minutes daily and there's lots of crime-era memorabilia to buy. Chicago's *Hard Rock Café* shares the block with *Capone's Chicago;* you can't miss the bright neon arrow pointing skyward. Stand in line, if you wish, for juicy hamburgers and teeshirts (also see *Eating Out* in THE CITY).

This walk continues north along Clark Street, a recently gentrified area. At Chicago Avenue, turn left and walk a block back to where you began.

Walk 5: North Michigan Avenue

Though the soul of Chicago is still the Loop, the city's spirit has gradually been moving across the Chicago River to North Michigan Avenue. Until *Water Tower Place* was built in 1974, Michigan Avenue was a tree-lined boulevard of individually owned shops, office buildings, and art galleries; its commerce was more cultured than that of the bustling Loop. Now "Boul Mich" has more law firms than art dealers; family-run shops are giving way to classy, high-end stores, many of them branches of international chains. Once a street of stately and modestly scaled graystone buildings, North Michigan Avenue has become an exhibition of architectural one-upmanship. Although the street is said to have the world's densest concentration of upscale retailing, it still retains some of the quiet elegance befitting a thoroughfare known as the Magnificent Mile (a nickname developer Arthur Rubloff gave it some 25 years ago).

Our walk begins at the intersection of Michigan Avenue and Wacker Drive. On this spot stood *Fort Dearborn,* the trading outpost that grew into the city. Until 1835, when all the area's Native Americans were required by treaty to move west of the Mississippi, this post primarily traded with the tribes that lived along the lakeshore. Stroll across the river on the Michigan Avenue Bridge. To the north and on the left is the *Wrigley Building,* the skyscraper that chewing gum built; on the right is the *Tribune Tower,* home of the *Chicago Tribune.* Behind the bright, white *Wrigley* towers is the *Sun-Times Building,* home of the city's other daily newspaper, and a pleasant terrace with a *McDonald's.*

The *Tribune Tower,* a Gothic tribute to the power of the press, was designed by the firm of Hood & Howells, who won a 1923 competition for the commission. Some of America's greatest journalists have worked out of this building. Also from here came *Dick Tracy, L'il Orphan Annie,* and the "Dewey Beats Truman" headline.

Walk between the *Tribune Tower* and the modern *Equitable Building* to *Channel Gardens,* the pedestrian entrance to the *NBC Building.* Head north along the garden-centered street known as CityFront Place and look east toward the lake. From here, *Navy Pier* is visible. This 1916 structure extends a half mile out into the lake and, when its current reconstruction is completed this year, it will again host numerous exhibitions and festivals. Also visible is *Lake Point Tower,* a 70-story cloverleaf-shape apartment building, the world's tallest purely residential building when it was built in 1968 (to date, no one has come forward to top its claim).

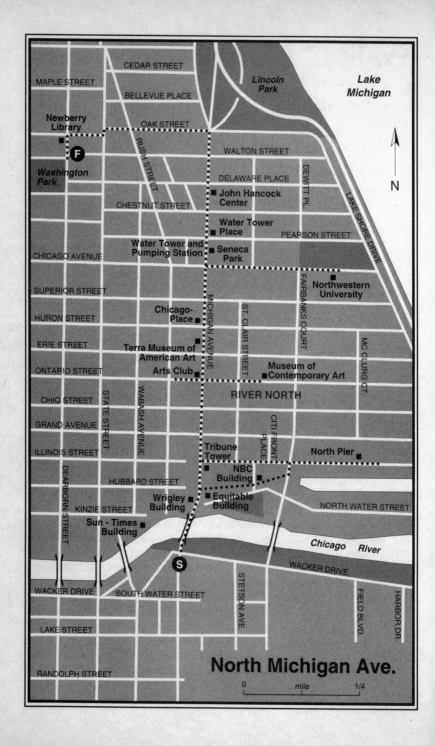

North Michigan Ave.

0 mile 1/4

For a pleasant (though hardly brief) detour, go through the *NBC Building* and walk a half-block north to Illinois Street, and then two blocks east to *North Pier* (435 E. Illinois St.). This former riverside warehouse has been transformed into several floors of delightful shops and restaurants. It also has *BattleTech Center,* a state-of-the-art "virtual reality" video game parlor. On a warm, sunny day, there's no better place for a cool beer or soft drink than one of the numerous spots along the water's edge at *North Pier,* looking back on the city. Ice cream and more substantial fare are available as well.

If you didn't take the detour, follow CityFront Place behind the *Tribune Tower* until it turns west at upper Illinois Street. On the right is the *Inter-Continental* hotel. This architectural fantasy, built in 1929 to house the *Medinah Athletic Club,* moves from Assyrian to Renaissance themes, incorporating a little Moorish here, a bit of Celtic there, and touch of Byzantine just for good measure. If it's a chilly afternoon, stop in the lobby for afternoon tea (also see *Checking In* in THE CITY). For an interesting side trip, take any one of the staircases down to Lower Michigan Avenue. News junkies might want to stop at the *Billy Goat Tavern* (430 N. Michigan Ave., lower level), where reporters (including venerable columnist Mike Royko) hang out. (Also see *Eating Out* in THE CITY.)

Along this stretch of Michigan Avenue there are several office buildings, the *Chicago Marriott* hotel (540 N. Michigan Ave.), a branch of *Kroch's and Brentano's* bookstore (516 N. Michigan Ave.; phone: 312-321-0989), plus a choice of chi-chi cookie and yogurt stores. Three blocks north of Illinois Street is Ontario Street. Turn right on Ontario for a visit to the *Museum of Contemporary Art* (237 E. Ontario St.; phone: 312-280-5161), or just look around at the interesting mix of old townhouses and modern office towers standing side by side. The museum is closed Mondays; there's no admission charge on Tuesdays (also see *Special Places* in THE CITY). Return to Michigan Avenue, then walk a half-block west on Ontario to the *Arts Club of Chicago* (109 E. Ontario St.). This is a private club, but visitors are allowed inside to look at two of its showpieces: an elegant stairway designed by Miës van der Rohe, and Alexander Calder's *Red Petals.*

At the corner of Erie Street and Michigan Avenue is the flagship *Crate & Barrel* housewares store (646 N. Michigan Ave.; phone: 312-787-5900). Its modest five stories, in glass and white aluminum, buck the trend toward overpowering Michigan Avenue with towers. North of Erie Street on the east side of Michigan Avenue are two not-to-be missed additions to the avenue: the *Sony Gallery of Consumer Electronics* (663 N. Michigan Ave.; phone: 312-943-3334), which showcases and sells the latest in electronics; and the exciting *Nike Town* next door (669 N. Michigan Ave.; phone: 312-642-6363), a three-level emporium offering the latest in its name brand apparel.

Proceed north on Michigan Avenue, passing the *Terra Museum of American Art* (666 N. Michigan Ave.; phone: 312-664-3939), one of the few museums devoted solely to American art and artists. It's closed Mondays; there's an admission charge (see *Special Places* in THE CITY). On the next block is the vertical mall at *ChicagoPlace,* home to *Saks Fifth Avenue,* numerous other shops, and a handsome eighth-level food court. Notice the two-story murals on either side of the entrance to *ChicagoPlace.* Mrs. O'Leary's cow (peeking out from behind the prairie grass) is just one of the symbols of Chicago's past depicted in this delightful artwork.

Continue walking north toward the arched, rose-colored granite entrance to *Neiman Marcus* (737 N. Michigan Ave.; phone: 312-642-5900), on the east side of the street. Across the street is Chicago's recent experiment in retail architecture, the *Banana Republic* store (744 N. Michigan Ave.; phone: 312-642-0020), designed by New Yorker Robert A. M. Stern.

The curious-looking castle with the tower poking up in the middle is the *Water Tower* (it's visible all the way up the avenue). This building and the matching *Pumping Station* (across Michigan), are the only downtown survivors of the Great Chicago Fire. The first floor of the *Water Tower* now houses the *Chicago Office of Tourism.* A pleasant park surrounds it, and horse-drawn carriage rides leave from here.

At the *Water Tower Pumping Station* is *Here's Chicago* (phone: 312-467-7114), a sound-and-light show in which a mechanical figure of Abe Lincoln, who began his political career in Illinois, comes out to explain his connections to Chicago and to introduce a film of a magnificent helicopter tour of the city's skyscrapers. Right outside the *Pumping Station* is *Untouchable Tours* (phone: 312-881-1195), a two-hour bus ride through neighborhoods once frequented by the likes of Frank Nitti, Earl "Little Hymie" Weiss, and Dion O'Banion, as well as the most notorious of them all, Al Capone. (In winter, tours are held only on Wednesdays and weekends.)

Though the vertical mall at *Water Tower Place* beckons, take a roundabout route to it by walking south on Michigan Avenue to Chicago Avenue, turning left behind the *Pumping Station.* A little beyond the most charming fire station in the city is *Seneca Park,* a great rest stop. The park's lovely play lot was built with money raised by the community and is named for the late restaurateur who concocted *Eli's* cheesecake (his restaurant, *Eli's, the Place for Steak,* is across Chicago Avenue; also see *Eating Out* in THE CITY). Grown-ups might want to sit a while and meditate on Deborah Butterfield's sculpture, *Horse* (1990). The major construction project east of the park is a new home for the *Museum of Contemporary Art.*

For a longer side trip, wander east on Chicago for two blocks to *Northwestern University*'s downtown campus. Its medical center and law school are here; headquarters for the *American Dental Association* and the *American Hospital Association* (after Washington, DC, Chicago is the nation's association capital) are nearby.

Now it's time for *Water Tower Place,* a site nearly everyone who comes to Chicago visits at least once. *Water Tower Place* pioneered the concept of the vertical shopping mall in Chicago and there's almost nothing that isn't available here. The mall also has several places to eat and a movie theater, and the building is open until long after the stores close. Families won't want to miss the freestanding *F.A.O. Schwartz* store across from *Water Tower Place* (840 N. Michigan Ave.; phone: 312-587-5000); it's a visual delight, offering the latest in extravagant playthings. Bibliophiles will want to explore elegant *Waterstone's,* around the corner facing Chestnut Street (840 N. Michigan Ave.; phone: 312-587-8080).

Just north of the *Water Tower* is "Big John," the *John Hancock Center.* Once the world's tallest building, it is now shadowed by the *Sears Tower,* the *Amoco Building,* both in the Loop, and New York's *World Trade Centers One and Two.* The *Hancock,* however, is the only one that has residential apartments. Across Michigan Avenue from "Big John" is the *Fourth Presbyterian Church* (126 E. Chestnut St.; phone: 312-787-4570), a Gothic Revival structure built in 1912. During the summer, the church offers concerts in its cloistered garden. If the church is open, visit the sanctuary, a harmonious retreat of carved wood and stained glass amid the neighborhood's glass and steel.

Mammon reigns north of the church at the shops at *900 North Michigan,* the most elegant and upscale of the avenue's malls. *Bloomingdale's* (phone: 312-440-4460) anchors this one, and there are numerous other shops (many of them European imports) in which to indulge. Across the street is the 1930 *Palmolive Building* (919 N. Michigan Ave.), from which Hugh Hefner ran his bunny empire. (His daughter, Christie, now is in charge, and she moved Playboy Corp. to Lake Shore Drive.)

Between Walton and Oak Streets on Michigan Avenue is a composition of three hexagonal granite and glass tubes called *One Magnificent Mile.* The building houses shops, offices, a movie theater, and apartments, as well as *Spiaggia* (980 N. Michigan Ave.; see *Eating Out* in THE CITY), one of city's most pricey and intriguing restaurants.

From One Magnificent Mile, you can either walk west on Oak Street, Chicago's intimate street of one-of-a-kind shops, or embark on a tour of the exclusive Gold Coast neighborhood (see *Walk 6: The Gold Coast*).

Oak Street offers a delightful collection of shops selling an assortment of goods from leather to linen, fur to feathers. For a movie, stop at the 1937 *Esquire Theater* (53 E. Oak St.; phone: 312-280-0101). The building's clean Art Deco streamlining was a marked contrast to the Moorish palace-style movie houses that preceded it. Oak Street's shopping area ends at Rush Street, where it intersects with State Street. Either get a downtown-bound bus here or walk one block farther to Dearborn Street and one block south (both very short stretches) to Walton Street. A public elementary school is on one side of the street; on the other is the 1892 *Newberry Library,* keeper of maps and genealogical and historical archives. The library faces *Washington Square* (also known as *Bughouse Square*), the city's first public park and once a forum for orators and rhetoricians of all political persuasions. To get back downtown from here, either hail a cab or walk back to State Street and catch a bus.

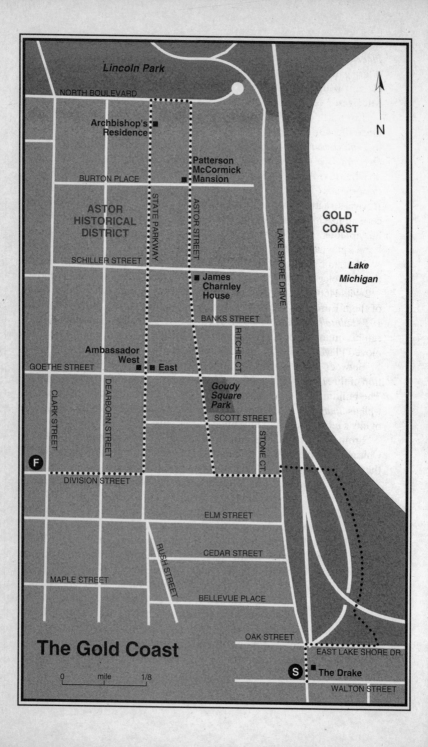

Walk 6: The Gold Coast

The Gold Coast is a mere wedge of land six blocks long and three blocks deep, but the amount of wealth concentrated here in the neighborhood's heyday was nothing short of stupefying. Potter Palmer was the first of Chicago's businessmen to build here, in the late-1880s, and his presence drew many others. Though millionaire fur trader John Jacob Astor never lived here, the most attractive street in the area was named for him. As time goes on, the Gold Coast mansions are increasingly hemmed in by the high-rise luxury apartments of the city's envious nouveaux riches, but the grand old homes, built in the late-19th and early 20th centuries, that made this *the* place to live are undiminished by the comparison.

This walk begins, appropriately, at the grande dame of Chicago hostelries, the *Drake* (140 E. Walton St.; see *Checking In* in THE CITY). Since its opening in 1921, it has provided lodgings for many dignitaries, among them Queen Elizabeth. If it happens to be mid-afternoon, stop in for tea at the *Oak Terrace* before strolling down block-long East Lake Shore Drive, the most exclusive of Chicago addresses. The park on the street's north side boasts a gazebo, lovely landscaping, and very inviting benches.

Amble along the lakeshore north toward Division Street. On the west side of Lake Shore Drive are the apartment buildings that form a sort of front-yard fence for the Gold Coast. Two blocks north of Oak Street, mansions begin to appear amid the apartment towers. Once, the drive was lined with such magnificent houses.

Cross Lake Shore Drive via the underpass at Division Street to get to the heart of the Gold Coast. Walk past Stone Court to Astor Street and turn right. This tranquil, six-block-long street is lined with marvelously well-maintained private residences, many of them dating from the turn of the century. At 1308-12 Astor are a series of ivy-covered row houses designed by John Root (who lived at 1310) of the architectural firm Burnham and Root. At Goethe Street is lovely little *Goudy Park*, recently redone thanks to a $350,000 contribution from neighborhood residents.

A little farther along, at 1335 Astor Street, is where Irna Phillips, the writer who created television's first soap operas, once lived. Nearby is *Court of the Golden Hands* (1349-53 Astor St.), which was built by lumberman William Goodman (the city's famed *Goodman Theater* is named for him). At 1406 Astor Street is the home built by steel magnate Joseph Ryerson; the Georgian house with a formal side garden was built by William McCormick Blair, founder of the investment firm of the same name.

The *James Charnley House* (1364 Astor St.) was designed by Louis Sullivan, with an assist from his young protégé, Frank Lloyd Wright. While Sullivan's decorative hand has adorned the building's façade, Wright's influence can be seen in the roofline of the three-story house. Its appearance is a sharp contrast to the other houses on the street, which were built around 1892.

At the corner of Astor Street and Burton Place is the *Patterson-McCormick Mansion,* built by one of the daughters of *Tribune* founder Joseph Medill and later altered by heirs of the McCormick reaper fortune. In the late 1970s, it was converted into several spacious condominiums.

Continue walking along Astor Street until it ends at the southernmost end of *Lincoln Park,* and then turn left on North Boulevard to North State Parkway. *Lincoln Park* is the largest oasis in Chicago, covering 1,200 acres of lakefront property. It also is the location of the *Chicago Historical Society* (N. Clark St. and North Ave.; phone: 312-642-4600) and the *Lincoln Park Zoo* (2200 Cannon Dr.; phone: 312-294-4660). The historical society is closed *Thanksgiving, Christmas,* and *New Year's Day;* there's no admission charge on Mondays. The zoo is open daily; no admission charge. (For additional details on both, see *Special Places* in THE CITY.)

At State Street, turn south again. On the left is the Queen Anne–style *Archbishop's Residence* (1555 N. State Pkwy.), the oldest building in the Astor Historical District. Since 1885 it has been the home of the Roman Catholic Archbishop of Chicago. On a more secular note, 1340 North State Parkway was once the *Playboy Mansion,* home of Hugh Hefner.

At the corner of State and Goethe Streets, the *Ambassador East* and *Ambassador West* hotels face each other. Booth No. 1 in the *Ambassador East*'s restaurant, the *Pump Room* (see *Eating Out* in THE CITY), once was the most important place to be seen in Chicago. Among those who have sat at this choice spot to the right of the bar are Gertrude Lawrence (setting a record at 90 consecutive nights), Frank Sinatra, Salvador Dali, David Bowie, and even Morris the Cat. The restaurant serves continental food with a price tag appropriate to the neighborhood.

Continue south to Division Street. Quick-change artist that the city is, it has gone from elegance and tranquillity to the honky-tonk of Division Street's bars in two short blocks. If you didn't dine in Booth No. 1, try *P. J. Clarke's* (1204 N. Clark St.; phone: 312-664-1650), popular with singles and owned by a man said to "run" the Near North neighborhood (the only thing he really runs is an insurance agency by that name). *Yvette* (1206 N. Clark St.; phone: 312-280-1700) is a tad tonier; pizza, the Chicago standby, is available at *Edwardo's* (1212 N. Dearborn St.). Buses down State Street are readily available from here, and there's a subway stop at Clark and Division Streets.

Walk 7: Lincoln Park

Lincoln Park is one of Chicago's most affluent neighborhoods, and it's also rich in historic districts, fine restaurants, interesting shops, and tree-lined streets. It began, however, as a working class neighborhood that attracted European immigrants in the 1800s, particularly to the area around North Avenue. Farther north, the neighborhood along Fullerton Parkway was decidedly upscale, as the restored brownstones here indicate. During the nation's early experiments with urban renewal, the area weathered considerable chaos as feisty residents, many of them artists, successfully fought the wholesale destruction of the beautiful 19th-century buildings in Lincoln Park. They argued, and proved, that renewal could result from preservation as well as from demolition.

This lakefront neighborhood has *Lincoln Park*, Chicago's largest park, as its eastern border. The 1,212-acre linear park is larger than New York's *Central Park*. It was designed, in part, by the landscape architect Jens Jensen. The Swedish-born Jensen saw poetry in the Midwestern prairie of his adopted homeland and incorporated it into his park designs.

The Lincoln Park area stretches from North Avenue up to Diversey Parkway and west to Racine Avenue. This walking tour begins at the heart of the Lincoln Park neighborhood, at the intersection of Halsted Street, Fullerton Parkway, and Lincoln Avenue. At this crossroads are *Children's Memorial Hospital* and *De Paul University*. To reach this area from the Loop, catch a Howard Street Line train heading north. Get off at Fullerton and walk one long block east along this parkway, past lovely brownstones and churches, to Halsted Street and Lincoln Avenue. Buses go to Lincoln Park as well; the best choice is the No. 11 Lincoln Avenue bus, which stops in the Loop along State Street. This tour is best made without a car; it ends several blocks from where it begins and parking is at a premium here.

Begin by heading north up Lincoln Avenue. The street, which runs through the neighborhood on a diagonal, starts the day sleepily (some shops don't open until nearly noon), and really comes to life at night. Farther up the block is a microcosm of urban living. The people who stroll up and down this thoroughfare are as diverse as the city: politicians, television stars, socialites, lots of quite ordinary folk of all ages, as well as hippies and a bag lady or two. Move with the crowd (the sidewalks are narrow), and you'll feel right at home.

On the left just north of the intersection where the tour begins is the *Three Penny Cinema* (2424 N. Lincoln Ave.; phone: 312-935-5744), a theater with grimy charm and good popcorn. Across the street is the *Biograph* (2433 N. Lincoln Ave.; phone: 312-348-4123), the legendary movie house where G-men tracked down their number one enemy, bank robber John Dillinger. He and his treacherous female companion, known as "the lady

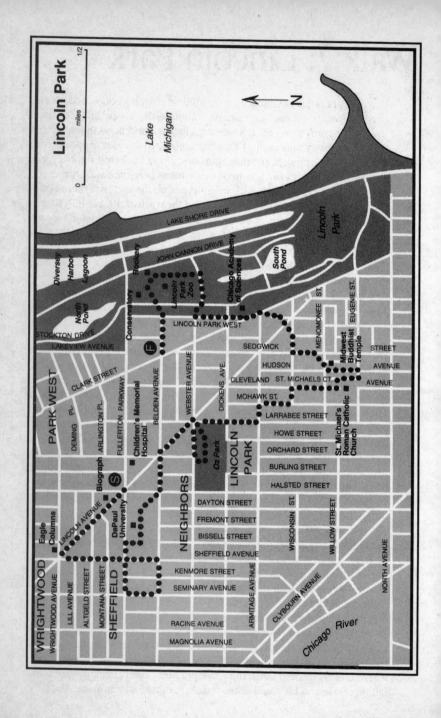

in red," attended a 1934 screening of *Manhattan Melodrama*. She had clued the lawmen that she and her sweetheart would be there, and as the two of them left the theater, Dillinger was riddled with bullets. Some crime buffs say that the man that was killed wasn't really Dillinger, and that the criminal quietly retired to Indiana.

For the music-minded, this block offers a choice of avant-garde clubs: *Lounge Ax* (2438 N. Lincoln Ave.; phone: 312-525-6620); *Lilly's* (2515 N. Lincoln Ave.; phone: 312-525-2422); and *Irish Eyes* (2519 N. Lincoln Ave.; phone: 312-348-9548). Though *Earl's Pub*—run by the legendary "Earl of Old Town," a crusty barkeeper with a soft heart who fed many struggling would-be singing stars—closed in 1993. However, newer venues like *Kasey's Tavern* (2462 N. Lincoln Ave.; phone: 312-544-3232) are establishing their niche in the neighborhood.

The shops here are as eclectic as the music and the population. *Uncle Dan's Army & Navy Store* (2440 N. Lincoln Ave.; phone: 312-477-1918) offers everything for the urban camper. *Kongoni* (2480 N. Lincoln Ave.; phone: 312-929-9749)—the name means "antelope" in Swahili—is run by two staunch conservationists; every item is authentically African and has been selected with environmental preservation in mind. *Omiyage* (2482 N. Lincoln Ave.; phone: 312-477-1428), which sells baubles for children of all ages, is also a delight.

Bookworms love this area because the bookshops stay open late—most at least until after the movie houses' last shows have begun. Start at *Booksellers Row* (2445 N. Lincoln; phone: 312-348-1170), loaded from ceiling to floor with used books on every imaginable topic. It's the epitome of an old-fashioned neighborhood bookstore, complete with invitingly cluttered shelves and the slightly musty aroma of old tomes and wooden bookcases. Also eminently browse-able are *Dan Behnke Booksellers* (2463 N. Lincoln Ave.; phone: 312-404-0403), which specializes in used books; *The Children's Bookstore* (2465 N. Lincoln Ave.; phone: 312-248-2665); and, a few doors up, *Rohe & Sons, Booksellers* (2603 N. Lincoln Ave.; phone: 312-477-1999).

If you've worked up an appetite, consider the bright red storefront sporting the Union Jack, the *Red Lion Pub* (2446 N. Lincoln Ave.; phone: 312-348-2695). Founded by a Brit (noted architect) John Cordwell, it's one of the few places in town that advertises authentic British cooking. Other nearby eateries include *Lucille's* (2470 N. Lincoln Ave.; phone: 312-429-0660), which has taken over the *Earl of Old Town's* space, and the casual *Pasta Cucina* (2461 N. Lincoln Ave.; phone: 312-248-8200). Several lively coffeehouses add warmth (and aroma) to the block as well.

Lincoln Park is an umbrella community; within it are a number of distinct, smaller neighborhoods—Sheffield, Wrightwood, Lincoln Central, and Old Town among them—and each has its own neighborhood association. Separately, these quasi-governmental groups determine the course of development within the neighborhoods; together, they fight City Hall on common issues, like parking congestion, rowdy bars, and high taxes. (For example, the stretch of Lincoln Avenue that you have just explored is part of an area known as Wrightwood. Every July, this neighborhood sponsors a *Taste of Lincoln Avenue* festival and uses the proceeds to help improve the area's schools, parks, and public areas.)

Continue up Lincoln Avenue to where it intersects with Wrightwood and Sheffield Avenues. To the right are the *Eagle Columns,* a trio of bronzes created by local sculptor Richard Hunt. (This is truly public art; residents here spent five years raising the money for this sculpture, and then treated themselves to a huge block party for its 1990 unveiling.)

From here, walk south down Sheffield Avenue. Hunt's studio is at the corner of Lill and Sheffield Streets. Next door is the *Lill Street Gallery* (1021 W. Lill St.; phone: 312-477-6185). The gallery operates a cooperative exhibition space and provides a workshop for potters who fashion sculptures, functional pots, and almost everything else you can make with clay.

Continue south, walking along Sheffield Avenue to De Paul, a neighborhood named for the university at its center. The first stop is the *De Paul Bookstore* (near the intersection with Fullerton Pkwy.; phone: 312-341-8423); student dorms are above this store, a converted factory building.

Once primarily a commuter school, *De Paul University* is attracting a growing number of students from elsewhere around the country. A major renovation and expansion of its campus currently is under way. For a sense of the campus, walk two blocks west on Fullerton Parkway to Seminary Avenue and turn left; then walk one block south. A classroom and office building is on the left and a student union is on the right; both were constructed within the last 20 years. At Belden Avenue, turn left, stopping at Kenmore Street, the next corner. Look south to the graystone townhouses, many of which have been converted to university buildings.

De Paul is part of the Sheffield neighborhood, and is known for its exquisite gardens, which are shown off in mid-July during the *Sheffield Garden Walk.* South of the university, along Seminary Avenue, Kenmore Street, and Sheffield Avenue, are the private homes—dating from the turn of the century—that give Lincoln Park its charm; many of them are stops on the annual garden walk. After exploring this community, head back to Fullerton Parkway on either Kenmore Street or Sheffield Avenue to continue the tour.

The next part of this walk goes down an alleyway that offers an opportunity to peek into some picturesque backyards; it is a concealed pathway that even some people who have lived in the neighborhood for years haven't yet discovered. Walk east on Fullerton Parkway under the El tracks, and at the first driveway on the right, enter the iron gates; walk about 100 feet to a brick alley and turn left. Here look for architectural salvage pieces, now used as yard ornaments, and for artwork and sculpture among the shady gardens. At the intersection of another alley, look up and to the left to see an iron totem sculpture attached to the second story of a brick house at 901 West Fullerton Parkway. This yard is full of sculptures and iron work. Continue east down the alley for one more block. A giraffe made of car bumpers that have been welded together—a sculpture by Lincoln Park artist John Kearney—is on the right.

At the end of the alley, turn right to explore the McCormick Row House Historic District. These 19th-century brick residences once comprised the *McCormick Theological Seminary,* a Presbyterian institution that erected one of the neighborhood's first buildings. To the left, with a sculpture in front, is *De Paul Concert Hall,* which originally was the seminary chapel. Exit the campus onto Belden Avenue and Halsted Street.

Cross Halsted Street and go straight east two blocks, where Belden Avenue intersects Lincoln Avenue. Across the street is a 100-year-old pub called the *John Barleycorn Memorial Pub* (658 W. Belden Ave.; phone: 312-348-8899), after the limey lush of legend. There's beer, music, and continuous slides of classic paintings; the hamburgers are huge, and the atmosphere is welcoming. (During Prohibition, the pub became a "Chinese laundry," where it was the patrons and not the shirts that got washed.)

From here, it's off to see the wizard: Walk one long block down Lincoln Avenue, and at Webster Avenue, turn right into *Oz Park,* the area where writer Frank Baum lived when he created his famous children's books. Named in honor of his beloved fantasy land, this park boasts a castle-like playground that delights youngsters of all ages. Designed by Robert Leather, it's similar to installations he's done around the country.

Walk along Larrabee Street, which is the park's eastern border. This area is known as Lincoln Central, and, like the other area neighborhoods, it is managed by its own quasi-governmental neighborhood association. Cross Dickens Avenue and walk one more block south to Armitage Avenue. Notice the relatively recent construction here, a shift from the 19th-century brick buildings that have peppered this walk. This area is one of the sections of Lincoln Park that was demolished for urban renewal in the 1960s, before residents made a concerted push for preservation.

Turn left at Armitage and walk east one block to Mohawk Street. Turn right and go south one block to West Wisconsin Street, then turn left and walk another block to North Cleveland Street and head south (right). You'll be wandering among the variety of houses and apartments in a neighborhood known as Old Town. About a block down North Cleveland is *St. Michael's Roman Catholic Church* (1633 N. Cleveland St.), built to serve the German immigrants who first populated this area. From the cul-de-sac in front of the church, look up to see its elegant spire. The church was built between 1866 and 1869, but part of it was destroyed by the Great Chicago Fire of 1871 and rebuilt later. Step inside to see the high vaulted ceilings, the brilliant stained glass windows, and the sword-wielding figure of St. Michael. Listen for the chimes. Local lore has it that if you can hear the bells of St. Michael's, you are in Old Town.

The famous *Old Town Art Fair* is held along Wisconsin and Menomonee Streets during the second weekend in June, as it has been for more than four decades. Each of the area streets has its own special charm; take your pick and explore them at leisure.

Old Town was the first section of Lincoln Park to be revitalized after World War II. The original residents had begun to abandon the area for the suburbs, leaving room for dedicated urbanites to move in, changing the neighborhood's character from aging working class to what's now referred to as gentrified. From *St. Michael's,* walk a short block east on Eugenie Street. At Hudson Avenue, turn left and, as you go around the corner, notice 1700 North Hudson Avenue, the home of architect Walter Netsch and his wife, Dawn Clark Netsch, who for many years was a state senator and comptroller for the state of Illinois. Netsch's rooftop design studio is above the garage.

Continue north on Hudson Avenue for one block to another house of worship, the *Midwest Buddhist Temple* (435 W. Menomonee St.), a pagoda-type structure surrounded by oriental gardens; you'll be coming at it from the rear. Go west along Willow Street a few steps and turn right into a walkway that runs along the western edge of the Buddhist temple. Stand back and contemplate its tranquillity amidst all this urban bustle. Across the street from the temple to the northeast is a pedestrian mall—actually a little park—with stone tables inset with boards for playing chess or checkers. Follow this path past two more of John Kearney's bumper sculptures, a pair of horses.

The path ends at Sedgwick Street. Turn left and go one-half block to Wisconsin Street, then turn right. At the corner of Sedgwick and Wisconsin Streets is a community conversation area next to the *Church of the Three Crosses,* a low, modern building that provides a sharp contrast to *St. Michael's.* Catercorner from this spot is a residential townhouse development, the award-winning *Belgravia Terrace,* where townhouses sell for about $1 million each. Formerly the site of a hospital, this is one of the last parcels of land reconstructed under urban development.

Walk east along Wisconsin Street to Orleans Street and angle through the commercial mall to Lincoln Avenue. Stop by *Ranalli's Pizza* (1925 N. Lincoln Ave.; phone: 312-642-4700) to try one of more than 100 imported beers. This is also the place for some of Chicago's best pizza; it opens out to a delightful terrace in the summer.

Just ahead, across Lincoln Park West, is the *Chicago Academy of Sciences* (2001 N. Clark St.; phone: 312-549-0606; closed *Christmas*). The *Chicago Historical Society* is two blocks down Clark Street to the right (N. Clark St. and North Ave.; phone: 312-642-4600; closed *Thanksgiving, Christmas,* and *New Year's Day*). Both museums are worth a visit (they have no admission charge on Mondays), but first stroll through the park for which this community is named, beginning with the famous (and free) *Lincoln Park Zoo.* (For details on all three, see *Special Places* in THE CITY.)

Walk into the park at Armitage Avenue, in front of the *Chicago Academy of Sciences.* Then walk behind it and a block north to the *Café Brauer* (phone: 312-280-2724), an exquisite piece of Prairie School architecture designed in 1905 by Dwight Perkins, who also designed many of the city's public schools and fought for the establishment of the forest preserves, the large areas of greenery that surround the city. Café diners can order several light dishes and enjoy them outside by the small lake; rowboats can be rented under the bridge to the south. The zoo begins here, just across the bridge east of *Café Brauer.*

Wander through the zoo; then follow signs to the *Rookery,* a rock garden designed in 1936 by the late curmudgeon Alfred Caldwell, a student of Jens Jensen and past dean of Chicago's landscape architects. A faithful restoration of this lovely place, where all manner of waterfowl are free to come and go, was completed in 1991. *Lincoln Park Conservatory* (Stockton Dr. at Fullerton Ave.; phone: 312-294-4770) is three acres of greenhouses and gardens. The glass-walled conservatory building itself is a marvel, with a tropical jungle at its center and constantly changing displays in other rooms. It's closed *Christmas;* no admission charge (also see *Special Places* in THE CITY).

Leaving the conservatory, walk west a short distance to Clark Street. From here, any bus goes back to the Loop; taxis also frequently pass here as well.

Andersonville and Clark Street

BRYN MAWR AVENUE

GLENWOOD

LAKEWOOD AVENUE

N

BALMORAL AVENUE

BOWMANVILLE

BERWYN STREET

■ **Swedish American Museum**

FOSTER AVENUE

SHERIDAN ROAD

WINNEMAC AVENUE

RAVENSWOOD

St. Bonifaccius Cemetery

UPTOWN

LAWRENCE AVENUE

Chase Park

DAMEN AVENUE

RAVENSWOOD AVENUE

WILSON AVENUE

■ **Truman College**

MONTROSE AVENUE

ASHLAND AVENUE

■ **Getty Tomb**

LINCOLN AVENUE

Graceland Cemetery

BERTEAU AVENUE

BROADWAY

IRVING PARK ROAD

CLARK STREET

GRACE STREET

LAKEVIEW

■ **Wrigley Field**

ADDISON STREET

0   mile   1/2

Walk 8: Andersonville and Clark Street

Clark Street runs parallel to Lake Shore Drive from the city's northern boundary to 23rd Street, near McCormick Place on the South Side. Historically, Clark Street has been a magnet for recent immigrants. Earlier this century, for instance, it provided a new home and renewed hope for generations of Italians, Swedes, and other Europeans. Since the early 1970s, however, a new generation of immigrants has established a beachhead here that is evident in the ethnic crazy-quilt of its restaurants. The area also has an extraordinary outdoor museum, *Graceland Cemetery,* and the nation's most gracious ballpark, *Wrigley Field,* home of the *Chicago Cubs.*

The segment of Clark Street between 5600 and 5200 North is the main street for Andersonville, Chicago's vigorous Swedish enclave and one of the most concentrated Swedish neighborhoods in America. Major Swedish festivals held in Andersonville include a colorful mid-June street fair, featuring costumed folk dancing and choral singing, and *St. Lucia Day* (mid-December), with *Christmas* caroling and the traditional crowning of the Queen of Light.

This walk down Clark Street begins at Bryn Mawr Avenue in Andersonville (5600 North) and ends at Addison Street (3600 North), where every loyal North Sider's favorite team plays ball. This tour can be done by car or on the Clark Street bus, which runs the entire length of the street. To get to the starting point by car, head west from Lake Shore Drive on Bryn Mawr Avenue (5600 North). To get there on public transit, take the Howard Street train to Bryn Mawr Avenue and walk over to Clark Street (about a 10-minute trek). From Bryn Mawr Avenue, head south through the wonderful assortment of boutiques, specialty bookstores, offbeat second-hand shops, and eateries and grocery stores that serve or sell the makings of just about every kind of ethnic fare imaginable.

To sample the ethnic mix, begin at *Machu Picchu* (5427 N. Clark St.; phone: 312-769-0455), one of the few Peruvian eateries in the Midwest. Choose from among eight appetizers, including lobster soufflé and potato stuffed with a mixture of onions, beef, tomatoes, raisins, olives, boiled egg, and herbs. Entrées include a popular pork dish served with a lively peanut sauce, duck in amaretto sauce, and filet of chicken accompanied by a potato prepared with a two-cheese sauce. The restaurant does not serve liquor, but patrons are invited to bring their own.

If pastries are a weakness, walk another block to a huge hand-painted medieval-style mural with princesses and knights. It graces the front of the *Swedish Bakery* (5348 N. Clark St.; phone: 312-561-8919), a haven for tempting bread (including limpa and potato), pastries, cookies, muffins, and 20 different kinds of coffee cake—all at reasonable neighborhood-bakery prices. The genteel decor of the interior—pretty white wallpaper, a wooden bench, and a revolving cake stand—is reminiscent of a village tea shop. The sales staff wears traditional Swedish costumes.

Just ahead is the *Tipanan* restaurant and cocktail lounge (5402 N. Clark St.; phone: 312-784-1802). The restaurant, with an easily recognizable red-and-white façade, prepares Szechuan and Mandarin Chinese, as well as Philippine, dishes; they also have live entertainment in the evening.

Across the street is *Calo* (5343 N. Clark St.; phone: 312-271-7725), specializing in Italian food and good wine (and locally renowned for its pizza). *Calo* offers live entertainment, featuring popular music, with dancing on Wednesdays, Fridays, and Saturdays to help diners work off the calories. A few doors down is *Okee Chee's Wild Horse Gallery* (5337 N. Clark; phone: 312-271-5883), a gallery/boutique dedicated to Native American culture, offering art, books, weavings, and handmade toys. Also on this block are the *Kopi Café* and *Jalan Jalan Boutique* (5317 N. Clark St.; phone: 312-989-5674), offering up a heady combination of espresso, soups, and travel books. The *Fiery Clock Face* bookstore (5311 N. Clark St.; phone: 312-728-4227) specializes in cookbooks and out-of-print children's books.

From here, walk to the hand-me-down haven of *Camden Passage Antiques* (5309 N. Clark St.; phone: 312-989-0111). This shop has vintage clothes, jewelry, and lots of odds and ends. It competes with the nameless second-hand shop on the other side of the street, which offers an array of inexpensively priced clothes, furniture, and bric-a-brac. At Berwyn Street is the *Landmark* (5301 N. Clark St.), a collection of shops specializing in Swedish gifts and housewares along with distinctive clothing.

Food is the highlight of the next block, starting with the *Baskin-Robbins* ice cream shop (at the corner of N. Clark and Berwyn Sts.). Beyond that is *Andie's* (5253 N. Clark St.; phone: 312-784-8616), with tantalizing Greek and Lebanese food, and *Reza's* Persian restaurant (5255 N. Clark St.; phone: 312-561-1898). This last is an unusually good-looking neighborhood restaurant, with smart hardwood floors, vases filled with fresh pink carnations, and pretty Iranian prints adorning its brick walls. Try the yogurt-based appetizers, beef kebabs, and char-broiled combinations of shrimp, beef, chicken, scallops, and vegetables.

Down the street is *Svea I* (5330 N. Clark St.; phone: 312-275-7738), a Scandinavian eatery that serves hearty breakfasts and lunches featuring sausages, ham, roast beef, and corned beef, along with seafood and salads. If you've a craving for herring, try *Wikstrom's* Scandinavian-style deli (5247 N. Clark St.; phone: 312-878-0601). *Wikstrom's and Erikson's,* another deli across the street (5250 N. Clark St.; phone: 312-561-5634), offers a veritable smorgasbord of Scandinavian goodies, including Swedish potato sausage, Danish brie, and Norwegian jarlsberg, along with lutefish, packages of potato dumplings, sacks of yellow peas, and an assortment of Scandinavian chocolate and candy.

In the next block are three stores catering to women, beginning with *Studio 90* (5239 N. Clark St.; phone: 312-878-0097), which offers handmade and handknit clothing. The colorful display at *Womanwild* (5237 N. Clark St.; phone: 312-878-0300) only hints at the delights within. Offering what it calls "treasures by women," this shop sells gallery-quality textiles, pottery, and jewelry. These imaginative and often brightly colored items are all original designs; they make great and unusual gifts. Next door is the city's best feminist bookstore, *Women and Children First* (phone: 312-769-9299). In addition to books, the shop offers diverse merchandise, including small gift items, unusual T-shirts (with readers and feline fanciers in mind), note cards (both whimsical and profound), and a selection of jewelry.

Resale goods are the highlight of the next block. *Right Place* (5219 N. Clark St.; phone: 312-561-7757) has a variety of circa-1950 items—gaily colored clothing and plastic goods. Across the street at *Books off Berwyn* (5220 N. Clark St.; phone: 312-878-9800), a small bright storefront has been turned into a card and bookshop with a particularly good selection of children's books. The *Swedish American Museum* (5211 N. Clark St.; phone: 312-728-8111) will give you a glimpse of Swedish culture, both past and present. The museum is closed Mondays; admission charge (also see *Museums* in THE CITY).

Ann Sather (5207 N. Clark St.; phone: 312-271-6677), a Chicago landmark, offers heavenly Swedish waffles, piled high with whipped cream and strawberries, thin pancakes smothered with tart lingonberries, and a side order of mild potato sausage, served with a hot buttery cinnamon roll. You can order a combination breakfast plate that lets you sample both pancakes and waffles. Three-egg omelettes are popular breakfast fare, and this also is a good and inexpensive spot for hearty lunches and dinners, such as meatballs, roast duck, loin of pork, pan-fried chicken liver, and a Swedish sampler platter. It most definitely is a family place; a series of murals along the wall chronicle a Swedish fairy tale, and the restaurant presents readings of children's classics on Wednesday mornings (also see *Eating Out* in THE CITY). Across the street is a new shop called *One Touch of Nature* (5204 N. Clark St.; phone: 312-561-3300), catering to lovers of wildlife. A board by its entrance announces which unusual birds have been sighted in the area.

The next stop is *Graceland Cemetery,* a dozen long blocks south and, thus, worth the bus fare or returning to the car to drive. *Graceland* (4001 N. Clark St.; enter where Clark Street meets Irving Park Road) embraced the Victorian-age belief that cemeteries should be places where the dead could lay eternally in sweet repose and the living could enjoy a tranquil carriage ride through lush, groomed landscape. *Graceland* is the final home of George Pullman, Potter Palmer, Philip Armour, Cyrus McCormick, Marshall Field, and many other luminaries (at least the Protestant ones) who built this city. Not only are many of the city's architects buried here (Miës van der Rohe, Louis Sullivan, and Daniel H. Burnham among them), they also designed some of the tombs. (Architectural historians cite Sullivan's *Getty Tomb* as the beginning of modern architecture in America. To build it, he looked not to models from the past, but to his own vision of what American architecture could be.) The *Chicago Architecture Foundation* (phone: 312-922-3432) gives tours of *Graceland* on Sunday afternoons in the spring and fall. The foundation also sells a self-guided tour.

Move on to Addison Street and *Wrigley Field,* where the Chicago *Cubs,* those guys who "just love to break your heart," play ball. The gloomy statistics: The *Cubs* haven't been in a *World Series* since 1945, and the last time they won was 1908. This neighborhood is called Wrigleyville, and its residents fought the Chicago Tribune Company (a formidable foe in this town) for a decade over the issue of night games. The Trib eventually won and the lights went on in 1990, but on the neighborhood's terms. A warning: If it's game time, don't park here (assuming there's an available spot). One of the promises the neighborhood extracted from the city in return for approving night games is that residents get stickers for their cars; those without them get towed on game nights.

There are several places to eat a hot dog around here even if the team isn't playing. For atmosphere, try the *Cubby Bear Lounge* (1059 W. Addison St.; phone: 312-327-1662). Those interested in more ethnic fare might want to try *Moulibet* (3521 N. Clark St.; phone: 312-929-9383), a long block south. This is an Ethiopian establishment specializing in lamb, chicken, and vegetable dishes. Tej, a sweet honey wine, makes a good accompaniment to this very spicy food.

The Howard Street train stops at Addison Street (if there's a game, many people take advantage of its convenience). Hop on for an elevated ride through Lincoln Park on the way back to the Loop.

Walk 9: Argyle Street and Little Saigon

Argyle Street, named for a Scottish duke, is now, oddly enough, the center of a neighborhood known as Little Saigon. The area, a few brief blocks between Broadway and Sheridan Road at 5000 North, has become an eclectic mix of Asian nationalities, particularly Vietnamese. Many shops have signs printed both in English and in the native tongue of the owner.

Getting here is easy: Hop on a Howard Street subway train in the Loop and head north. If it's rush hour, get on an "A" train; it's the only one that stops at Argyle Street (at other times of day, all Howard Street trains stop there). The station, decked out in green and red, is hard to miss. The train comes out of its subway tunnel at 2000 North and provides views of Lincoln Park, Lake View, and *Graceland Cemetery* along the way. Get off the train and head east toward Sheridan Road.

If you are taking this tour on a weekend, begin at the tiny, storefront *Vietnam War Museum* (954 W. Carmen Ave.; phone: 312-728-6111; see *Museums* in THE CITY), a reminder of the controversial war that drove the local Vietnamese people from their homeland. The museum is filled with uniforms and equipment, maps, photos, and other memorabilia. Open weekend afternoons only; no admission charge.

Head back toward Argyle Street. The *Superior* gift shop (1006 W. Argyle St.; phone: 312-271-0253) has everything its window promises and then some: from vases to party decorations. The *Pho Xe Lua* Vietnamese restaurant (1021 W. Argyle St.; phone: 312-275-7512), a little farther down the street, offers delicious and inexpensive lunches in a no-frills setting. For something with more atmosphere, cross Argyle again to another Vietnamese restaurant, *Nhu Hoa Café* (1020 W. Argyle St.; phone: 312-878-0618), which also offers Laotian dishes. Distinguished by lions guarding the door and the neon palm trees in the window, it's known for crunchy egg rolls and fiery curry dishes.

The tumult of activity along Argyle Street is reminiscent of a Far East city. People preoccupied with shopping zigzag though the bazaar of exotic shops; delivery trucks loaded with pungently scented foods line up along the curb; and the air rings with the sing-song music of the Vietnamese language. There are dozens of restaurants, gift shops, and grocery stores along this three-block stretch; to choose a restaurant, look to see how busy it is and check reviews and menus in the window. There are also several video stores, jewelry shops, and a newsdealer along these few packed blocks. If you are in the market for a new timepiece, try *New World Watch* (1050 W. Argyle St. at Kenmore Ave.), which advertises discounts of 30% to 70%.

FOSTER AVENUE

WINONA STREET

UPTOWN

Vietnam
■ War Museum

S

CARMEN AVENUE

WINNEMAC AVE.

Hue ■   Superior
Nhu Hoa Cafe ■   ■

ARGYLE STREET

F

Viet Hoa ■   ■
Market   Pho Xe Lua

SHERIDAN ROAD

LITTLE SAIGON

AINSLIE STREET

CASTLEWOOD TERR.

MAGNOLIA AVENUE

BROADWAY

WINTHROP AVENUE

KENMORE AVENUE

GUNNISON STREET

LAWRENCE AVENUE

LAKESIDE PLACE

RACINE AVENUE

N

Argyle Street and
Little Saigon

0   mile   1/8

Directly across Argyle Street is a food market popular with locals who load up here for a week's supply of groceries. Called the *Viet Hoa Oriental Grocery* (1051 W. Argyle St.; phone: 312-334-1028), it's crammed with fresh and frozen fish, exotic spices, oriental vegetables, spiced tea, and flavored rice, as well as an array of hand-painted teapots, Vietnamese cooking utensils, and inexpensive ceramic bowls. If *Viet Hoa* is too crowded, there are a half dozen other grocery stores to choose from.

The bustling scene continues in the next block with more shops, including necessities for the neighborhood's residents: mortgage companies, hair salons, and several dentists. The *Vinh Tho Grocery Store* (1112 W. Argyle St.; phone: 312-275-2985) offers ginseng and herbs. *Thai Vin* (1113 W. Argyle St.), despite its name, serves Vietnamese cuisine—noodle dishes, quail, and frog's legs are specialties—in two very bright and busy rooms. The *Sun Wah Bar-be-que* (1134 W. Argyle St.; phone: 312-769-1254) offers both Filipino and Vietnamese foods, to take out or eat in. Roasted chickens and a whole pig adorn the front window.

Argyle turns into a residential area west of Broadway. Vietnamese families live in the decrepit-looking brownstones and narrow wooden houses of this neighborhood. Yet in just a decade and a half, these refugees have carved out a distinct and self-sufficient community here. The area now boasts its own brand new strip mall on Broadway just south of Argyle Street, with still more food, jewelry, and video stores.

To return to the Loop, walk back to the train station where you arrived and head south.

Devon Avenue

WHIPPLE

SACRAMENTO

RICHMOND

S

Globus Gourmet Foods ■ ■ Chicago Hebrew Bookstore
Rosenblum's
FRANCISCO   Judaica ■ ■ Hashalom

MOZART

CALIFORNIA

FAIRFIELD

■ First Cook
   Community Bank
WASHTENAW

■ Jai Hind
   Foods and Video
TALMAN

Gandhi India ■ ■ Kamdar Plaza
ROCKWELL

GLENLAKE

ROSEMONT

DEVON

ARTHUR

ALBION

NORTH SHORE

MAPLEWOOD

CAMPBELL

ARTESIAN   K-Econo ■

Parthenon-Gyros ■
       Greek
WESTERN

F

CLAREMONT

OAKELY

BELL

HIGHLAND

LEVITT

GRANVILLE

HOYNE

HOOD

SEELEY

N ⟶

0   mile   1/4

Walk 10: Devon Avenue

Elderly Jewish men shopping at a kosher butcher; Indian women with caste marks on their foreheads looking at colorful fabric; Russians, Greeks, Palestinians, and a growing number of Koreans. You'll find them all along Devon Avenue, where every few blocks Chicago's diverse ethnic communities come together like bands in a rainbow. Once strictly a Jewish enclave, many of the original residents—now senior citizens—remain, surrounded by flourishing Eastern European bakeries, Middle Eastern groceries, Indian markets, and even a Croatian community center.

This walk starts at 3000 West Devon Avenue, at the intersection of Sacramento Avenue, and heads east. To get here, either drive or take a train and bus. By car, take the Kennedy Expressway northwest to the Diversey Street (2800 North) exit and head north on Western Avenue to Devon Avenue (6400 North). Devon Avenue is about a 15-minute drive from the exit. The tour actually ends here and begins a dozen short blocks west. You'll want to leave your car on a side street before embarking on this walk: Traffic just crawls along Devon Avenue and parking there is impossible. To get here by train, take the Howard Line to Howard Street, walk downstairs to the bus terminal and get a No. 155 Devon Avenue bus.

One block east of Sacramento Street is Richmond Street; note that the street signs here call Devon Avenue "Golda Meir Boulevard"(when the shops become predominantly Indian five blocks east, Devon Avenue is labeled "Gandhi Targ"). A Mandarin restaurant at this corner marks the beginning of the rich ethnic mix here. On the west side of Devon Avenue, the *Fruit Wagon Produce and Deli* (2958 W. Devon Ave.; 312-338-2296) advertises Tabachnik soup and hand-sliced lox. Nearby, the books that line the shelves at the *Chicago Hebrew Bookstore* (2942 W. Devon Ave.; phone: 312-973-6636) reflect the ethnic group that predominated here from the 1920s, when farmlands became blocks and blocks of bungalows, until the 1970s, when Indian families began to arrive. More recently, Russian and Ukrainian immigrants, mainly Jewish, have come. This block also includes the *Thai Lai-Kram* restaurant (2916 W. Devon Ave.; phone: 312-973-2221), advertising little-known Thai specialties along with various curries.

In *Globus Gourmet Foods* (2909 W. Devon Ave.; no phone), you get a real sense of the neighborhood's Russian and Ukrainian residents. In the long lines at the back of the store, shoppers repeat a habit learned at home; much socializing is done while queuing up for food. Sausages hang from the walls, canned goods bearing labels with Cyrillic letters line the shelves, cheeses are stacked in refrigerated cases, and a display near the door features luscious cakes from the *Kiev Bakery* in Brooklyn, New York. Like many other stores, this one also carries a good selection of Russian-language videos for sale. Next door, Arabic letters announce the *Zabiha Meat*

Market (phone: 312-274-6700); its interior offers other treats: pita bread, falafel, spring roll pastry, savory leaves, yogurt dip mixes, an aromatic mix called garam masala, pomegranate seeds, and a host of other Middle Eastern goods.

Rosenblum's Judaica (2906 W. Devon Ave.; phone: 312-262-1700), a book and gift store, features Hebrew cards, religious gifts, and a selection of special children's books with such titles as *How Uncle Murray Saved Seder.* In the window are silver menorahs, a magnetic spelling board with Hebrew characters, and ceramics of stern elders and studious rabbis.

Across the street is the popular *Hashalom* (2905 W. Devon Ave.; phone: 312-465-5675), a storefront restaurant with baskets and tapestries decorating its plain white walls and blue vinyl covering its tables. Its deliciously authentic Middle Eastern food combines Moroccan and Israeli preparations. Popular dishes include couscous, *bourekas,* and falafel. Another specialty of the house is *shakshouka,* a classic Israeli dish made with fresh tomatoes, onions, peppers, tomato sauce, two eggs sunny-side up, and pita bread. Top off the meal with rich Israeli coffee.

Heading east, note the huge *Croatian Cultural Center of Chicago* (2845 W. Devon Ave.), a long, flat, unattractive cement building that is windowless and decorated with horizontal red, white, and blue stripes across its façade. Peek inside its cool, dark interior at walls adorned with portraits of Croatian kings and paintings of coastal scenes; perhaps its heavy chairs and tables are decorated for an upcoming wedding.

The shopfronts along Devon Avenue boast a diversity of goods and services worthy of an international bazaar. The windows at *Ted's Fruit Market* (2840 W. Devon Ave.; phone: 312-743-6739) advertise an eclectic feast of kosher salami, Greek olives, cooked ham, and fuji apples; travel agencies along the street suggest trips to Guatemala, Israel, Mexico, and Russia; a cosmetology school has a sign in Korean. One of the oldtimers along this block is the *Kosher Karry Deli* (2828 W. Devon Ave.; phone: 312-973-4355), which provides knishes, *kugel,* and other fare for bar mitzvahs, as well as bakery and deli goods for neighborhood patrons. On the north side of Devon Avenue, the *Three Sisters Delicatessen* (2854 W. Devon Ave.; phone: 312-973-1919) offers Russian groceries, including a variety of smoked fish—shad, herring, mackerel, sable, and sturgeon.

Striking an incongruous note is the First Cook Community Bank (2720 W. Devon Ave.), with its brick colonial architecture featuring dormers and white shutters. Outside is the *Spirit of the Fighting Yank,* a statue of a grenade-wielding American GI. The building houses a family medical center and *Jewish Community Service* office.

"Little Bombay" begins in earnest along the stretch of Devon Avenue immediately east of Washtenaw Street, at 2700 West, where Devon is labeled Gandhi Targ. In fact, many of the Indian and Pakistani restaurants in this section of Devon Avenue advertise singers and musicians "direct from Bombay." *Jai Hind Foods and Video* (2658 W. Devon Ave.; phone: 312-

973-3400) is typical of the food markets that vie for business along the next few blocks. Shoppers in saris peruse jars of chutney, tandoor paste, and sacks of rice to the omnipresent chant of Indian pop music and the pervasive aroma of pungent spices. An entire wall is stacked high with a variety of beans, curry and other powders, and seeds such as mustard and cumin. A small dining area in the rear offers a buffet of South Indian specialties and sticky desserts. A jewelry store offering mainly pieces in pure gold is a recent addition to this growing emporium.

Along the next section of Devon Avenue, each block seems to give over to a particular kind of merchandise. First there are several grocery stores, then a block where each merchant seems to be selling saris, another block is mainly restaurants. But the groceries are seldom just food stores—jewelry, videos, and saris are as likely to be sold as are beans and lentils. And the organization in each will appeal to even the most fanatic closet straightener; unlike the Russian shops where various goods are unappealingly lumped together, the stock in the Indian stores is neatly arranged, and all are labeled carefully in English.

Kamdar Plaza (2646 W. Devon Ave.; phone: 312-338-8100), an Indian grocery, opens onto yet another reasonably priced sari store, which has floor-to-ceiling shelves crammed with bolts of cloth in a rainbow of colors with the ubiquitous Indian music playing in the background. Across the street, *Sharda Saree Center* (2629 W. Devon Ave.; phone: 312-338-8193) displays its filmy saris in a kaleidoscope of color on mannequins with delicate Indian features, their hands gracefully folded. Selections of saris also can be found at *Indira Fashions* (2625 W. Devon Ave.; phone: 312-338-4900) and *Sari Sapne* (2623 W. Devon Ave.; phone: 312-338-7274).

The *Gandhi India* restaurant (2601 W. Devon Ave.; phone: 312-761-8714) is typical of the eateries in the neighborhood's colorful Indian enclave. Although it may lack atmosphere, there's ample compensation in the good, inexpensive food. A daily, all-you-can-eat buffet is a bargain. The punjabi bread is delightful, and the tandoori chicken and vegetarian dishes are tasty. Even if you don't opt for a full meal, take a short break and sample the combination appetizer plate and a glass of Taj Mahal beer.

A few doors down and across the street you'll see the *Viceroy of India* (2520 W. Devon Ave.; phone: 312-743-4100), an airy, elegant restaurant with a daily all-you-can-eat lunch buffet. Its specialties include tandoori cooking, yogurt marinades, and mulligatawny soup. Several other Indian restaurants in the area are *Taj Mahal* (2502 W. Devon Ave.; phone: 312-338-4000); *Kanval Palace* (2501 W. Devon Ave.; phone: 312-761-7270); *Tandoor Indian Restaurant* (2548 W. Devon Ave.; phone: 312-761-4546), which specializes in clay-oven cooking; and the *Udupi Palace* (2543 W. Devon Ave.; phone: 312-338-2152), which serves only vegetarian meals. All offer an inexpensive luncheon plate; to decide where to eat, read the reviews and menus in the windows.

A block farther, the neighborhood's delightful ethnic mix offers yet another food option: gyro sandwiches, spinach pie, *saganaki,* and baklava at the *Parthenon-Gyros Greek* restaurant (2447 W. Devon Ave.; phone: 312-761-6550). Scattered among the restaurants are several video stores; the *Bombay* (2634 W. Devon) advertises tapes in a dozen south Asian languages, a reminder that Bombay turns out more movies than Hollywood did in its 1930s heyday.

On the southwest corner of Devon Avenue and Artesian Street, *K-Econo* (phone: 312-274-0658) is the sort of discount emporium where transistor radios can be found among samurai swords, soccer balls from Pakistan, even a wall clock laminated with a picture of John Wayne. It's also a sign that the stores are about to change category again. At Western Avenue, and continuing for a few blocks east, electronic stores dominate, beginning with the two-story *Gandhi Electronics* (2358 W. Devon Ave.; phone: 312-973-7667). Though the proprietors here are Indian, some of the smaller shops are run by Koreans, heralding yet another change in Devon Avenue's rich mix.

The tour ends here, at Western Avenue. Either pickup a Devon Avenue bus to take you back to the train, or retrace your steps to your car.

Walk 11: Halsted
The World on One Street

Locals claim it's possible to live an entire life without ever leaving Halsted Street, and they're probably right. A tour of this street can take a day, a week, a month, or more. This miniature universe stretches for 20 miles through metropolitan Chicago, from 4000 North to 12000 South. The busy thoroughfare is lined with hundreds of ethnic restaurants, as well as night-clubs, theaters, several ethnic neighborhoods, a university, a peddlers' market, and the *Union Stock Yards,* source of much of Chicago's early wealth.

Named for two Philadelphia brothers who financed the real estate acquisitions of Chicago's first mayor, William B. Ogden, Halsted Street shoots straight south through Lake View, Lincoln Park, West Loop, Greektown, *Hull House,* Maxwell Street, and from there into several ethnic enclaves, ending near historic Pullman. To get the full flavor of Chicago's variety, this is the tour to take. You can do it by bus, getting on and off to explore selected sites, or hoof it, arriving and departing by train. The No. 8 bus runs the full length of Halsted Street, starting at 3700 North. The Howard Street train stops at Addison Street, three blocks from where the tour begins, and at North and Clybourn Avenues, about midway through the tour. (The station at North and Clybourn Avenue is currently closed on weekends, which means you have to take a North Avenue bus east if you want to end the tour there.) A car is an impediment on the northern end of Halsted Street; it's not a problem from North Avenue south.

An excursion down this lengthy boulevard is easily broken into two parts if there isn't time to do it all at once. The first leg starts at the northern end of Halsted Street and runs south to the off-Loop theater district near North Avenue. A separate tour can be made of the downtown section of Halsted Street, starting at Madison Street, cutting through Greektown, and passing the *University of Illinois at Chicago* and *Hull House.*

Just south of the bus terminal at 3700 North Halsted Street, where this tour begins, are two aromatic spots catering to sybarites: the *Graceway Corners* (3751 N. Halsted St.; phone: 312-348-4612) and *Coffee Tree and Tea Leaves* (3752 N. Halsted St.; phone: 312-871-7818). Across the street is one of those unexpected architectural treasures that abound in Chicago, the *Chicago Park District Storage Building* (3640 N. Halsted St.). The extraordinary terra cotta work on the façade seems unwarranted for such a commonplace, utilitarian structure.

Like so many major American cities, Chicago has seen the growth of an open, activist gay community since the early 1970s. Over the past two decades, that community established a center along North Halsted Street. Today, in the 3600 block, the *Brown Elephant Resale Shop* (3641 N. Halsted

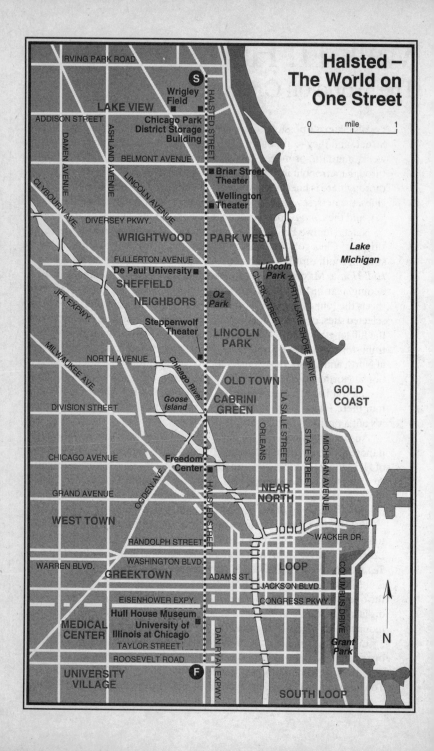

Halsted –
The World on
One Street

0   mile   1

IRVING PARK ROAD

S

Wrigley
Field

LAKE VIEW

ADDISON STREET

Chicago Park
District Storage
Building

BELMONT AVENUE

■ Briar Street
Theater

■ Wellington
Theater

DIVERSEY PKWY.

WRIGHTWOOD

PARK WEST

*Lake
Michigan*

FULLERTON AVENUE

*Lincoln
Park*

De Paul University ■

SHEFFIELD

*Oz
Park*

NEIGHBORS

Steppenwolf
Theater

**LINCOLN
PARK**

NORTH AVENUE

Chicago River

**GOLD
COAST**

OLD TOWN

**CABRINI
GREEN**

*Goose
Island*

DIVISION STREET

CHICAGO AVENUE

Freedom ■
Center

**NEAR
NORTH**

GRAND AVENUE

WEST TOWN

RANDOLPH STREET

WASHINGTON BLVD.

WARREN BLVD.

GREEKTOWN

ADAMS ST

LOOP

EISENHOWER EXPY.

JACKSON BLVD.

CONGRESS PKWY.

**MEDICAL
CENTER**

Hull House Museum
University of
Illinois at Chicago ■

TAYLOR STREET

ROOSEVELT ROAD

*Grant
Park*

F

N

**UNIVERSITY
VILLAGE**

SOUTH LOOP

(street labels on map:) HALSTED STREET, DAMEN AVENUE, ASHLAND AVENUE, LINCOLN AVENUE, CLYBOURN AVE., JFK EXPWY., MILWAUKEE AVE., OGDEN AVE., DAN RYAN EXPWY., CLARK STREET, NORTH LAKE SHORE DRIVE, LA SALLE STREET, ORLEANS, STATE STREET, MICHIGAN AVENUE, WACKER DR., COLUMBUS DRIVE

St.; phone: 312-549-3549)) sells its warehouse full of previously owned items to benefit an AIDS clinic. *Vortex* (3631 N. Halsted St.; phone: 312-975-6622) is one of several gay bars and dance clubs in the area.

At the corner of Addison and Halsted Streets is the *Town Hall* (23rd District) *Police Station*. The building was originally the *Town Hall* for a community named Lake View. In the 19th century, this was a resort area, far from the city's heat (the lake was a lot closer to Halsted Street than it is now). But by 1890, Chicago had expanded to the borders of Lake View and the community was annexed, as were many others over years of relentless growth. Across the street is *Checkers Restaurant* (3601 N. Halsted St.; phone: 312-296-0326), a 1950s-style diner popular with the area police.

The next few blocks are loaded with restaurants, among them are: *Bangkok* (3542 N. Halsted St.; phone: 312-327-2870), offering authentic Thai decor and food; *Ooh La La!* (3335 N. Halsted St.; phone: 312-935-7708), a tempting mix of French and Italian dishes; *Yoshi's Café* (3257 N. Halsted St.; phone: 312-248-6160), a pricey Japanese spot with a French accent (see *Eating Out* in THE CITY); *Chicago Diner* (3411 N. Halsted St.; phone: 312-935-6696), a vegetarian delight; and *Nookies Tree* (3334 N. Halsted St.; phone: 312-248-9888), for quick but quality dining. At Cornelia Street, just around the corner, is *Cornelia's* (750 W. Cornelia St.; phone: 312-248-8333); its classic Italian dishes are frequently served with herbs grown on the nearby sidewalk, and a side order of classical music is included at no extra charge.

Fine antiques stores also are abundant on the 3400 block of North Halsted Street. Though you may not be in the market for a chifforobe, intriguing smaller items also can be found at the *Brokerage* (3444 N. Halsted St.; phone: 312-248-1644) and *Formerly Yours* (3443 N. Halsted St.; phone: 312-248-7766).

Step into *Caffè Pergolesi* (3404 N. Halsted St.; phone: 312-472-8602), a bright yellow coffeehouse, and step back into the 1960s. In addition to the inevitable coffee, it offers solid fare like lox and bagels and hearty vegetable stews. Next to the bright red phone booth (a refugee from a London street corner) is *Roscoe's* (3356 N. Halsted St.; phone: 312-281-3355), a popular gay nightspot. *Town Hall Pub* (3340 N. Halsted St.; phone: 312-472-4405) is another great 1960s folk place. And art lovers will enjoy browsing in the *Art Mecca Gallery* (3352 N. Halsted St.; phone: 312-935-3255) and *Gallimaufrey Gallery* (3345 N. Halsted St.; phone: 312-348-8090).

Fans of mystery writer Sara Paretsky, who has become a role model to a growing group of Chicago authors that set whodunits in their hometown, may recognize the corner of Belmont Avenue and Halsted Street as the place where private investigator V. I. Warshawski lived when her apartment was torched and she just missed going up along with it. Across Halsted Street (and just around the corner to the right) is *Victorian House Antiques* (806 W. Belmont Ave.; phone: 312-472-0400). This lovingly restored, if not too elegant, "painted lady" is as renowned for its hauntings as for its household goods.

The area of Halsted Street between Belmont and Fullerton Avenues is best visited at night, when the streets come alive with people looking for some of the best entertainment in town. Chicago has long been known as a place where actors can make their mark, and today that often means working in this neighborhood. At 3133 North is the *Briar Street Theater* (phone: 312-348-4000), which began life as a stable, then became a sound stage and, finally, a theater. It hosts revivals, experimental productions by established playwrights, plus dance and jazz troupes. Nestled between Halsted and Clark Streets at Wellington Street is the *Wellington Theater* (phone: 312-975-7171). Once called the *Ivanhoe* (hence the crenelated façade), this theater languished during the 1980s and was rejuvenated in 1990.

Before the show or after, refuel at any one of the many fine (and exotic) restaurants along here. They can't all be listed, but among the more unusual is *The Helmand* (3201 N. Halsted St.; phone: 312-935-2447), which offers Afghan food in a somewhat upscale environment. The 2600 block is jammed with an international lineup of restaurants, including *La Llama* (phone: 312-327-7756) for Peruvian food; *Arrivederci* (phone: 312-528-3854) for Italian fare; *Uncle Tannous's* (phone: 312-929-1333) for Lebanese food; *Szechwan Kitchen* (phone: 312-348-5599); and *Stevie B's Rib Café* (phone: 312-471-7513). Stuffed? Get a little exercise (very little) at the billiard parlor *Corner Pocket* (2610 N. Halsted St.; phone 312-281-0050). If the wail of Chicago blues is in the cards, two of the city's best clubs are in the 2500 block: *Kingston Mines* (phone: 312-477-4646) and *B.L.U.E.S.* (phone: 312-525-8371); also see *Nightlife* in THE CITY.

During the day, you may want to hop a cab or bus from Belmont Avenue to Fullerton Avenue, where Halsted Street is more hospitable to daytime activities. Between Webster Street (2200 North) and North Avenue, the street is loaded with the kind of shops that appeal to the neighborhood's residents: young urban professional families who can afford upwards of $800,000 to purchase the utterly charming old houses lining the area's side streets. This is the place to buy something for the kids at home, the grandparents who are staying with them, or even the boss who gave you a few extra days off. The stores are too numerous to mention; if what's in the window is appealing, walk in and have a look around.

In the 1800 block, there's a delightful array of domestic architecture: squat wooden Chicago cottages, townhouses, brick cottages, a few brownstones, plus some refurbished four-story walk-ups. Though the first floors of many have been converted to storefronts, some remain private dwellings.

A few restaurants in this area deserve special mention. One is *Café Ba-Ba-Reeba!* (2024 N. Halsted St.), a *tapas* bar where an entire evening can speed by amid the hot and cold appetizers (*tapas*) popular among Spaniards after their afternoon siesta (see *Eating Out* in THE CITY). Traditional *Carlucci*

(2215 N. Halsted St.; phone: 312-281-1220) offers elegant regional Italian dishes in a sleek setting. Innovative and reasonably priced, *Relish* (2044 N. Halsted St.; phone: 312-868-9034) provides updated American classics with unexpected combinations of flavors and textures, partially a result of their stock reductions, in a welcoming atmosphere. Neighborhood standby *Café Bernard* (2100 N. Halsted St.; phone: 312-871-2100) has long offered French country dishes in a comfortable bistro surrounding. This neighborhood's other outstanding restaurant is *Blue Mesa* (1729 N. Halsted St.), featuring authentic Southwestern cooking and tortillas that transport the soul to the land of canyons and cactus (see *Eating Out* in THE CITY).

The gala opening of the *Steppenwolf Theater* (1650 N. Halsted St.; phone 335-1650) in 1990 got as much press attention in New York as it did in Chicago. That isn't all that surprising, since the company had previously sent acclaimed productions of *Balm in Gilead* and *Grapes of Wrath* to Broadway, the latter went on to win several Tony awards. *Steppenwolf* also launched the careers of such renowned actors as John Malkovich, Glenne Headley, and Gary Sinese, all of whom are still involved with the group. The building has a 500-seat main stage, as well as a smaller stage for experimental works (also see *Theater* in THE CITY). Across the street from the *Steppenwolf* is the two-theater *Royal-George* complex, which also has a cabaret and wine bar to round out an evening's entertainment.

At Halsted Street and North Avenue are several renovation/construction projects; one, the renovated *Yondorf Hall,* harks back to the neighborhood's early days. Once a community center with a two-story theater and numerous meeting rooms, it dates from when this was a heavily German manufacturing district. Later it housed a discount liquor store, then became a dilapidated eyesore until the area began to change and a Canadian banking group restored the building to its current state.

On the west side of Halsted Street is a shopping center anchored by the *Crate & Barrel Outlet Store* (900 W. North Ave.; phone: 312-787-4775). Now a national institution, the chain got its start on Wells Street, a dozen blocks east of here.

There's lots going on at this rather chaotic intersection. To the east, along North Avenue, are several new or refurbished townhouse developments; to the southeast are a housing project for senior citizens and, in cheerfully colored glazed brick, a *YMCA* that serves both the upscale Lincoln Park area to the north and the poverty-stricken residents of Cabrini-Green to the south. On the west side of Halsted Street, beyond the *Crate & Barrel Outlet,* is the brightly lit *Byron's Hot Dogs* (850 W. North Ave.; phone: 312-266-3355), a 1950s-style diner. Across North Avenue is a sprawling and rather wild new Tex-Mex place called *La Hacienda Mexicana* (4821 W. Irving Park Rd.; phone: 312-283-1555) and an equally large furniture outlet, *John M. Smyth's Homemaker's Furniture* (phone: 312-649-5500). South on Halsted Street, where it meets Clybourn Avenue, is the *Golden Ox* (1578 N. Clybourn Ave.; phone: 312-664-0780), established 70 years ago when this was a working class area. It still serves hearty bratwurst, strong beer, and other German fare.

The bus goes past renovated lofts housing offices and galleries to the right and, south of Division Street (1200 North), is Cabrini-Green, the housing project frequently cited as the worst example of a bad idea. Just south of here the street crosses the tip of Goose Island, at the intersection where the North Branch of the Chicago River splits into two channels. The huge Material Service complex is to the right (gravel and building materials); beyond that are old manufacturing and warehouse buildings now advertising expensive lofts. On the left at Chicago Avenue (800 North) is the massive *Freedom Center* where the *Chicago Tribune* is printed. At Randolph Street, look west to see Chicago's central market, where fresh produce is brought in each morning and distributed to stores and restaurants.

To the east, between Halsted and Desplaines Streets, was the locus of one of Chicago's most notorious public brawls, the Haymarket Riot. The fracas began when John Bonfield, an overzealous police inspector, sought to break up a meeting of socialists and anarchists in the Haymarket Square. The assembly had been called to protest the slaying of six men several days earlier at the McCormick works. When the police intercepted the Haymarket crowd as it left the square near the corner of Desplaines Street, someone in the crowd tossed a bomb, killing seven policemen and wounding many others. A brief gun battle followed, and large numbers of civilians and police were injured. Seven men, all associated with the anarchist newspaper *Arbeiter Zeitung,* were executed for the crime, though the real culprit in the bombing may have escaped.

Stay on the bus until the neighborhood changes again—this time to lively Greek restaurants and nightspots. If you want to walk around Greektown, get off the bus at Monroe Street or Adams Street, 100 or 200 South. This neighborhood is chock-full of great places to eat, and any choice you make is sure to be a good one (don't be shy about walking in, looking at a menu, and walking out; proprietors are used to browsers here). Some suggestions: *Greek Islands* (200 S. Halsted St.; phone: 312-782-9855), decorated with blue-checkered tablecloths and popular with *University of Illinois* faculty; *Rodity's* (222 S. Halsted St.; phone: 312-454-0800), somewhat rougher, considerably noisier, and popular with locals; and the *Courtyards of Plaka* (340 S. Halsted St.; phone: 312-263-0767), definitely the most upscale, with an extensive wine list.

Also along this part of Halsted Street are other Greek establishments such as the *Athenian Candle Company* (300 S. Halsted St.; phone: 312-332-6988), which sells soaps, creams, and incense. The *Athens Grocery* (phone: 312-454-0940), in the same block, offers plump Greek olives floating in vats of oil, crumbly feta cheese, and halvah, a sweet treat made of ground sesame seed and honey (sometimes with chopped dried fruit and pistachio nuts). For a magnificent selection of airy Greek pastries, try the *Pan Hellenic*

Bakery (phone: 312-454-1886) next door; in addition to baklava and various cakes dripping with honey, there are round and flat breads and marvelous cheese and spinach pies, a meal by themselves.

For after-dark amusements (this neighborhood bustles until 11 PM or so), try the *Parthenon* (314 S. Halsted St.), where cries of "opaa" (hooray) accompany flaming platters of *saganaki*—a popular cheese appetizer that was actually invented in Chicago (also see *Eating Out* in THE CITY). There's belly dancing at *Neon Greek Village* (310 S. Halsted St.; phone: 312-648-9800) and a few other locations along here. There's plenty of parking nearby, and restaurants and nightclubs will validate tickets from any of the lots on the east side of Halsted.

Just south of Greektown is the Eisenhower Expressway, a main artery for traffic heading in and out of the Loop. To end the walk here and head back downtown, hop on the train that runs down the middle of the highway.

If you continue walking, pause at the top of the overpass to take in the view of the *University of Illinois at Chicago* to the southeast. Since the campus was constructed nearly 30 years ago, its "brutalist" architecture has been frequently criticized as too harsh for what should be a nurturing environment. The dorms just south of the expressway were an attempt to soften the visual effect.

When the university was built, the area was still composed of several large brick turn-of-the-century buildings collectively known as *Hull House*. One of Chicago's more successful attempts at social engineering, *Hull House* was the nation's first settlement house, an institution that provided English courses, crafts workshops, health care services, and job training for generations of immigrants. Founded by early feminists Jane Addams and Ellen Gates Starr, *Hull House* served the Greek neighborhoods to its north, the Italian community to its west, and the Jewish market area to its south, as well as several other ethnic enclaves. The settlement was named for Charles J. Hull, the previous owner of the "country home" Addams acquired in 1889 to begin her experiment in urban welfare. That original 1854 building still stands at 800 South Halsted Street, in jarring contrast to the buildings surrounding it. Maintained by the university as a museum, it contains many exhibits about the work of *Hull House*. It's closed Saturdays; no admission charge (phone: 312-413-5353).

The next street south is Taylor Street. Two blocks east and one block south is DeKoven Street and the site where Patrick O'Leary's barn stood until October 8, 1871. According to city folklore, a clumsy cow kicked over a kerosene lantern that night and ignited the blaze that torched the entire city. The Great Chicago Fire killed at least 300 of the city's residents and left one third of the rest homeless. Another result of the fire, however, was that Chicago redesigned itself and changed the face of American architecture in the process.

This walk concludes at Taylor Street, 1100 South, but from here a side trip worth considering is a stroll through Chicago's largest Italian community, which is chockablock with restaurants, as well as street vendors selling Italian ices. To get there, walk three blocks west on Taylor Street.

Halsted Street continues south beyond the city's border and other historic neighborhoods line it. One is Pilsen, which begins at 18th Street and continues south and west for several blocks. Once a Bohemian neighborhood, Pilsen is now largely Mexican, and has a thriving artists' community. At 32nd Street, Halsted Street becomes the main street of Bridgeport (home to two Chicago mayors named Daley), 10 blocks farther on are the old stockyards (now a struggling industrial park; no meat has been butchered there since the late 1960s) and the old *Chicago Amphitheater,* site of several presidential nominating conventions. To return to the Loop, go north again on Halsted Street, back through Greektown, and east on Jackson Boulevard or Monroe Street, crossing the expressway and Chicago River on the way. If you're on foot, buses run regularly on both streets.

Walk 12: Chinatown

Chinatown insiders always seem to know something the rest of us don't, like how to shop for seaweed, who sells the best squid, or how to order dim sum. Fortunately, Chicago's Chinatown, like the city itself, is fascinating and comprehensible, perhaps even more accessible than its counterparts on either US coast. From the Loop, pick up a red line (Dan Ryan) train on the elevated Wabash tracks, and after passing over old railyards, get off at Cermak Road, which is also marked Chinatown. If you are driving, Chinatown is just northeast of the junction of the Dan Ryan Expressway and Adlai Stevenson Expressway, Cermak Road/Chinatown exit. If you are driving from the Loop, head south along State Street to Cermak Road (2200 South) and turn right; there's a large parking lot at Cermak Road and Wentworth Avenue. (Be sure to leave your car here; parking anywhere else in Chinatown verges on the impossible.)

You'll know you're in Chinatown when you see the portal that arches across Wentworth Avenue at Cermak Road. Though relatively new (it was erected in 1975), this imposing structure is akin to porticoes in China dating back at least to the 10th century. Like similar entries in other cities, this is more than a gateway to a city within a city, it is a spiritual gateway, connecting the immigrant Chinese population with its historical roots. Notice particularly the way the transverse beam linking the heavy posts turns up like a tongue of fire at each end.

The tourist area of Chinatown fans out north, south, and west of the Cermak Road–Wentworth Avenue intersection. If you are ready to eat, there are two restaurants catering to tourists at this corner. *Haylemon* (phone: 312-225-0891), on the southeast corner, offers a regular menu in its bright and open, red-laquer-decorated dining room, plus dim sum, the popular and tasty dumplings filled with a variety of meats, vegetables, and fruits. On the northwest corner is *Three Happiness,* which occupies two floors of a ramshackle building and is also known for its dim sum. Inside harried and generally indifferent waiters and waitresses push carts laden with goodies in and out of cramped spaces, stopping here and there to disburse duck feet steeped in star anise, steamed rice noodles, and upwards of 50 other succulent dainties (also see *Eating Out* in THE CITY).

The best way to explore Chinatown is just to wander down the streets, stopping in any appealing-looking shops, and buying or not as you wish. Before entering the portal at Wentworth Avenue (once the main street of Chinatown), you might want to wander west along Cermak Road, where many changes are taking place. Chief among them is Chinatown Square, an upscale-looking strip mall with many new shops, restaurants, and a pleasing dragon-bedecked central plaza. To see it, walk one block west on Cermak Road to Archer Avenue, which comes in on a diagonal from the northeast.

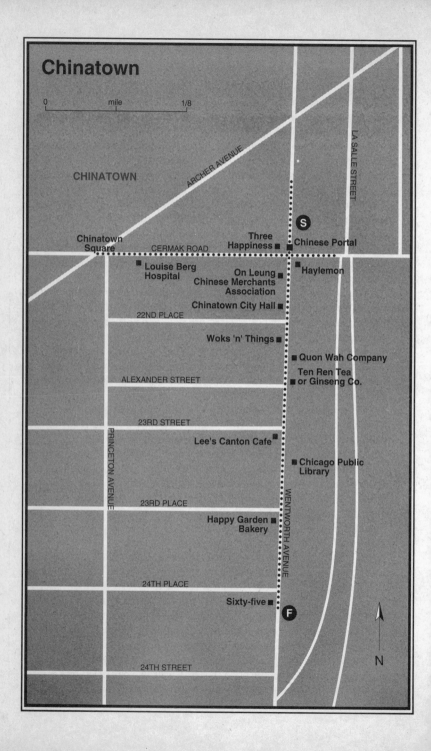

You can't miss Chinatown Square, with its pale red-brick buildings and sea-green accents. Rising behind the mall is a 600-unit residential development.

From there, cross Cermak Road and walk east along it, passing another group of shops. There are those who rate *Hong Min's* (221 W. Cermak Rd.; phone: 312-842-5026) dim sum even more highly than that of *Three Happiness*. Pork buns and fresh noodles with seafood have been singled out for particular praise. *Yee Wau Tong* (211 W. Cermak Rd.; phone: 312-326-1883) is a fairly spacious grocery with prices well marked and reasonable; pick up some baby peanuts or a bottle of oyster sauce. *Bark Lee Tong* (229 W. Cermak Rd.) does a brisk business in herbs and traditional home remedies.

Continue east to Wentworth Avenue, turn right, pass under the portal, and stroll down the center of Chinatown. At 2216 is the *On Leung Chinese Merchants Association,* scene of more than one gambling raid. Red-and-green pagoda towers rise at each end of the building. Between them, a glossy green tile roof stretches over two tiers of colonnaded balconies.

For cookware sufficient to whip up an emperor's banquet, visit *Woks 'N' Things* (2234 S. Wentworth Ave.; phone: 312-842-0701). This kitchenware emporium stocks knives fine enough to skin a frog and cleavers hefty enough to dismember a whole pig. Bamboo steamers, ladles, woks, and all the attendant paraphernalia can be found here. Several doors down, *Oriental Boutique* (2262 S. Wentworth Ave.; phone: 312-842-3978) sells kimonos and Susie Wong dresses, and *Sun Sun Tong* (2260 S. Wentworth Ave.; phone: 312-842-6398) mingles postcards and appealing plaster figurines with royal jelly and herbal remedies. *Doug Kee Co.* (2252 S. Wentworth Ave.) spreads canned and dried foods, trinkets, and oversize woks through three large rooms without the clutter ordinarily found in such establishments.

Across the street is *Quon Wah Co.* (2241 S. Wentworth Ave.; phone: 312-842-6614), a no-frills grocery store. In this store's chaotic jumble of goods is everything from litchi nuts in syrup to octopus. *Frida's Bakery* (2228 S. Wentworth Ave.; phone: 312-808-1113) is one of several along the street that offers American-style baked goods. For a moderately elegant meal, stop at the *Mandar Inn* (2249 S. Wentworth Ave.; phone: 312-842-4014), popular with suburbanites. *Emperor's Choice* (2238 S. Wentworth Ave.; phone: 312-225-8800) excels at soups; 14 are listed on the menu, ranging from an aromatic meal-in-a-bowl called "Eight Treasure Winter Melon" to the refined and expensive shark's fin with crab.

Serious tea drinkers will find it difficult to resist a stop at *Ten Ren Tea & Ginseng Co. of Chicago* (2247 S. Wentworth Ave.; phone: 312-842-1171). While the merely curious tend to buy fragrant hibiscus tea, well-heeled connoisseurs go for the aptly named king's tea, priced at nearly $120 a pound.

Lee's Canton Café (2300 S. Wentworth Ave.; phone: 312-225-4838) offers a varied menu at reasonable prices. The *Chinese Christian Union Church* on the corner of 23rd Place, an otherwise straitlaced affair of tan brick, flaunts a handsome green pagoda roof at its northern end and red-lacquer doors and window frames.

Chang Ying Ginseng Hong (2314 S. Wentworth Ave.; phone: 312-791-1525) is made for souvenir hunters: Among its collectibles are imported toy cars, fat plaster Buddhas, Chinese movie posters, decorated chopsticks, and soapstone carvings.

New Hong Kong Bakery & Café (2824 S. Wentworth Ave.; phone: 312-808-0088) offers Western and Chinese pastries, a red bean freeze, and cold soybean juice. The Chinatown branch of the *Chicago Public Library* (2353 S. Wentworth Ave.; phone: 312-747-8013) has three display cases devoted to ceramics and Chinese costumes. It's in another block-long strip of shops, all in pale red brick with vaguely Chinese accents. Shops here look a bit more familiar to Westerners; if you have children along, you might visit the *Crystal Palace Aquarium* (2351 S. Wentworth Ave.; phone: 312-808-1838), which displays a healthy selection of exotic sea life. *Happy Garden Bakery* (2358 S. Wentworth Ave.; phone: 312-842-7556) makes both bean paste and lotus moon cake pastry, as well as flaky coconut puffs. *Mei Wah* (2401 S. Wentworth Ave.; phone: 312-225-9090), across the street, displays glistening carp and red snapper on shaved ice.

Three of the best places for Hong Kong-style ("westernized") food are at this end of Wentworth Avenue. The large and somewhat garish *Evergreen* restaurant (2411 S. Wentworth Ave.; phone: 312-225-8898) serves sautéed dried squid, chicken steamed with black mushrooms and savory Chinese sausage, and huge clams steamed with black beans. *House of Fortune* (2407 S. Wentworth Ave.; phone: 312-225-0880) offers white tablecloths, a varied menu, and a bit of refinement. Between them is the *Sixty-five Bakery,* with an incredible selection of Chinese baked goods (phone: 312-842-7253); directly across the street is a restaurant of the same name, considered to have the best seafood in Chinatown (2414 S. Wentworth Ave.; phone: 312-225-7060).

While window shopping, keep an eye open for events along the street. During the *Chinese New Year* (four weeks or so after January 1) some energetic young men slip into a gaudy fabric dragon to wriggle the length of Wentworth Avenue, scaring bad luck away. Shopkeepers along the route pass small money gifts wrapped in lucky red through the creature's mouth, and watchers can help the evil spirits on their way by tossing sputtering firecrackers about with abandon. The streets are less explosive during the rest of the year, but you never know what you might see: The brass band you pass may be playing for a funeral at the Bowman Funeral Home (2236 S. Wentworth Ave.).

Return to the Loop via the same route you took to get here.

Walk 13: Hyde Park

The *University of Chicago,* and its tradition of intellectual and architectural excellence, dominates Hyde Park. At last count, 63 Nobel laureates had been associated with the university, which celebrated its centennial in 1992 and has distinguished itself as a bastion of economics and the social sciences. The university has fostered much of the urban renewal in Hyde Park and some of the city's great architects have designed buildings for the campus. The university neighborhood is a fascinating community in its own right: It's the most successfully integrated area in the city, and its residents, whether associated with the university or not, maintain parks, lakefront, and flora, as well as schools and bookstores.

Hyde Park today is an architectural compromise between tradition and the forces of redevelopment. Whole blocks of shops, bars, and apartments have been torn down to keep the district from deteriorating. Nonetheless, many fine old homes and businesses have been lovingly maintained. A walk through Hyde Park and Kenwood is a safe and delightful trip through a college town in the middle of a large city. Neighborhood residents, like U of C students, tend to be intellectual, ideological, and idiosyncratic.

Hyde Park stretches from the lakefront west to *Washington Park,* and from 60th Street north to Hyde Park Boulevard at 51st Street. The most convenient way to get to Hyde Park is to drive; street parking is limited but available. It is also accessible by public transportation: Take the downtown No. 6 Jeffery Express bus from State Street or take the *Metra* train south from stations underneath *Grant Park.* Whether traveling by bus or train, get off at Hyde Park Boulevard (the conductor might call it 51st Street) and walk three blocks west to Dorchester Avenue. The following walk is about 2 miles long and takes about two hours, making a few stops along the way.

Walk half a block north on Dorchester Avenue and go through the iron gate on the west side of the street. This is Madison Park, a private, cooperative, ethnically mixed area that stretches two blocks. Walk west and watch children run and play down the grassy strip in the center. The houses and apartments on either side help separate this small community from the city just outside it.

When you've ambled the length of Madison Park you'll be on Woodlawn Avenue. Walk north to 49th Street. This is Kenwood, a neighborhood of landscaped boulevards lined with spacious estates and wooded gardens. Most of these architectural gems were built between 1890 and 1910. On the northeast corner of 49th Street and Woodlawn Avenue is the secured compound of Louis Farrakhan, the controversial leader of the Nation of Islam. (His private security force guards the house and the area around it.)

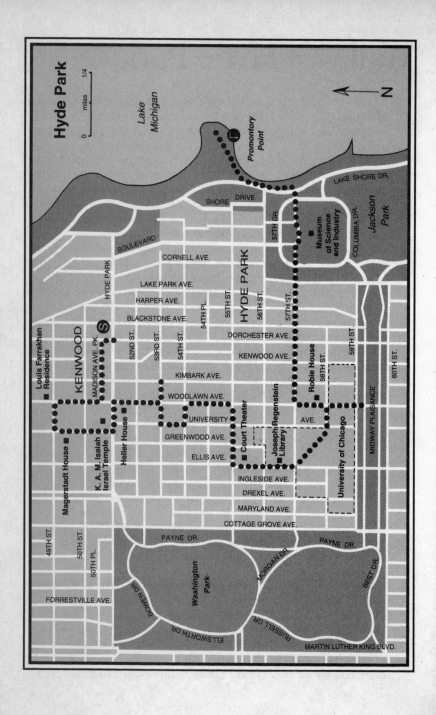

Hyde Park

Lake Michigan

Jackson Park

Promontory Point

0 1/4 miles

N

SHORE DRIVE

LAKE SHORE DR.

Museum of Science and Industry

57TH DR.

COLUMBIA DR.

BOULEVARD

CORNELL AVE.

HYDE PARK

HYDE PARK

LAKE PARK AVE.

HARPER AVE.

BLACKSTONE AVE.

54TH PL.

55TH ST.

56TH ST.

57TH ST.

KENWOOD

Louis Farrakhan Residence

MADISON AVE. PK.

S

52ND ST.

53RD ST.

54TH ST.

DORCHESTER AVE.

KENWOOD AVE.

Robie House

58TH ST.

59TH ST.

KIMBARK AVE.

WOODLAWN AVE.

UNIVERSITY

Heller House

Court Theater

Joseph Regenstein Library

AVE.

University of Chicago

MIDWAY PLAISANCE

60TH ST.

GREENWOOD AVE.

ELLIS AVE.

Magerstadt House

K. A. M. Isaiah Israel Temple

INGLESIDE AVE.

DREXEL AVE.

MARYLAND AVE.

COTTAGE GROVE AVE.

49TH ST.

50TH ST.

50TH PL.

PAYNE DR.

PAYNE DR.

MORGAN DR.

BEST DR.

Washington Park

FORRESTVILLE AVE.

BOWEN DR.

ELLSWORTH DR.

RUSSELL DR.

MARTIN LUTHER KING BLVD.

Go west on 49th Street to Greenwood Avenue, then turn south. The *Magerstadt House* (4930 S. Greenwood Ave.) is a massive brick private residence designed by a contemporary of Frank Lloyd Wright. Its wide overhang and horizontal thrust recall Wright's Prairie style. A 1968 remodeling restored the house to its original 1906 appearance.

Continue south on Greenwood Avenue back to Hyde Park Boulevard (or 51st Street). The massive Byzantine structure on the northeast corner is *K.A.M. Isaiah Israel Temple.* K.A.M. stands for Kehilath Anshe Maarav (Congregation of the Men of the West). Founded in 1847, it is the oldest Jewish congregation in the Midwest. The synagogue was designed by Alfred Alschuler, a prominent Chicago architect, in 1924.

Stroll east on Hyde Park Boulevard one block to Woodlawn Avenue, then turn south. At 5132 South is Frank Lloyd Wright's *Heller House,* also a private residence. Though it was built in 1897, the projecting eaves and spacious feel hint at the typical design of Wright's later residences. The Prairie style, as it came to be called, used a bold horizontal sweep to evoke the Midwest's dramatic openness and natural beauty. Head south to 53rd Street.

East of Woodlawn Avenue on 53rd Street is an eclectic shopping district full of small boutiques and interesting ethnic restaurants. This is where the neighborhood comes to shop and stroll. If time permits, walk over and join them. Retrace your steps to 53rd Street and head south on University Avenue, one block west. The houses along this block are renowned for their gardens. At 54th Street, between University and Woodlawn Avenues, note the colorfully decorated graystone houses of local artists.

At Woodlawn Avenue, proceed south to 55th Street. East of the intersection (from 1300 to 1500 E. 55th St.) are contemporary row houses designed by I. M. Pei. Once a popular bohemian neighborhood of artists and intellectuals, this part of 55th Street was one urban renewal project that some area residents felt unnecessary. Nonetheless, such projects have helped keep Hyde Park stable, integrated, and safe, while other areas of the South Side deteriorated.

The *Woodlawn Tap and Liquor Store* on the corner of Woodlawn Avenue and 55th Street (phone: 312-643-5516) is a neighborhood institution, as is owner Jimmy Wilson, who has tended bar near the *University of Chicago* campus for 50 years. His tavern opened in 1948 and has periodically expanded into adjoining rooms. *Jimmy's,* as it is familiarly known, is a favorite hangout for philosophers, poets, and construction workers, who, in Chicago, are as good as philosophers. Jimmy keeps an encyclopedia behind the bar, as well as Greek and Latin dictionaries and the complete works of Shakespeare to settle arguments. Stop in for a cheeseburger and a beer; in the afternoon, Jimmy might be sitting at the end of the bar smoking a cigar and helping himself to the stock.

Just west of *Jimmy's* on 55th Street is a fire station. In the 1950s, in a ramshackle building that stood here, a group of comics calling themselves the *Compass Players* started an improvisational troupe. These mixed nuts, among them Mike Nichols and Elaine May, went on to establish *Second City,* now located on Wells Street, north of the Loop.

Continue west on 55th Street for three blocks to Ellis Avenue. Dozens of bars and nightspots featuring jazz and blues used to line this street, but when they started to go to seed in the 1950s, the university bought them up and tore them down. When you reach Ellis Avenue, go south. On the left is the modern *Court Theater* (5535 S. Ellis Ave.; phone: 312-753-4472), a professional company that presents first class performances. One block east of the theater is the university's *David and Alfred Smart Museum* (5550 S. Greenwood Ave.; phone: 312-702-0200), showcase for an impressive collection of visual and decorative art. The museum has a bit of everything, from the classical to the contemporary. It's closed Mondays; no admission charge.

The next block south on Ellis Avenue is dominated by the modernistic and angular *Joseph Regenstein Library,* which attracts scholars from around the world and also is the campus's busiest social center. But this block once held a large athletic field. The *University of Chicago* is perhaps the only school in the world that could graduate professional football's first coach (Amos Alonzo Stagg) and have the temerity to tear down the football stadium named in his honor to build a library. Even more daring than that, in 1942 the university allowed Enrico Fermi and a group of scientists nicknamed the "suicide squad" to use the field house to conduct a risky experiment in nuclear fission. The result was the world's first self-sustaining nuclear reaction. For good or ill, the atomic age was born on this spot in December 1942. The event is commemorated by Henry Moore's looming sculpture *Nuclear Energy* (at 5631 S. Ellis Ave.).

Continue south on Ellis Avenue to 57th Street, where the university's mix of architectural styles becomes most apparent. *Hitchcock* and *Snell Halls,* the Gothic stone buildings on the left, are undergraduate dormitories. To the right is the modern *Kersten Physics Teaching Center.* Behind *Kersten* is the *John Crerar Library,* the Midwest's largest medical library. Also on the right is the brutalist-style *Hinds Geophysical Sciences Building* and its taller cousin, the *Cummings Life Sciences Center.* The more traditional red brick building at the corner is the *University Bookstore,* which has, in addition to its extensive stock of books, a small and very busy deli.

On the other side of Ellis Avenue is the limestone *Administration Building.* When it was erected in 1947, it was the first campus building to break with the university's customary neo-Gothic architecture. In 1969, when a popular instructor was denied tenure, radical students staged a sit-in here. Unlike such protests at other universities around the country, officials did not call on the police to put an end to it; they simply allowed the demonstrators to stay in the building for two weeks.

Head east through the *Administration Building* and wander through the university's main quadrangle. Students study, relax, and occasionally march on the grass in the summer, but the quad is beautiful year-round, surrounded by towering trees and imposing neo-Gothic buildings that create an academic oasis. Notice particularly the snaggletoothed gargoyles, U of C's unofficial mascots, that stare down from every rooftop.

Walk east across the quad and exit between the tennis courts at the corner of University Avenue and 58th Street. Across the street to the right is the *Oriental Institute* (1155 E. 58th St.; phone: 312-702-9521), a branch of the university that is one of the world's foremost sponsors of archaeological digs in the Near East. The institute's museum showcases the history and art of the ancient Middle and Near East. Among its treasures are Sumerian and Assyrian statues, Persian jewelry, and Egyptian mummies. The museum is closed Mondays; there's no admission charge (also see *Special Places* in THE CITY).

Across 58th Street from the *Oriental Institute* is the *Chicago Theological Seminary* (5757 S. University Ave.). In the basement of the building is the *Seminary Cooperative Bookstore* (phone: 312-752-1959), internationally acclaimed and simply the best academic bookstore to be found anywhere. Professors in town for colleagues' funerals have been known to skip visiting the deceased's family in favor of browsing through the store's cozy aisles—and the family usually understands.

Stay on 58th Street and head east to Woodlawn Avenue. On the right is the *Rockefeller Chapel,* an imposing limestone pile with stained glass windows in grand Gothic-cathedral style. Named for John D. Rockefeller, who donated the millions necessary to found the university in 1892, it is and will always be the tallest building on campus according to the terms of Rockefeller's bequest.

To the left across the street is *Robie House* (5757 S. Woodlawn Ave.), the most famous and influential of Frank Lloyd Wright's houses. Built in 1909, its sweeping eaves and horizontal lines make it one of the best examples of the Prairie style. Wright also designed the interiors of his buildings, including the furniture and carpeting, and these have been lovingly maintained by the University's *Alumni Association,* which uses the house as its offices. Free tours are given Mondays through Saturdays at noon.

Walking south from here on Woodlawn, you'll come to 59th Street and the *Midway Plaisance.* Today this is just an undistinguished strip of urban greenery, but in 1893 it was the glittering midway of the *World's Columbian Exposition,* a celebration of the 400th anniversary of Columbus's landing in the New World.

Return north on Woodlawn Avenue to 57th Street and turn right. This quiet, tree-lined stretch of 57th Street is a hodgepodge of apartments, restaurants, and bookstores. If the kids are along, there's also a large park and playground on the north side of the street. *57th Street Books* (1301 E. 57th St.; phone: 312-684-1300) is a branch of the *Seminary Co-op* that features a large children's area, as well as a wide selection of periodicals from around the world. Farther east is *O'Gara & Wilson Ltd.* (1311 E. 57th St.;

phone: 312-363-0993); the oldest bookstore in the city, it's a homey shop with towering shelves of used volumes and a fluffy gray cat that prowls the aisles.

East of here there is a trio of restaurants: *Edwardo's* (1321 E. 57th St.; phone: 312-241-7960) is part of a local chain that serves a delicious Chicago-style deep-dish pizza, as well as other Italian entrées (see *Eating Out* in THE CITY). *Medici Pan Pizza* (1327 E. 57th St.; phone: 312-667-7394) is a favorite college hangout serving pizza, hamburgers, and desserts in a dark, casual atmosphere—the kind of place where customers feel free to scratch their names into the tabletops and write graffiti on the bathroom walls. Even if you don't stop in, check out the stone carving of gargoyles eating pizza and drinking coffee on the exterior. *Ann Sather* (1329 E. 57th St.) offers delicious, reasonably priced Swedish specialties; be sure to try a cinnamon roll (also see *Eating Out* in THE CITY).

Farther east is *Salonika* (1440 E. 57th St.; phone: 312-752-3899), an economical Greek-Mexican-American restaurant that's a favorite with cash-strapped students, as well as local policemen and residents. Another block east is *Powell's Book Store* (1501 E. 57th St.; phone: 312-955-7780), a two-story paradise of used books that opens early and closes late.

Directly east of *Powell's* is the *Metra* Electric viaduct, where you can walk four blocks north to catch a train back to the Loop. The next street east is Stony Island Street, a stop for the No. 6 Jeffery bus back to the Loop. Looking southeast from this corner, you'll see the *Museum of Science and Industry* (S. Lake Shore Dr. at 57th St.; phone: 312-684-1414), located in what was the *Columbian Exposition*'s *Palace of Fine Arts.* The museum, one of the city's most popular, is closed *Christmas Day* only; there's no admission charge on Thursdays (also see *Special Places* in THE CITY). If you chose to save the museum for another day, you might want to walk just a little bit farther east, across Lake Shore Drive to Lake Michigan. Stroll along the beach to Promontory Point, where you can sit and contemplate the view of the downtown skyline.

Walk 14: Pullman Historic District

The nation's first planned industrial community, the town of Pullman was built in the early 1880s by George M. Pullman, industrialist and founder of the Pullman Palace Car Company. The company manufactured railroad sleeping cars, a necessary luxury for those who could afford it in the days when a cross-country trip by rail could take four or five days. The premise of the town of Pullman was the enlightened theory that workers who lived in pleasant and hygienic surroundings would be more productive. Pullman added his own twist to the theory: Since it was an investment, the town also had to turn a profit.

Built on a marshy piece of land 14 miles south of the Loop, the workers' village was designed by noted architect Solon S. Beman and landscape architect Nathan F. Barrett. It was a nominally utopian plan, with a bank, a hotel, and a marketplace—plus a church, schools, and a library, a gas works, and (novel at the time) separate storm and sanitary sewers. With its clean, gas-lit streets and pastoral setting (in those days it was surrounded by farmland), it was far from the squalor of most Chicago neighborhoods. It was a pedestrian-scale community that was pleasing to the eye and nourishing for the spirit.

But it didn't last long. An economic depression in 1893 caused railroads to cut back drastically on new car orders. George Pullman responded by cutting back on his work force and lowering wages for the remaining workers. He did not, however, lower the rent or utility bills of Pullman residents. When a grievance committee went to him and appealed for such relief, the members were fired. In May 1894, the unionized employees went on strike, leading to one of the most contentious chapters in American labor history. Eventually, other railroad workers across the country staged sympathy strikes, refusing to move trains carrying Pullman cars. Since those same trains also hauled the US mail, President Grover Cleveland eventually called in federal troops to break the strike and the union. Strike leader Eugene V. Debs wound up in jail and became a cause célèbre, and in 1897 Pullman died one of the most hated men in America.

By an order of the *Illinois Supreme Court,* the company sold all its properties not relating to the railroad car business, including Pullman. This was accomplished by the early years of this century, when the company deeded Pullman to the city and the *Chicago Park District.* The neighborhood went into a long decline, and by the mid-1950s it was on the verge of becoming a slum.

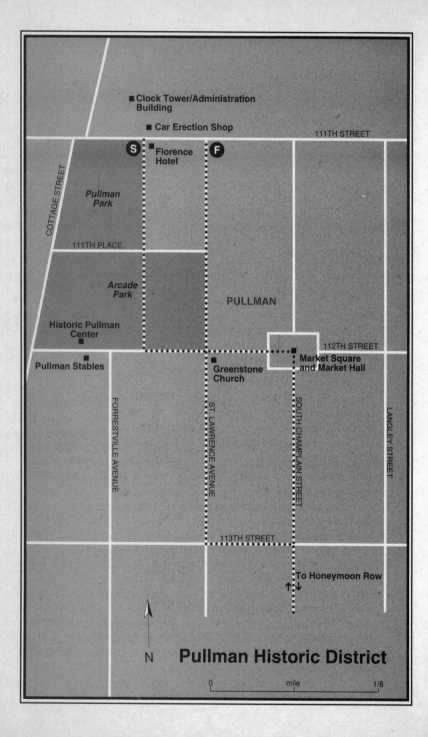

Clock Tower/Administration Building

Car Erection Shop

S Florence Hotel **F**

111TH STREET

COTTAGE STREET

Pullman Park

111TH PLACE

Arcade Park

PULLMAN

Historic Pullman Center

Pullman Stables

FORRESTVILLE AVENUE

ST. LAWRENCE AVENUE

Greenstone Church

112TH STREET

Market Square and Market Hall

SOUTH CHAMPLAIN STREET

LANGLEY STREET

113TH STREET

To Honeymoon Row

N

Pullman Historic District

0   mile   1/8

In the past 20 years, however, Pullman has experienced a renaissance. Designated a city, state, and national landmark because of its town-planning and historical significance, Pullman is being restored with public and private initiatives, mainly through the efforts of the *Pullman Civic Organization* and the *Historic Pullman Foundation.* To get to the village, take the Dan Ryan Expressway (I-94) south to the 111th Street, Pullman exit; head west to the second stoplight. Pullman also is accessible by *Metra* train; pick one up at the underground station near Randolph Street and North Michigan Avenue and get off at 111th Street (it's a 30-minute ride).

This walk begins at the *Florence* hotel (Cottage Grove Ave. and 111th St.), named for Pullman's favorite daughter. In 1975, the *Historic Pullman Foundation* saved the building from destruction and restored much of it, including Pullman's own suite on the second floor. The Queen Anne–style building, with gables, turrets, and a 200-foot verandah, had the district's only bar in George Pullman's day—and its use was restricted to hotel guests. Today the *Florence* hotel restaurant and bar are open for lunch on weekdays, for breakfast and lunch on Saturdays, and for the restaurant's modest but famous brunch on Sundays (phone: 312-785-8181 for reservations, as well as for information about the variety of tours provided by the foundation; maps and other materials about Pullman are available in the hotel lobby).

Across 111th Street from the *Florence* hotel are the most prominent remaining structures of the Pullman Palace Car Company: the *Car Erection Shop* (1881–1907) and the *Clock Tower/Administrative Building,* which is better seen from Cottage Grove Avenue at 110th Street. The original hand-wound clock and bell still keep time, chiming on the hour. Pullman's palace cars were finished in the *Car Erection Shop* before being shipped off to robber barons, captains of industry, and others who could afford them. In 1991, the State of Illinois purchased these buildings and the *Florence* hotel, intending to develop them into the *Pullman State Historic Site,* a museum about the railroads and transportation.

From the *Florence* hotel, walk south through *Arcade Park,* once an elaborate flower garden, to 112th Street. The squat, architecturally undistinguished building in the center of the park now houses the *Historic Pullman Visitor Center* (1141 S. Cottage Grove Ave.; phone: 312-485-8901). Visit it to learn more of the town's history. Directly south of it at 112th and Cottage Grove Avenue are the *Pullman Stables,* which also housed the village fire department. Two carved horse heads adorn the entrance. For sanitary reasons, all the town's horses were boarded at these stables. Residents could rent a horse and buggy here for picnics or errands in the city.

Walk one block east along 112th Street to St. Lawrence Avenue and the beautifully restored *Greenstone Church,* now owned by the United Methodists. Built of green serpentine stone from Pennsylvania, the Gothic Revival building was designed to enhance the town's architecture rather than to serve any particular congregation. Pullman leased it to whatever denomination could afford to pay the rent. The village's founder initially ignored the requests of Catholics and Lutherans for their own houses of worship, but he relented in 1888 and leased a plot of land to Swedish workers so they could build a Lutheran church. A year later, *Holy Rosary Roman Catholic Church* was built on vacant land west of the town.

Walk east along 112th Street to the intersection of South Champlain Street and *Market Hall,* originally the town's only shopping area. Its first floor consisted of 16 stalls where fresh produce was sold; on the upper floor were a dance hall, gymnasium, and meeting rooms. Greatly in need of restoration, *Market Hall* had its top floor removed half a century ago; the rest was damaged by fire in 1974. Market Square is surrounded by four arched, colonnaded apartment buildings, which George Pullman had built for some of his guests attending the 1893 *World's Columbian Exposition.*

From Market Hall, walk south to 113th Street along South Champlain Street, noticing how the housing designs vary. The more important one's job at the car company, the larger one's house. Farther down South Champlain Street, you'll see a full block of townhouses south of 114th Street. Modest in size, they're called *Honeymoon Row* houses, because newlyweds tended to rent them.

From here, walk a block west to St. Lawrence Avenue and stroll north to 111th Street where Pullman's executives lived. The houses here are built on a much grander scale than the workers' housing in other parts of the village.

The end of the Pullman tour is just a block from the *Florence* hotel and the train station, where you can catch a train back to the Loop.

Index